For my grandfather

Raymond L. Stairs, Jr.

And for his son, my uncle,

Raymond Stairs

Two sweet men taken too soon by cancer.
May their souls swim in the disease free oceans of heaven.

My grandfather Raymond Stairs playing on the beach
with his sister Alice in Hull, Massachusetts, in 1927.

Thank you

First, I need to thank my endocrinologist, Dr. Sol Jacobs, M.D. This adventure began the day he discovered my lump. I am forever grateful for his dynamite detective work. Next, I have to thank the finest surgeon in the world, Dr. Gregory Randolph, M.D. Every time I use my voice to bring positive change to the world, I celebrate his craft. To Danny, Jane, Danny and Phil: Cancer launched our relationship to a higher level. I hope we continue to soar! To my friends: You are the low-carb whipped cream on a no sugar added hot fudge sundae! Thanks for making my life delicious! To Paige, Tyler, Taylor, and Trey: If only pharmacies sold your type of medicine! Thanks for the laughter. To Elizabeth and Tahlia: Thank you for seeing, accepting, and loving me. To my mother Wanda: Thank you for taking care of me. You define family and love. To my husband Roger: **Oxygen**...Back at 'ya!

Contents

The Ides of March

HE STRAPPED MY FEET AND WRISTS to the sides of the bed, wrapped a blanket around me and said, "Remember, don't move. I'll see you in forty-five minutes." The full body scan would prove to be a crucial tool used to mark the effectiveness of my radioactive iodine radiation treatment. The results would serve as the tracking system to monitor recurring malignant cells.

I had been in the entertainment industry for over fifteen years. This was the first time my performance was upstaged by fear and panic. This was my first time sharing the set with claustrophobia. Up until my thyroid cancer diagnosis, I considered myself to be one of the toughest and most self sufficient girls on the block. I was rugged in a girly *girl power* way. The clout of a rockin' lipstick and potency of implausible hair products helped me weather life's storms. Somewhere between a cancer diagnosis and a complete thyroidectomy, all of that changed. The girl who could conquer anything in a great pair of shoes was being ruled by a fear of small spaces.

I should have been more mindful of my dislike of being enclosed. I sleep with my feet outside of the covers at night. I bathe with the shower curtain only three quarters of the way closed with the bathroom door ajar. I keep the passage ways to each room in my house open. The French doors in my living room and the pocket doors leading to my bedroom are purely decorative. They have never been closed shut. Most days I have a hard time wearing a turtle neck.

Somehow the fright I felt in the body scan was new to me. I've been performing for years and have never experienced stage jitters. I walked out onto the field at Fenway Park to sing our national anthem without so much as an elevated heart rate. As an on camera acting coach and casting associate for the largest casting company in Boston, I have spent a decent amount of time in front of the camera. My time on the scanning bed waiting for my pictures to be taken was rapidly turning into the nastiest shoot of my life. Unlike all other gigs in my career, my future literally depended on how I did in front of the camera that day. Cast and crew on set were in search of a clear take, free of hot spots and leftover cancer.

Within seconds in my locked-down, imprisoned coffin-like state, all judicious thoughts vanished. My mind kept repeating the same thought: *I have to get out of here!* As I tried to settle my limbs on the bed, I couldn't help but question why I was strapped in so tightly. While waiting for the procedure to begin, I found it increasingly more difficult to, in the words of the tech, "relax." I kept telling myself *you have to do this test. This is the first stage of the before and after shots taken to mark the progress of the treatment. Skipping this step is not an option. The cancer can come back. We have to kill the leftover cells.*

Just then, the tech explained how the bed was going to move *very slowly* under the photo canopy of the scanning table. Again, he asked me not to move or talk and reiterated checking back on me in three quarters of an hour.

Before the machine began to move, my heart began to pound. Just when it seemed as if my insides were under ambush, an earsplitting reverberation engulfed my head. All at once, every street artist I had ever heard banging on five gallon buckets was inside of my body bashing on my lungs, ribs and heart. My mind was screaming *I have to get out of here!* As the deafening noise permeated throughout my chest cavity, the pounding inside became more than I could stand.

"Remove the straps from my legs and hands, please! I need to sit up, **now**! I need you to tell me <u>exactly</u> what is going to happen." The artist in me craved a dress rehearsal or technical run through before the actual *show*. "Is it possible for you to <u>quickly</u> bring me under the canopy so I, <u>free of restraints</u>, can get a sense of precisely what I am in for?" The tech agreed to my hysterical request.

I took a deep breath and tried to prepare my psyche for the ride into the scanning machine. I heard the motor of the bed kick on. I was going in head first. While my seemingly boiling breath fogged the frigid top lid of scanning camera, my body (trapped beneath equipment) tried to float away to a place of serenity and peace. *Your mind is strong enough to block out your fear, Lorna...focus on the ocean...take your body to the sea and allow it to drift down the shore...you can <u>do this.</u>* Despite my efforts to psychologically regain control, once again the imaginary street musicians struck their drums sticks on my body. The *rat-tit-tit-tat, rat-tit-tit-tat, rat-tit-tit-tat, rat-tit-tit-tat, rat-tit-tit-tat, rat-tit-tit-tat, rat-tit-tit-tat, rat-tit-tit-tat* beats were so consuming I began to weep.

The blanket which swaddled my body locked in the rhythms of the drum core bashing around inside of me. The top of the machine was lowered closer to my nose as my body remained prisoner under the canopy. *Rat-tit-tit-tat, rat-tit-tit-tat, rat-tit-tit-tat, rat-tit-tit-tat, rat-tit-tit-tat, rat-tit-tit-tat, rat-tit-tit-tat, rat-tit-tit-tat.* Just then my mind went to my strapped hands and feet. *Am I being executed or cured? I have got to get out of these restraints. Rat-tit-tit-tat, rat-tit-tit-tat, rat-tit-tit-tat, rat-tit-tit-tat, rat-tit-tit-tat, rat-tit-tit-tat, rat-tit-tit-tat, rat-tit-tit-tat.*

The drum sticks were bashing all the way up to my skull. Every inch of my body was pulsating to the roar of my heart. I couldn't catch my breath, move, talk, cough, or clear my brain of all that was zipping through it. Everything became murky. In a loud voice I said, "So I am expected to be in here for nearly an hour? I anticipated an X-ray or CT scan. No one told me about this type of scan." *Rat-tit-tit-tat, rat-tit-tit-tat, rat-tit-tit-tat, rat-tit-tit-tat, rat-tit-tit-tat, rat-tit-tit-tat, rat-tit-tit-tat, rat-tit-tit-tat.* In a louder voice I went on to say, "My mind isn't *my own* these days. I'm extremely hypothyroid. I'm <u>exhausted</u>. I don't think I can do this." *Rat-tit-tit-tat, rat-tit-tit-tat, rat-tit-tit-tat, rat-tit-tit-tat, rat-tit-tit-tat, rat-tit-tit-tat, rat-tit-tit-tat, rat-tit-tit-tat.*

Suddenly tears began to gush out of my head as I barked, "I do not deserve to go though this today! I've already been through enough." *Rat-tit-tit-tat, rat-tit-tit-tat, rat-tit-tit-tat, rat-tit-tit-tat, rat-tit-tit-tat, rat-tit-tit-tat, rat-tit-tit-tat, rat-tit-tit-tat.*

On the verge of a breakdown, I cried out to be set free. "I need you to get me out of here right now!" This snap in sanity, this ultimate state of panic and vulnerability occurred in the cold, lonely, and uncaring environment I had become all too familiar with—a hospital room.

The sound of the machine backing out of the chamber brought pause to my frenzy. At last, I was out of the tunnel! The tech walked over to my side and said, "Miss, did you bring anyone with you today? Is there someone I can get for you? Someone you'd like me to call?"

For the first time since our rancid scanning rendezvous ensued, I heard compassion in the tech's voice. In a tearful ramble, I told him that for thirty-five days I'd been exhausted, freezing, forgetful, itchy, achy, emotional, desperate and fragile. I *wanted* to say that I felt like a vacant shell. I *wanted* to say that I could feel my soul expiring. "Roger." is what came out of my mouth. "Get my husband. He's in the waiting room."

When Roger walked in, I was overcome with the urge to run. Not to him. Just to *run*. Sprinting wasn't an option, so I clutched on to him soaking his shirt with hypothyroid tears of anger, fear, exhaustion, and frustration. The harder I cried the louder the piercing tones of the street drummers rocked through my cranium. *Rat-tit-tit-tat, rat-tit-tit-tat, rat-tit-tit-tat, rat-tit-tit-tat, rat-tit-tit-tat, rat-tit-tit-tat, rat-tit-tit-tat, rat-tit-tit-tat.*

It was my first real melt down since the surgery. I had wanted to cry so many times… really, *really* cry. Bawling my eyes out invoked an intense amount of pain near my neck incision. On top of that, I knew I wouldn't be able to blow my nose adequately. I didn't want to engage all of the muscles in my throat associated with sobbing and snout honking.

The Diva in me didn't want to risk making my scar ugly by tugging it while wailing like a colicky baby.

Pre-cancer I'd never been much of a crier, or hugger for that matter. I rolled with life's punches, and emerged one damn strong boxer. Since the moment my doctor suspiciously ran his fingers across my neck, that street-smart and savvy chick had been replaced by a sappy, sorry ass, cream puff of a girl. A girl I hardly knew.

I cried the day my doctor found the lump on October 21, 2004. The water works continued pretty consistently through December 15, 2004, when I got the news confirming my Papillary Thyroid Cancer diagnosis. Subsequent to hearing my diagnosis, I cried straight through February 2, 2005, when the disease was expelled from my body. From February 2, 2005, through the March 15, 2005, body scan, mild whimpers were all I could muster up. Ladylike non-taxing sniffles were my only catharsis.

The events that took place in the hospital that day released a deluge of unearthed post-surgical sentiment. I couldn't help but wonder if my claustrophobia was really my first panic attack or a case of misdirected anger. Deep down inside I was pissed off at God for giving me cancer. Every needle stabbed into my arm, every lab, test, scan, appointment, prescription, tear, and sleepless night reminded me of my unfinished business with my higher power. I will say this, in the maddening moments in the scanning room I took great comfort in being able to stand my ground. That <u>one single decision</u> to refuse to endure another moment of distress in the scan empowered the panties off of my pink, plus-sized ass. After months of feeling powerless, I was regaining control over my life.

March 15, The Ides of March, is the day Julius Caesar was slaughtered. As I sat on the scanning bed holding my husband, the ghost of my pre-cancer street savvy self whispered a poignant question in my ear; *do you want to end up like Caesar today? Do you want cancer to slaughter you? Or do you want to slaughter your cancer? YOU ARE IN CONTROL HERE. The tech is not your Brutus. He isn't here to kill you. He is here to help you KILL CANCER. Have the scan your way...take back your life.*

In a determined voice I told the tech exactly what I needed in order to complete the scan. After listening, he said, "Let's try this whole thing another way. We can put you in *feet first* rather than *head first*. We'll skip the foot and wrist straps but you <u>have to hold still</u>. We can stop in between photos. You can get up, walk around…go to the bathroom. Your husband can stay. Once we finish the head and neck photos, your head will be out of the scan. I'll let you know when it's OK to talk to him. How does that sound?" *Torture verses compassion…how do you think it sounds?*

"Great. Let's do this." was my response. Then with gentle eyes and a tender voice the tech said, "I'm sorry, Miss. I didn't realize you were having such a…hard time. I should have asked. Please accept my apology." Just then I realized the pounding had subsided. My chest was still.

Turns out neither strapping my hands and feet down, nor putting my head under a canopy for nearly an hour is a medical necessity. Does the medical world just assume that we are incapable of remaining still during a scan? Do the higher ups train the techs to tie us down like cattle to save time and money? I have known cats and dogs that received better medical treatment than I did those first few horrifying minutes in the scanning room.

At the risk of sounding like a whiner: Being hypothyroid is unbearable. It is one of the worst times to be treated like a nameless, faceless number. As much as I love sweets, I'm not going to sugar-coat this, folks. To prepare for the radiation following thyroid cancer, patients need to become hypo. While hypo, our bodies try to function without the help of any thyroid meds to winch them up. Menial tasks (like hair brushing) require a post-resting period to muster up enough energy to make it through the day. While hypo, our minds are dull and our bodies are lifeless. Days are coated with a fuzzy film. The world seems to be moving around at the speed of lightning as the hypos remain stuck in molasses. Hell, when hypo even my libido was lounging in someone else's lingerie.

One can imagine how wearisome it is to dress, drive to the city, and trek through a mammoth, maze-like hospital, only to park your frozen buns in the chilliest room on the Nuclear Medicine floor.

(Hypothyroidism brings new meaning to the word cold.) But until hypothyroidism sets up camp in your body, you have no idea how intense life can become. On the subject of intensity, who in God's name named the Nuc Med department? As a sick person the term Nuclear Medicine scared the power plant pants off of me!

As patients, our medical options should be clearly mapped out for us. It's our right to decide what route is best. Why did it take thirty minutes of personal agony before the tech decided to use a different method? Why aren't all of the scans done the easy way?

I am a full scholarship, conservatory-trained artist. Was my brave act the reason why the tech didn't notice my apprehension? To receive medical empathy, must we wear our emotions on our sleeves? The truth is, people who undergo diagnosis and treatment are encouraged to be strong. *Be strong, be brave, you can do it, you can beat it,* they say. I find it ironic that it's the very act of trying to be brave that keeps us from receiving the empathy and compassion we so desperately need. By trying to remain stoic about the scan, I ended up getting hurt. I sent the message that I was fine, but that was in part to keep myself composed. I wasn't fine—and that façade is why the tech spared me the immediate empathy I deserved.

The Ides of March, 2005, is the day I stopped being a voiceless victim of cancer and became a spoken woman fighting her way back to wellness.

Ave Maria

WAVES WERE DANCING ON THE SHORE of my favorite vacation spot in Dennisport, Massachusetts when I got the call from an old acquaintance. Her father had passed away. She wanted me to sing the funeral mass at our church. The morning of the service was sweltering. It was the last Saturday of August 2004. Humidity in New England can be brutal and this was one of the most oppressive days yet. As I entered the church, I was overwhelmed by the smell of lilies. Fragrant and powerful, lilies are lovely in a garden. For a singer with seasonal allergies, it can be tricky to sing along their side in an enclosed space. I was to the left of the altar with all of the flowers. Surprisingly enough, I seemed to be okay. No watery eyes or nose.

My first piece was "Ave Maria." I've sung the song for countless weddings and funerals without a problem. That hot August afternoon, during the more demanding section of the song, I noticed a strange sensation on the left side of my throat. It felt as if someone was pressing a finger on my neck. I had never felt that before. That feeling stayed with me for the duration of the mass. I left church blaming it on the lilies.

A few weeks later, I was in a voice lesson with a student. As we were warming up, I noticed the same feeling in my throat. Again, I assumed it was allergies. I had fallen out of my weekly allergy shot routine and ragweed was flourishing outside. Remembering my allergist's warning about how potent those weeds can be, I ignored the lump in my throat and continued to sing. Assuming all would be well once the golden-haired pests dried up, I refilled my allergy meds.

A month later, on October 21, 2004, I was in Boston at a routine exam with my endocrinologist whom I'll call Dr. Smith. Years prior, he had diagnosed me with Poly Cystic Ovarian Syndrome. Each year he checks my thyroid by pressing his hands on my neck while I drink a cup of water. He asks me to swallow as he feels around my neck. That day, he stayed in one spot longer than usual. He said, "Have you been having any trouble? Any neck pain? Anything different?"

As I tried to recall how long the *knot* had been there, my doctor said, "I'm sure it's nothing, but do you have any history of cancer in your family?" Instantly, body went numb. On February 9, 2002, we lost my uncle Ray to pancreatic and liver cancer. Many of us assumed my uncle's illness was a result of lifestyle rather than heredity. As a police officer, electrician, and father of three, he had a boatload of stress in his life. Diet and exercise weren't very high on his *to do* list. The women in my family lived to be in their late eighties. My mother shared impressive stories about her 94-year-old great-grandmother from Sicily walking up and down the streets of Watertown, Massachusetts dressed in black and sharp as a tack. Most of the girls in my family only visited the hospital to have babies. None of us had a history of major surgeries or illnesses.

"Like I said, it's probably nothing to worry about," Dr. Smith said, adding that only a small percentage (less than 5%) of nodules or lumps end up being cancerous. "What if it is?" I asked. "What's plan B?" After a pause he said, "We'll start with a fine needle aspiration, or biopsy." He went on to describe the various methods of treatment for positive and negative nodules on the thyroid. "But, Lorna, I'm *sure* it's nothing."

As I made my way to the parking lot, fear rushed in like a harsh New England storm. I called my husband from the car. As always, he was unruffled and said, "Babe, just make the appointment for the ultrasound. We'll take it from there. It's going to be alright." My polar opposite, my husband is always calm and level-headed. I heard *cancer*. He heard that I needed to take some tests. An only child brought up in a quiet household, Roger's life could not have been more different from mine. I am the oldest of three girls. My loud Sicilian household was filled with high emotion. Everyone spoke at full volume, all the time.

Most days, I thanked my lucky stars for my husband's calming manner. As his wife, I never had to worry about his getting angry or yelling at the top of his lungs. I could rest knowing that threats or warnings would never fly out of his mouth. That was a true slice of heaven for me because there was a lot of yelling and verbal abuse from the men in my home as a child. Whenever my husband was really upset, he was as silent as a stone. I admired that restraint and tried to emulate it.

The first available appointment for an ultrasound was close to Thanksgiving. Rather than wait that long, I decided to call in a favor. I had performed in a few shows with a technician who worked in radiology on the south shore. He made a few calls and got me in on November 2nd. It was also the 2004 Election Day. I was working the polls for a state rep friend of mine running for re-election. I arrived at the polls at 10:00 AM, and spent the entire day talking about the Bush/Kerry race and local politics. No matter how heated the conversations became, my mind kept reverting to my ultrasound. Colleagues of mine implied that the radiation tech would be able to tell whether or not the screen looked good or bad. I expected all of my worries to subside once the ultrasound tech said, "It looks fine. No need to stress."

Throughout the day, several of my friends showed up to hold election signs. Typically, I am open about my feelings. I talk about everything, from sex to nuts. That day, I said very little about my appointment. My unwillingness to chat about the ultrasound was my first indication that I was afraid. At the time, my husband was working evenings. He offered to skip work and accompany me to the hospital. My friends and family offered to take me, too. I declined all of the offers, brushing the appointment off as no big deal.

Although I'm an avid talk radio fan, I drove the whole way to the appointment in silence. I turned the heater in my Jeep Grand Cherokee on my toes and opened the sunroof to feel the crisp November air. The gentle scents of woodstove fires and autumn in Massachusetts swirled around me. The sunset was magnificent. I drove beneath a gazebo of shades of ginger, lavender, sapphire, and pink. -A moment of serenity. Taking in all of the beauty, I stood in the parking lot of the hospital looking at the sky. On the pavement, I said a prayer to the Blessed Mother Mary for strength.

I walked into the radiation lab, said hello to a few familiar faces, and sat down to watch TV. George Bush was ahead in the polls, and was being declared the winner. Despite our Democratic state, no one in the room had anything to say. I remember laughing to myself thinking *another four years with a Republican in office and no one in this room has anything to say?* As a registered undecided voter, with a totally right-wing father and left-wing mother, I normally love to debate. At that moment, I was trying to focus on staying calm. I'm guessing all of the people in the waiting area were in the same swift boat because no one was talking. (Couldn't resist the John Kerry pun.)

A woman's voice called out, "Lorna Brunelle?" She walked me to a small, dimly lit room. All business, she skipped the small talk and instructed me to remove all of my clothes from the waist up. I got on the table as she explained what was going to happen. She began by applying jelly to my neck area. From there she pressed a devise on my throat. I was shocked by how deep and uncomfortable the pressure was.

Eagerly waiting for the proverbial, "Everything looks good," I tried to make eye contact with the tech hoping for a sign. When she asked how I was doing. I replied, "Okay, but it seems to be taking a lot longer than I expected. Is everything alright?" "I am not authorized to say." She said. *Well, you pretty much just said it all.* I thought to myself. I refused to walk away empty handed. I called on my *how to play a scene to win* conservatory training—a skill that had been drilled into me all four years of college. My acting teacher scared us into winning. His bellowing English accent still fresh in my mind, I heard him say "If what you try the first time doesn't work, you must try another tactic! Don't ever give up. Play to win!"

First, I brought up the Red Sox. They had just won the World Series. The tech was a huge fan. I told her that I sang the National Anthem at Fenway Park. It was the year before Curt Shilling joined us. He was playing for the Arizona Diamond Backs against the Sox the day I sang to a sold-out crowd of 34,000 fans. Still trying to pull her in, I explained my concern about my voice if the lump was cancerous. Focused on her work, the tech remained friendly, but wouldn't give me what I wanted.

I tried again. This time I mentioned that I worked for a large casting company in Boston. I told her that we needed hundreds of extras to be in the Fenway Park scenes for the movie *Fever Pitch*. She seemed very interested, but still wouldn't leak out any information about my ultrasound. I gave her the website for the company, told her how to register as an extra. For my final tactical choice, I brought out a prop. I looked at my watch and said, "Wow, I've been in here almost an hour. Is this normal?" "Every ultrasound is different." she replied. *Wait for it… wait for it…she's going to give you a sign that you are okay…* Nothing. I walked out empty-handed. My professor would not approve.

This was not a game in acting class. This was the threat of cancer. Technicians are not allowed to make a diagnosis. Even if the woman suspected that I had cancer, even if she suspected that I'd have to remove my entire thyroid, even if she suspected that the disease had spread into my lymph nodes, she could have lost her job for sharing that information with me. That kind of victory wasn't worth winning the scene.

From the hospital I drove to the celebration for my state rep friend who had been re-elected. Too wrapped up in the ultrasound to fake enthusiasm about political victory, I left the party minutes after I arrived. My voice had felt funny for months, the radiation tech hadn't thrown me a bone, and I had to wait to hear from my doctor about the results. For a girl who likes instant rewards, this was torturous.

That night panic and thirst brought me from my bed to the kitchen. I walked by a magnet I've had for years. The Mahatma Gandhi quote reads *"There is more to life than increasing its speed."* I couldn't help but wonder if that was one of my lessons to learn. I normally wouldn't even have noticed the amazing sunset on my way over to the hospital. I would have been enveloped in some heated talk radio discussion or on my cell phone. For years I had been living in the fast lane, becoming more and more out-of-touch with the simple joys around me.

I went back to bed ready to face whatever health issue was being tossed my way. I said a prayer asking God to be kind during his tutorials. I concluded my cerebral email with a request for a tremendous amount of strength to pull me through. In that moment, I made a pillow promise to slow down enough to live a healthy and fabulous life.

Don't Move

My PHONE RANG ABOUT THREE TIMES. I remember dashing to my pocketbook and yanking out the contents to find my cell. Dr. Smith's voice sounded uneasy as I heard him say, "I'm not satisfied with the ultrasound."

That was the moment I thought I had cancer.

Dr. Smith very calmly said, "I've reviewed your ultrasound, and I'm recommending a fine needle aspiration. Remember, 95% of the time, this is nothing to worry about. We just want to be sure. The quickest appointment is about five weeks from now on December 13." *Breathe… Six tiny letters spell the word cancer, Lorna. You are stronger than six tiny letters.*

The morning of the biopsy Rog and I left our home at 6:00 A.M. It was bitterly cold and I was bitterly cranky. I'd never been much of a morning person. My maiden name may be the root of my pre-dawn dislike. Sleeper. As in Lorna Jayne Sleeper. -Enough said.

The commute was very quiet. My husband knew that I wasn't up for chatting. As we drove past the Dorchester Yacht Club, I was amazed to see a repeat of the colors I saw the night of my ultrasound. The same lavenders, pinks, gingers, and sapphires, blazed across the sky. Only this time it was sunrise. I couldn't remember the last time I watched the sun come up. Suddenly my panic lifted and I felt peaceful, grateful, grounded and strong. I felt as if an angel had joined us in my Jeep. The feeling was different from any feeling I had ever experienced in church.

As an adult, I sang in the church choir. Despite all of my involvement in the church, I only felt close to God twice during church-related activities. The first occasion was during my confirmation (a sacrament and important rite of passage for Catholics) when I was asked to do a reading. After the service, the Cardinal approached me. He lifted my chin, looked into my eyes and said, "You were given your voice for a reason. It is a gift from God. Do *great* things with it." I felt like my feet were lifting off of the ground. It was as if God himself was looking at me through the Cardinal.

The second time I felt the presence of God, I was miles away from a place of worship. Our C.Y.O. group took a church field trip to New Hampshire over Columbus Day weekend. Together, my fellow parishioners and I climbed Mt. Monadnock. The foliage was spectacular. At the top of the mountain, our priest said, "This is God's house, his church; take in the beauty and splendor of this moment. Whenever you doubt the power and presence of God, remember this day." From that point on, I have associated all things beautiful in nature with God.

I wish I could say I get out of bed every Sunday to attend mass, or that I don't gossip or swear. I support a woman's right to choose and unequivocally believe that women should be priests. I'm nowhere near the poster child for Catholicism. But I know what it feels like to experience God's magnificence in nature. The sunset on the evening of my ultrasound and the sunrise the morning of my biopsy brought me back to that feeling of inner peace. The exquisite colors in the sky reminded me of how I identified God's presence though beauty in my life. On the road to my biopsy, I became reacquainted to God.

We signed in at the hospital, and I waited to hear my name called. Although we hadn't discussed it, I knew my husband wanted to come in with me for the biopsy. I decided to leave the decision to invite Roger up to the nurse. If she said, "Lorna Brunelle...Oh would you like to come in, Sir?" then I'd agree to it. I figured if she didn't invite him in, it was for a good reason. As a performer, I find it easier to stay "ON" in front of strangers. I am a lot stronger when I am alone. I knew that if I brought my husband into the room with me, I'd be more apt to fall apart. Moments later, a nurse called my name. She didn't ask about my husband. I followed her into the room alone. Surprised by how many staff members were in there, I waited for someone to give me direction. Each member of the team introduced themselves to me. I met a few nurses and then a beautiful woman said, "I am here to hold your hand if you need me, nothing more." Her face was lovely and her smile warmed my chilled psyche.

The doctor joined us and explained what was going to happen. The team initiated the small talk that I had so longed for in my ultrasound. The doctor had the team prop my neck up on top of several rolled towels. The position felt very odd. My head was back and my neck was sticking up toward the ceiling. A singer is taught never to hyperextend their neck in fear of taxing the crucial muscles in that region. My first thought was *I'm not supposed to have my neck this way; it's awful for my voice.* My second thought was *if you have cancer you may never sing again Lorna, get over yourself and just deal with the unpleasant situation for a few moments.* Just then my body became freezing cold. *Did they give me a shot of something? Is this nerves? Why am I so cold?*

The doctor started going over the rules with me. "Once I insert the needle for a pass, you cannot talk, clear your throat, cough or move. You have to stay very still. I will be doing several passes this morning." I think she did eight in total. "I am removing fluid from your nodules. I see one larger nodule and a galaxy or cluster of little nodules around it. In between each pass I will let you know when you can swallow and speak. It is <u>very important</u> that you stay very still. Whatever you do, DON'T MOVE."

Knowing my intense hunger for information, Dr. Smith had given me strict orders not to go online for information about thyroid cancer. He said on line research isn't always accurate and can mislead patients.

Believe it or not, I obeyed his request. I'm sure that is why my next question for the doctor was so hard to formulate. "Am I at risk for vocal damage during this procedure?" Rather than giving me a straight answer, the doctor said, "This is a good time to go over these forms." She read a few legal sentences stating that I understood the risks associated with the biopsy. The risks included vocal damage.

The hand holder smiled and said, "You are going to be fine." I noticed a Blessed Mother medallion on the chain around her neck. It was luminous, beaming toward me. From that point on, I focused on the hand holder and the image of Mary. The doctor applied a freezing cold gel to my neck and began the process. Now every woman reading this book knows what it means when the gynecologist says, "You'll feel a little pressure," but this was very peculiar. My neck felt heavy. No pain. After each pass, the doctor would say, "You can cough, speak or clear your throat." Then she'd say, "Okay, DON'T MOVE!" and she'd work the area again. I felt more pressure and weight each time she said, "DON'T MOVE!" This cycle repeated quite a few times.

"You're doing great," the hand holder said. I could tell she really meant it. I didn't realize I was crying until I felt tears moving down my face. My thoughts went back to my husband, sitting alone in the waiting area. I knew it would be hard for him to be left behind, but I was so glad he didn't join us. Lengthy needles were navigating my neck. It may have been frightening (and nauseating) to watch.

When the doctor was finished with the aspiration she bandaged my neck. She told me to expect soreness in my neck region and to take whatever I would normally take for pain. Then a nurse in the room said, "You should hear from your doctor within seventy-two hours." At that point, the doctor corrected her and said, "You should hear from Dr. Smith tomorrow." There was a strong emphasis on the word tomorrow.

That was the moment I knew I had cancer.

As a child, I had special abilities. I knew when the phone was going to ring, when people were going to stop over, and what a person's name was before he introduced himself. Occasionally, I heard people talking to me in an empty room. As a teenager, this hyper awareness, became so strong I had to use all of my might to block it out. As an adult, I supported paranormal behavior in other people, even produced shows for some famous mediums. Somehow I had managed to quiet my ability, keeping it out of my personal life. That morning at breakfast, I knew I had a lot more pain ahead of me. The consciousness or intuition from my childhood clouded over me. I sensed things were going to get a lot worse before they got better.

My neck continued to throb as the hours went by. The pain was piercing. Why do doctors use words like "uncomfortable" and "distracting" when the pain is downright brutal? Perhaps they should have to experience the procedures during med school so their vocabulary is more accurate. It was tremendously difficult to get comfortable in bed that night. I ended up on my back looking at the ceiling until I fell asleep. I woke up in pain each time I tried to roll over.

Having endured seven years of electrology treatments to combat my *Dude Looks like a Lady* five o'clock shadow, I like to think I have a pretty high threshold for pain. And while everyone's experience is likely a little different, over-the-counter pain relief didn't cut my post-biopsy discomfort. I recommend asking for a two-day supply of something a touch more powerful for pain. I also recommend scheduling your biopsy for a Friday. You won't want to go to work the next day.

I tried to keep myself busy as I waited for the phone to ring with my results. When my husband got home from work the next day, we headed to my mom's house in Buzzard's Bay for dinner. In her driveway at 5:30 P.M., I got the call from Dr. Smith. In a steady and stoic voice he said, "Lorna, I have the results from your biopsy. I'm <u>very sorry</u> to say that it is, in fact, cancer. I'm so sorry I have to tell you this. Normally, these things turn out fine." The next few sentences sounded like the voices of the teachers and parents in the Charlie Brown and the Peanuts cartoons. *Woah woahhhhhhhhh woowowoahhhhhh wowhhhhhhhhwooooahhooooo.* Then I heard him say, "Lorna, papillary thyroid cancer is a *VERY TREATABLE* cancer. It's the **good cancer,** one of the best to get. You are young and healthy. We expect a full recovery. This is not usually a terminal cancer. The odds of beating this are in your favor."

With Dr. Smith's voice in my ear, I walked through my mother's kitchen into her office. My sister Elizabeth and two of the four grandchildren were in the kitchen. "I know this is a lot, Lorna," he said, "Can you grab a pen?" He gave me the name of a surgeon, and the size of my nodule. He talked about the long-term treatment. -A life long relationship with replacement thyroid hormones. He walked me through the radiation options, (radioactive iodine) assuring me that things would be fine. His tone was even and precise.

"What about my voice?" I asked.

"Well, as you know, there are risks associated with this surgery, but they are rare. In some cases patients experience permanent hoarseness. In extreme cases, patients cannot speak above a whisper." My whole body went numb.

My husband, sister, and mom were reading the notes over my shoulder. My three-year-old niece asked me why I was upset. My sister explained, "Auntie is just having a bad day." My mother went into the kitchen and started talking about my Uncle Ray and how less than two years prior, he received the same news in her kitchen. Unlike my uncle's, "You have pancreatic/liver cancer and around six months to live" phone call, my doctor was saying that within six months to a year, I'd be on my way to feeling better.

"Here are the positives," he said, listing all of the good things in my corner. "You are a non smoker. You don't drink excessive amounts of alcohol. I don't have diabetes, high blood pressure or heart disease." Then Dr. Smith said, "We caught this in time." He recommended that we work quickly. As soon as he said the word <u>work</u> all of my thoughts jumped from cancer to my two jobs. *I've got to call my boss in Boston and tell my staff at the school. Dr. Smith needs to stop talking so I can tell my boss that I'll be missing work.* To be honest, I don't remember how our conversation ended. I heard my mother crying in the kitchen. I heard my sister Elizabeth on the phone with my sister Tahlia. I remained seated in my mother's office area. My husband tried hugging me. I felt totally anesthetized. Why was I so stunned? I had known since the biopsy that something was wrong. Suspecting and knowing are completely different animals in the cancer kingdom.

We sat at the kitchen table for a few moments without talking. By that point, Tahlia had arrived with her two boys. For the rest of the evening, I floated in and out of the conversation. I remember saying out loud, "Dr. Smith said this is the *good cancer*, this isn't like Uncle Ray's cancer. This is a good cancer. They can cure this."

No one in my family or circle of friends had even heard of thyroid cancer. We were familiar with the leaflets on every other cancer that sit in waiting rooms of doctors' offices, but none of us had ever seen anything about thyroid cancer. I had the unknown—and unpublicized—good cancer. I had recently seen a documentary on HBO entitled Chernobyl Heart. I was at least familiar with the term thyroid cancer, as most of the children exposed to radioactive fallout in that area of Russia were affected by it. Although Dr. Smith used the word GOOD to describe my cancer, I appreciated the potential of any cancer so close to the lymph nodes spreading throughout the body. I also appreciated the chance of a cancer so close to my vocal chords and recurrent laryngeal nerve, destroying my God-given instrument.

While Tahlia and Roger remained very quiet, Elizabeth called my grandmother Concetta (Connie) and my friend Reenie, a breast cancer survivor and my right-hand gal at work. I should have called them myself, but I was afraid nothing would come out of my mouth. Once the calls were made Elizabeth said, "Lorna, you, out of all of us, are strong enough to get through this. Whatever you need, just let us know. We are all here for you." Her offer was followed by an awkward silence in the room. In search of an ice breaker (and trying for a laugh) I said, "Tal, you can pass me the potatoes, I have cancer and don't really feel like getting up. Liz, can you get me a drink, after all guys, I do have cancer. Mom, can you give me a fork, I have cancer." Then I said, "Hey, you know how we all pulled names for Christmas this year? Well, since I have cancer, can all of you buy me a gift now? A girl with cancer should get more than just one name pull present, don't ya think?"

Within minutes, we were all laughing and joking around. We laughed so hard, we were crying. I knew instantly I was going to have to deal with everyone in that funny fashion. I had to put my illness right out there. Keep cancer light and on the table. As a family, we named that humorous approach to co-existing with cancer WORKING THE

"C"! My twelve-year-old niece Paige and eight-year-old nephew Tyler came up from the playroom to join us for dinner. I said, "Hey guys, I have to tell you something. I know you saw us crying earlier, and here is the deal; a part of my body is sick. A doctor needs to take it out. The part of my body that is sick has an illness or disease called cancer. **I do not have cancer**. **My thyroid has cancer**. The thyroid is right here in my neck". In search of a way to show how small the area of sickness was, I got a penny and said, "This is the size of the part of my body that is sick. The doctors are just going to take that out. It's not the bad cancer like Uncle Ray had. I have the good cancer. Anything you want to ask me?" One of them asked, "Are you going to die?" and I replied, "I don't think so. But I will tell you <u>everything you want to know</u> as soon as I find out. I promise."

Being open, honest, and even blunt about my disease was the only way I knew how to cope. I wanted the children to know that the word cancer doesn't have to be frightening and doesn't always mean death.

On the way home from my mother's house, we stopped in to see my friend Rose. Her sweet son Sean Michael had died unexpectedly nine months prior in a car related accident. This was her first Christmas without him. As we spoke, she remained very composed. Her sister is a nurse at a big hospital in Boston. She offered to run my information by her. During our conversation, she said, "You'll be fine and of course you know you have Sean up there watching out for you." No sooner than the words came out of her mouth, the light in the living room began to flicker. After a few seconds it began to stop. Then she directed another question to Sean. "Lorna will be okay, right, Sean?" The light began to flicker again.

Just then our husbands entered the room. Rose's husband said something about getting a second opinion. At that point, the light flickered on and off several times. Instantly, I began speaking to my friend on the other side and asked, "Do you think I should get a second opinion, Sean?" The light flickered wildly again. It was one of the most phenomenal moments of my life. I know the whole "other side" can of worms is another book for another time, but I need to report what happened and how it affected me. I felt support from a place we know very little about, yet put a ton of stock in each night in our prayers. I was ecstatic to know I had someone from TEAM GOD on the field with me. For the skeptics out there, it's worth mentioning that the light bulb did not need to be changed and the family does not have a problem with the wiring in the house. Sean continued to come to me throughout my journey with the same force he had that night.

Once I got home I decided to call my friend to share my news. She was born with spina bifida and has endured countless surgeries. I wanted to bounce a few of my questions off of her. Up until that point, I had never even slept in a hospital. Unfortunately, I got her answering machine. In a moment of inexcusably poor judgment, I left her a message along this line, "Hello, it's Lorna. Well, Dr. Smith called me tonight and I do have cancer. It's a good cancer though. He thinks I'll be fine. I'll talk to you soon."

At the time, I thought saying those words on her machine would be easier than saying them to her face. I realized how selfish my decision was when I retrieved my cell voice mail the next day. After midnight, she left me this tearful message, "Lorna, I am in your driveway but I don't see any lights on in the house. I called your cell because I didn't want to risk waking you up by calling the house phone. I'm here. I love you. I'm here. I'll wait outside here a little while. I love you." The sound of her sad voice made me want to kick something! Bottom line: I do not recommend telling people you love that you have cancer via voice mail.

They say timing is everything. I was diagnosed on December 15th and had three weeks off from school to wrap my brain around what was happening to me. I contacted my ear, nose, and throat specialist and my primary care physician to let them know. Each had great insight and questions to take to my surgeon.

I had about fourteen questions to ask during the consult. I printed out two copies, one for me to read to the surgeon and one for my mom to record his responses. That project kept me busy for a few days. While I was typing away at the computer, there was a knock at my door. It was a florist holding a huge plant wrapped in a big gold bow. The card said "WE LOVE YOU" Love, Kenny, Liz, (Elizabeth's nickname) Paige and Taylor. My sister Liz is the middle of three girls. I am the oldest. Our relationship has always been a bit strained, to say the least. As kids, I was closer to my little sister Tal, who's ten years my junior. Liz and I were only three and a half years apart. The gap in age with Tal created a different dynamic in our relationship. We never fought about blow dryers or bathroom time because Tal was six when I was sixteen. Liz was thirteen banging on the door to interrupt my 80s Aqua Net styling magic.

Like most sisters who grew up before cell phones, lap tops, and I PODS, Liz and I fought over time on the phone, the TV, who sat in the front seat of the car, and all of that other juicy sibling rivalry stuff. In all the years I've had Liz in my life I do not ever remember her using the word love in a sentence that had to do with me. She never said, "I love your shirt" or "I love your earrings." We never really did the *love* thing. She was always very aloof with the occasional, "Hey, where did you get that shirt?"

There, sitting in the picture window of my dining room, was an amazing voucher of her love. I had proof of her affection in writing.

My Shakespeare professor in college once proclaimed that no one ever cries alone. "We cry to get a reaction out of someone else. Crying is merely a tactic!" he'd holler to a room full of confused and disgruntled young artists. I remember my classmates roaring over his insane observations.

As I held the *I love you* card from my sister, crying all alone in my house, I thought of my professor. It was a poignant moment. My sister Liz actually loved me, and my Shakespeare professor was full of shit.

Retail Therapy

I HADN'T TOLD MANY OF MY FRIENDS about my diagnosis. I simply didn't know how. If only I could put all of them in a meeting room A.A. style and say in one quick sentence. "Hello, my name is Lorna, and I have cancer." I still felt guilty about leaving that unceremonious announcement on my friends' voice mail. I wracked my brain to think of a way I could tell a lot of people about my diagnosis with humor. With Christmas only days away, I knew it would be impossible to have them all over my house for a Yankee Swap/"I have cancer" party. I decided to write a funny tongue in cheek e-newsletter.

It went like this:

> "Hey friends, you all know how much of a unique non-conformist I am…Well, guess what? I landed a cancer only 5% of gals my age get. It's called Papillary Thyroid Cancer. Yes, the girl who has never smoked a cigarette, hardly ever eats sugar or processed foods, never drinks caffeine, never does drugs, (okay, I smoked a hit of pot a handful of times and I never really understood it) and has only been drunk

once when I turned eighteen on a camping trip (Green Monster Heffinrefer Beer chased by shots, -I DO NOT RECOMMEND IT!), has cancer!

Yes, here I am, the 33-year-old Catholic girl who lives like a Mormon landing the cancer less than <u>5 percent of folks ever score</u>. Guess what? That's not all; they say this is usually not a hereditary cancer but rather an environmental cancer. So, all of those afternoons spent playing at the power plant really paid off, huh, girls? Speaking of power plants, I get to have some radioactive iodine radiation post-op to kill any left over cancer cells. So for all of the environmentalists in my posse encouraging me to GO GREEN, I will finally really *be* green. I will be so green that my GLOW will be seen from a small aircraft. -Is that a power plant in your panties or are you just happy to see me? Can I get a drum roll please? I'll keep you all posted on the step-by-step process of this **lump** in my road. Would love to get together with you all soon."

That is how my friends found out. As I re-read my original emails, I realize how much anger is written between the lines. The e-blast was easier for me than calling everyone. After all, I was the one with cancer trying to find balance. My life became a struggle for order as I traveled down an all but familiar road of chaos.

I used to be one of those people who finished their Christmas shopping in July. I used to wrap all of my purchases immediately and put the gifts in bags for each household. My tree, window boxes, lights and decorations went up the day after Thanksgiving. And so because of this, I didn't have a lot to do on my vacation to keep my mind busy. I still had nine days to fill before meeting my surgeon. For the record, I wasn't sleeping at all. This is something I wish I'd talked to my doctor about. It turned out to be one of the many mistakes I made during my tribulations. I wished I had asked for a mild sleep aid. My mind raced all night into the dawn. The lack of slumber heightened my emotions, which resulted in a series of follies. Just ask my wallet how foolish things got.

I decided to buy birthday presents for everyone who had a birthday coming up. That morphed into purchasing gifts for everyone who had a birthday. Naturally, that included everyone I knew. On a mission to find perfect gifts, I purchased and wrapped birthday presents for my friends and family members. It kept my mind clear, but cost me roughly $2,000.00. I believe that behavior is called retail therapy.

My friend Reenie had always longed for a pewter collection. I hit almost every antique store in south eastern Massachusetts in search of pieces. I gathered a lovely display of plates, bowls, candlesticks, flatware and pitchers. I found everything right down to the cream and sugar bowl. Once the gifts were wrapped, I wrote out the cards. I wanted everyone to know how much I loved them and how important they were to me. Did I think I was going to die during that time? No. Things just felt differently. I so desperately wanted to be out of the NOW and in to the FUTURE. I wanted to press fast-forward and skip all of the hardship ahead of me. Purchasing and organizing gifts for the upcoming spring events (Mother's Day and birthdays) became an obsession. Each time I pulled the platinum plastic out out of my wallet I heard it say, "Lorna, what is going on? You are never this impulsive. What gives?" And I'd say, "We are planning for the future! Put your seatbelt on, we have more work to do." Have I mentioned that cancer also makes you a little crazy?

I'm sure on some level I wanted to be in control. With so much pandemonium around me, I wanted order, and I needed things to be neat and pretty. I searched out things to over power. I organized my closets, my drawers, my pocket books, my shoes, my jewelry, my car, my cabinets, my make-up, my pantry, my laundry room, my photo albums, my stationery and my note cards. I went on a cleaning frenzy. For those wondering, I'm not that girl who finds cleaning "therapeutic." I've never liked to clean. In fact, I've worked extra hours each week for a number of years just to hire a person help me around the house. But, at that time, cleaning scratched my itch. In the midst of all of my shopping, wrapping, writing, cleaning, and planning, we had quite a snowstorm in Massachusetts.

New England is downright handsome in the winter. The scenery is so striking it can take your breath away. Surrounded by winter splendor,

I kept hope for one of those astonishing moments wherein I felt God's presence through nature. It seemed beguiling to me that I couldn't conjure up spiritual reassurance when I needed it the most. Not to be all "Footprints in the sand," but I was praying for a sign. I wasn't looking for a reindeer to run across my yard. I wanted to feel God. I wanted to be comforted by the sensation I had the morning of my biopsy. Once I was officially diagnosed with cancer, I just couldn't tap in.

Our neighborhood goes Christmas caroling every year on December 23rd. The fifty plus year old Norman Rockwell-esque tradition began at my house with the former owners, the Walker family. Friends visiting from L.A. were joining us for the outing. As much as I tried to get excited about the party, I was dreading that day. The morning of the festivities, I was scheduled to meet my surgeon. Several days had passed since I got the cancer call from Dr. Smith. Wherever I was, the same question popped into my mind. How sick am I…<u>really?</u>

I'd be in the most mundane spot say, the grocery store, when all of the sudden I'd think *I have cancer!* Then I'd challenge my thoughts with, *do I really have cancer? I mean did the doctor say, "You <u>may</u> have cancer?" Maybe it was a <u>maybe</u>…I need to call him.* I'd run this denial (disguised as confusion) by my husband. His repeated response was, "Babe, <u>you</u> have cancer." For a moment, I'd confront him, get upset and yell. Eventually, I'd give in and feel as lost as I did the evening my doctor called with the news. I refer to that sense of disorientation as the cancer fog.

Retail therapy allows the sun to shine through the fog. But it doesn't last for long. Rather than max out your credit cards, I urge you to find another way to channel your cancer. Find a therapy that works for you. Take a walk, read a book, see a funny movie, have lunch with a friend or call an actual therapist. Although shopping provides instant gratification, nothing is worse than receiving the bill in the mail weeks later.

The Bow Tie Bastard

On "MEET MY NEW SURGEON EVE," I organized all of my questions, emotions, and paperwork. My file also included my 8x10 actor headshot. I wanted the surgeon to draw a line on the photo demonstrating his plan for the scar. Despite all of my preparation for the meeting, I woke up in a pissy mood. My morning workout consisted of being verbally abusive to my husband and short with my mother. I was totally put out by having to drive to meet the man who was going to cut open my neck. One would think I'd be thrilled to meet my doctor. After all, he was going to cut the cancer out of my body.

We parked on the street near the office. At exactly 11:30 A.M., the surgeon opened his door and brought us into his office. He was small in stature, with an English accent and a bow tie fixed tightly around his little neck. I will refer to him as The Bow Tie Bastard or B.T.B. for the duration of this book. He never acknowledged my husband or my mother. I was, once again, put out. This time it was by the surgeons' lack of manners. Everyone knows that cancer affects the entire family. I was taken aback when he didn't say hello to mine. As I was making my way to the chair, he blocked me in front of his desk. Before I knew it, he was snapping a camera in my face. He never mentioned the purpose of the photo.

We took our seats. He opened up the conversation by saying, "You have papillary thyroid cancer; it's a relatively *easy* surgery." He went on to explain the procedure. When he was finished, I said, "I'm not sure if Dr. Smith told you, but I am a professional singer. I am also a voice and acting teacher. What are the chances that I will lose my voice or end up with vocal damage?" He didn't respond so I went on to ask, "Will you be using a nerve monitoring system during the procedure?"

This practice helps prevent the surgeon from hitting the vital recurrent laryngeal nerve, which runs near the thyroid, and which, when damaged, can cause permanent vocal damage. From what I gathered, the monitoring device was similar to the doctor board game we played as children. If the physician gets too close to the nerves, the machine beeps. My request seemed to belittle the fine skillfulness of The Bow Tie Bastard. Rather than respond to my inquiry about nerve monitoring, he said, "Next question!" Yes, that's right. He ignored all reference to the nerve monitoring system. I think it's relevant to add that this man seemed incredible on paper. I actually paid eight bucks to download his report. I knew where he studied, what he had published, and how long he had been in practice. The only thing the profile failed to mention was that he had a very eccentric and bastardly bedside manner. He was like a wacky character on a David E. Kelly sitcom. Genius, I'm sure, but very quirky.

I asked if he, or I, could bring in a plastic surgeon to close my incision. Quite a few people I consulted with in the medical field said that was a legitimate question. "Absolutely not," he barked. "I'm not going to bring someone in to close a surgery I have done hundreds of times." He then went on to say that his scars are some of the best around. At that point I said, "I would love to see a photo of your work. Do you have a photo?" His face began to turn a slight shade of red. "I do not have any photos," he snapped. "It's rather an absurd request, really." Then he mumbled something about patient confidentiality or privacy regarding photos. All the while I was thinking, *I'd gladly allow someone to photograph my neck to help other patients; you just photographed my face and didn't even ask me. Get real, man. PS: Ever heard of fiber? You may want to try adding some to your diet.*

I bet hundreds of people would allow their post-op incision to be kept on file to ease the minds of people dealing with cancer.

Despite the lack of love in the room, I asked The Bow Tie Bastard a few additional questions. I'd never had surgery. I didn't know what to expect. And I didn't understand why the B.T.B. was so aggravated by my inquiries. When asked about the recovery, he said, "Of course, you cannot drive for a few weeks." He then went on to compare a total thyroidectomy with wisdom teeth removal. *I drove after my wisdom teeth were extracted, moron. How on earth are both surgeries similar?*

I asked about radioactive iodine radiation treatments and whether or not I'd be able to conceive a baby after the treatment. "That is a question for your gynecologist," he spouted. And to other subsequent questions, he continued to deflect them to my endocrinologist or my primary care physician. Finally, I asked one last question about my voice. His response floored me. "You know what, Miss? I think you need to be more concerned about your cancer and less concerned about your career."

I thought my head was going to explode.

I didn't have plan B. I merely wanted to know if I should consider signing up for the next real-estate license exam. I wanted to know how many singers and public speakers he had successfully worked on, how long it took them to use their voices again, and if any physical therapy or vocal rehab was necessary. Just then he said, "Naturally, whenever we are working in that area, the patient is at risk for vocal damage." *What the hell does that mean? Talk to me about facts, statistics. Tell me it's only happened to you once in your career. Say, "Less than 5% of the people with thyroid cancer have vocal damage." GIVE ME SOMETHING!*

Out of total frustration I said, "Give me the best and worst case scenario, please." He sharply replied, "**Best,** your voice will be the same with perhaps a little loss of range; **worst,** your speaking voice will have a permanent raspy sound and it may be difficult to project above a whisper." It was almost as if he relished that last part. As I was asking another question, he looked at his watch and stood up. "Right, thank you for coming in, you can see the front desk to schedule your surgery."

"When do I see you again?" I asked. "The morning of your surgery." He replied.

I had forgotten all about the gift (a wrapped box of Italian candies) I had brought in with me. As we were being ushered out of his office, I clumsily said, "I brought this for you." And he said, "Oh I wish you hadn't. I'll give it to the girls in the office." That remark sealed my burning hot loathing for him. Shocked by his offensiveness, I walked toward the receptionist area. "He is one odd duck isn't he?" I said to the woman behind the desk. If only I could have substituted the letter D with the letter F! "Here are some candies I brought. He didn't want them." The receptionist said that he was watching his weight. She went on to say that he was an amazing surgeon and that I could trust him. I wondered how many times she had to endorse her boss as potential clients walked out of his office looking baffled and appalled.

The entire meeting was a peculiar exchange of energy. As I made my way to the parking lot, I kept wondering if I really had to like my surgeon. I had been so spoiled up until that point. I generally liked all of my doctors. I joke with them, talk with them, and am never afraid to be myself in their company. Maybe that is rare? Halfway to the car, my mother asked me what I thought. "I think I'm going to shop around." I said. This distressed both her and my husband. They were more of the just get the cancer out of you school. I was more of the feeling comfortable in the hands of the person who cuts me open school. Their lack of support disappointed me. I became furious. That was the first time I cried out of pure anger. Roger said, "Lorna, you are crying because you don't want to be here. It's not that you don't like him; you just don't like the situation. It doesn't matter who the surgeon is; you are not going to LIKE him." For the record, I wanted to yank the parking meter out of the ground and smash it over his head. I was the one with cancer. I didn't need him or anyone else telling me why I liked, or why I disliked anything or anyone.

Earlier in the book, I remarked on how I wanted to emulate my husband's serenity and reason. At that moment I wanted to see a reaction on his face. I wanted to see him sweat. I wanted to <u>see</u> him <u>feel</u> one grain of sand-sized speck of what I was feeling. I wanted him to scream and get mad along with me. When you're in the throes of cancer, you want to know that someone has your back. There are moments when you want your partner to stand tall and flip God the bird on your behalf. As I approached my surgery, I wanted to see him throw his pen down or kick a piece of our furniture. I wanted him to commiserate with me by howling within the walls of our home. His animalistic instinct never surfaced. He never lost his cool. He was my lighthouse while I was being thrown about on a turbulent sea, engulfed in a cancerous fog.

I asked my mother if she found the surgeon to be as curt, removed, and rude as I. She said, "It's hard to say. He seems to have a very odd personality, I agree; but that doesn't mean he isn't a good surgeon. You were told he is the best at his hospital." She went on to say that I, too, was rude and that he may have been reacting to my poor attitude. For a moment I thought she had forgotten we are Sicilian. I couldn't believe the betrayal coming from her lips. We are <u>all about</u> defending family. (Tony Soprano would never have treated Meadow this way.) Why was my mom siding with the Bow Tie Bastard? I'm sure her feedback was accurate to some extent. Thing is, I went into the meeting as if it were an interview. My goal was to hire someone for a job. The position was very important. I needed the best candidate. It was *my* body. Settling for anything less than best was not an option.

I wanted to walk back into the doctor's office and tell him how severely he had screwed up our meeting. Having worked as an interview coach for contestants in the Miss America and Miss USA system, I can assure you, the Bow Tie Bastard interview was a sparkling example of how **not** to land the crown. There was no way I could move forward with the B.T.B. without some major explanations and an apology. In search of answers, I drafted a note to the person who recommended the B.T.B. -Dr. Smith.

The caroling party was only hours away. I tried to perk up. While we caroled through the streets of the historic Muttock area of our neighborhood, I was filled with emotion. The fusion of sentiment spun around in my head as the December air whipped through the trees. The little tornados of last season's foliage spinning around mirrored the twirling thoughts in my head. We walked from house to house singing "I'm Dreaming of a White Christmas." I was dreaming of a Christmas without cancer. During "Joy to the World" I developed a hard knot in my belly. I suspect the knot filled the space where my joy once lived. Singing about happiness and joy during my Christmas with cancer was torture. Even crueler, it may have been the last Christmas I could sing the carols.

We made our way to the nursing home at the end of my street. More than thirty of us wedged our bodies down the halls and into the rooms of the elderly residents. Several of them seemed incoherent. Our next stop was the cafeteria. I looked around the dining area and thought, *will I live this long? How many cancer survivors are in this room?* I wondered when my own death would come. I had to find the right doctor. I had to find someone who cared about my voice. I needed a surgeon who understood and accepted me, warts, questionnaires, idiosyncrasies, and all.

Just then the lyrics *May God bless you and send you a happy new year, And God send you a happy new year* rang through my body. God had blessed me with years of friends, laughter, love, health, success, and family. No matter what the new year had in store, cancer could not take away my past.

Canceristmas

WHEN STRESS TRIES TO GRAB ME by the throat, I cook. I spent all of Christmas Eve day in my kitchen. The amount of concentration it takes to prepare a dish was exactly what I needed to distract my mind. My therapeutic time around the stove seemed to beef up my low spirit, resulting in a five-star, Zagat-rated afternoon.

My goal was to make light of my Christmas with cancer. I asked my mother how she'd feel about me painting an outrageous cancer ice breaker on a T-shirt. We laughed over my slogan options. "Merry Canceristmas!", "Cancer = Great Presents", "Cancer on Board", "I have cancer, can 'ya pass the peas, please?", "Not now; I have cancer", "Don't ask me to help clean up- I have Cancer!", "I didn't buy you a gift because I have cancer", "I have cancer, try to top that one", "CANCER HAPPENS" or my personal favorite and consideration for the title of this book, "Does This Cancer Make My Ass Look Big?"

Ultimately, I decided to pass on the T-shirt idea. I wanted to put my cancer out there, laugh, and move on. The shirt would have visually invited cancer to spend the night with us. Shortly after I walked through mum's door, Tal and Liz started working the C. In true C workin' style, we joked about all things cancer. My grandmother seemed uneasy. "It's just too much," she said. "It's *not really* funny." Even my grandfather disapproved of our reindeer games. Having lost a son to cancer a few years prior, he found no comedy in my disease. If I had only known that my grandfather was sitting at the table with a grapefruit-size mass on his left lung with only eight months left to live, I **never** would have joked around. At the time, it was how **I** got by. Cancer humor was my shield protecting me from the disease.

A few days earlier, mum suggested that we visit the La Salette Shrine. It is divine place of pilgrimage a few towns over in Attleboro, Massachusetts. As children, we loved going to the holy place during the holiday. The shrine is named for the small hamlet in the French Alps where the Blessed Mother is said to have appeared to two shepherd children in 1846. The shrine in Massachusetts was built as a place of pilgrimage where people find healing and reconciliation. The grounds of the shrine are covered with beautiful lights. Hot apple cider is served outside. I cared most about the cider as a child. As an adult, I was moved by the history. James Soloman founded the shrine. He wanted to create a haven for people with cancer.

I longed for the innocence of my childhood. Bundled up in layers of clothes, my sisters and I would sprint toward the car. Face pressed to the back seat window, I'd linger with baited breath to catch sight of the endless sea of illumination. The lights seemed to stretch for miles. In my child mind, I was seeing a preview of heaven. Once there, we'd walk the stations of the cross, climb a flight of the holy steps on our knees, visit the manger, drink hot cider, peruse the gift shop, say a prayer, and light a candle. We would conclude our evening by walking over Rosary Pond on the large deck with a gazebo. The deck was designed like a fishing pier. The sides were outlined with huge rosary beads. At the edge, live goldfish and Koi swam under the ice. I was always amazed by their ability to survive in freezing water.

Now years later, I drove to the shrine in the front seat of the car.

Now years later, cancer ran through my cells on the commute. I couldn't help but think of the goldfish. Did I have what it takes to survive?

I heard the seatbelts on my niece and nephew click open before the car stopped. The beauty of the shrine was posted on their awestruck faces. As we approached the candles, mum explained the etiquette of prayer. "This is a time for you to think about what you *really* want. A time for you to ask God for something. Think about what you are *really* hoping for, make a wish, and light the candle." "Does your wish come true?" my niece Paige asked. "If it's meant to be, God will make it happen." mum replied. She went on to say, "God please watch over Auntie Lorna as she prepares for her surgery. Please make sure everything is okay." Then my mom asked my nephew Tyler what he prayed for. With big sincere brown eyes and all the simplicity of an eight-year-old he said, "I wished for a 4-wheeler." Expecting a more moving response, mum then turned to my niece Paige and asked, "What about you? What did you ask God for?"

The gorgeous, leggy 'tween with long curly brown locks replied, "A straight iron for my hair." Mum seemed a bit dismayed. The children missed the message about the candles and the power of prayer. I, on the other hand, instantly knew the kids were going to be fine. They didn't have to waste their prayer candles on my cancer. They had more important things on their minds. Quads and straightening irons. I wouldn't have wanted it any other way.

It was almost midnight and Christmas Eve 2004 was officially coming to a close. After several rounds of Christmas charades, (which somehow always end up x-rated) numerous plates of fabulous food, abundant trips down memory lane, and scores of moments wherein I felt the haze of cancer hovering over me, I decided to go home. A little voice inside of me said *you did it, Lorna! Now you just have to get through tomorrow.*

As always, I was the first one awake on Christmas. I made a cup of decaf English breakfast tea with cream and honey, and sauntered into the living room. The candles in the windows and the lights on the tree worked so well with the pink paint. The room had a warm and welcoming glow and smelled of balsam fir. I sat on the loveseat in the early Christmas morning quiet. I said a prayer for the strength to make it through the day with a smile on my face. A majority of the afternoon would be spent with my in-laws. I didn't want to ruin their holiday by behaving like Debby Downer. They knew me as the witty one with the warped sense of humor. I didn't want to introduce them to my new-found state of tears and jeers on Christmas Day.

My Christmas wish was to relax in every room of my home. With each sip of my tea, I fantasized about how I wanted to spend Christmas. We had just installed a woodstove in our hearth room. I wanted to plant myself in front of the fire in my leather wingback chair reading a magazine. From there, I wanted to watch a movie in the living room on the sofa near the tree. I wanted to eat hot oatmeal in the kitchen in my slippers. In the dining room, I wanted to email a few friends. In the bathroom, I wanted to take a long hot shower and cover my damp skin with lavender oil in my bedroom.

Then I thought about how much time I'd have to sit around during my recovery and radiation quarantine. Then I thought about my husband. As easygoing as he is, I was concerned that he would be upset if I skipped Christmas. Within half of an hour, I was in full make-up, hair and costume, ready to play the role of the girl at ease about having cancer on Christmas day.

There wasn't any laughter. There wasn't any deep conversation. There wasn't any joy. I remember eating and existing at the table. I was present in body but my mind drifted throughout the day. To make matters worse, my husband didn't buy me a gift. It's worth noting that years prior I had initiated the "let's not do gifts" conversation. I suggested a celebratory trip together rather than presents so for years we flew to a warm place. Working the "C" aside, this year, I really wanted a present. As all women know, men are not mind readers. *I* should have said, "This year, I'd like to exchange gifts. Let's celebrate our lives now, right here in our home rather than on a beach in a few months when I'm recovering." Alas, I didn't have the foresight to speak up. I didn't plan to experience self-pity over not getting a present on (for me) the most superficial day of the year. My vacillating cancer sparked emotions were all new to me. Prior to cancer, I loved that we avoided getting wrapped up in the "What did he get you?", "What did she get you?" craziness. I was the one who wanted things to be normal. I couldn't have it both ways. By not giving me a gift, he was just following the house rules. To prevent this from happening to anyone else, I want to go on record stating that when someone has cancer during the holiday season, they deserve a little gift every day just for getting out of bed.

The minute I walked in our house I got out of my clothes, washed up, and climbed into bed. All was tranquil on 96 North Street. I closed my eyes and prayed December 24, 2004, would be my last Christmas with cancer. I prayed that the cancer hadn't spread elsewhere. I prayed for strength.

Just then, a magnificent wave of assurance gently washed over my body. I felt a splendid sense of simplicity. My will to live a vast, disease-free, strong, happy, and spiritual life held precedence. My resolve was the only gift I needed. Call it what you will… an epiphany…a Christmas miracle…In that serene moment I realized that my relationship with cancer wasn't about temporarily escaping from my life. Unwrapping an object tied up in a bow is merely a quick fix. In order to evolve, I needed to permanently claim my inner strength. I needed to clutch everlastingly onto hope and faith.

On that night, that Christmas night, I closed my eyes. I visualized the spring butterflies, dragonflies, and hummingbirds do-si-doing around my gardens. I saw a strong image of my disease free body sitting in the grass. My new, gorgeous, and cancer-free life was only a few months away.

Hope and Hypothesis

Dr. Smith encouraged me to tell the Bow Tie Bastard how I was feeling about our appointment. B.T.B. was out of the country so I sent him an email. He responded within a day apologizing for seeming abrasive. He also mentioned that I was the second to last patient he was seeing the day before left for the holidays. He thanked me for the candy and offered to meet me once again before the surgery to clear the air. One would think the email exchange would have made me feel better. To the contrary, I felt more confused. My gut was holding on to the man I met. He was a lovely writer but when it came right down to it, I needed bedside manner. I couldn't rely on him passing me a note while I was wheeling into surgery. I needed more than, "You are going to be fine. Sincerely, Your Surgeon, Formally known as The Bow Tie Bastard."

The old me (the girl who didn't have cancer) would have forgiven The Bow Tie Bastard after his kind email. I'm not one to hold a grudge. I believe that holding negative energy creates a perfect breeding ground for cancer. Trouble is cancer made me a lot more selfish than ever before.

I wanted to love and admire my surgeon. Could I really warm up to The Bow Tie Bastard?

Earlier in the month, a friend at the casting company asked why I was taking a leave of absence. Turns out, she knew a lot about thyroid cancer. She, too, had her thyroid removed. I told her about my dilemma concerning The Bow Tie Bastard. Immediately, she locked in on my eyes and said, "Lorna, you have to like your surgeon. Shop around!" A few days later, she sent me the number for a rock-star plastic surgeon. I called him immediately. His receptionist was very hip and easy to speak with. I told her a little bit about my situation and asked how soon after surgery I could see the plastic surgeon. It was a baby step, but it was the first phone call that seemed to empower me. She asked for the name of The Bow Tie Bastard. Without saying his name, I filled her in on our meeting. Quickly she responded by saying, "Honey, if you don't like your surgeon, **do not** use him. We don't need to be spoken down to. A surgeon shouldn't belittle us." In quite a girl-power huff, she said, "I'll have the doctor call you back on his next break."

Within a few hours, the plastic surgeon returned my call. He listened to my entire story never asking for The Bow Tie Bastard's name. Then, in a most encouraging voice he said, "Lorna, if you are unhappy with your scar after surgery, I feel confident I can fix it. So find some comfort in that. Let me take that off of your mind. Most insurance plans do not cover it, but in lieu of your profession…the acting, singing and plus-size modeling work down the road, they may cover it for you. If not, it's about $2000.00 out-of-pocket depending on what you have going on. Every case is different. It may even cost less." As he spoke, I felt my ribs expand. He went on to say, "So tell me, what kind of singer are you? Do you sing at Karaoke bars? Do you sing at church or for fun in a band? What have you done?" I gave him the short list of my resume and ended with singing at Fenway Park and Gillette Stadium. Bare in mind, the Red Sox had just won the World Series and the Patriots were walking into their second Super Bowl victory.

His response was stern and focused. "You graduated from the Boston Conservatory? That is an excellent school. I'm going to give you a few names. They are, in my opinion, the best thyroid surgeons in North

America. If you are as talented as I think you are, you need to be with one of these guys. One of them is known around the world for his work with the nerve monitoring system. You'll definitely want this when you go in. The problem is they are most likely booking in the spring. I'll see what I can do. I've seen their work. If you get in with one of them, you may not even need me to touch up your scar. They both have been featured in a big Boston magazines and national publications as top thyroid surgeons year after year. Will you be at this phone number all day?" My heart was pounding. The plastic surgeon had just given away platinum advice for free.

Just as he promised, he called back within an hour. He said, "Dr. Randolph at the Massachusetts Eye and Ear Infirmary has an opening! He is the man who works with the nerve monitoring. He is one of, if not, the <u>best</u>." Forever grateful to the plastic surgeon, I vowed to refer him to all of my friends. His humanity restored my faith in the medical world. It was just what I needed after my bogus blind date with the Bow Tie Bastard.

As things were falling into place, I continued my quest for information about the thyroid and thyroid cancer. I wanted to know *how* I *got* cancer. Much to my surprise, exposure to radioactive fall out is one of the biggest connections to this type of cancer. Months prior to my diagnosis, I was fixated on the documentary CHERNOBYL HEART. After watching the near two hour special chronicling the aftermath of the largest peacetime radiation catastrophe that has ever occurred on this planet, (considered to be the worst manmade nuclear disaster in world history) I called everyone I knew urging them to watch the program. Until that film, I had never even heard of thyroid cancer. Thousands of people in the Chernobyl region had it and most of them were children. The scar left behind was actually referred to as the "Chernobyl necklace."

So many of the kids on the screen had patches over their necks. I'll never forget one doctor in the documentary who told a mother and father that their teenage daughter had thyroid cancer. The doctor decided not to tell the patient the whole truth about her condition. Would it have squelched her hope if she had been told the truth?

Hope had been on my mind for weeks. A friend of mine recommended the book <u>The Anatomy of Hope</u> by Dr. Jerome Groopman. The book is a series of stories or cases accounted by a Boston doctor who witnesses the results of patients whom were told the whole truth and the not-so-whole truth about their condition. It's an observation of what role hope plays in the mindset of a sick person. Hope is a commanding thing. Would I have been as high functioning after my diagnosis if the doctor said, "you have three to six months to live?" One can only imagine what goes through the brain of someone trying to process that news. It is a death sentence without the prison bars. My uncle received that report and elected to live as much as he could. He road his motorcycle, played golf, took his family to Niagara Falls, went to the movies with his wife, even contacted Canada for a supreme series of injections to prolong his life. By ordering that medicine from across the border, was he filled with hope?

On August 9th, 2001, he was told he had three to six months to live. He died on February 9th, 2002. <u>Exactly six months to the day</u>. So what does that tell you? Either the doctor had one damn good meter on the life expectancy of his patient, or my uncle was given a **DEAD**line, and his brain subconsciously absorbed that curfew and surrendered as scheduled. It seems to be too much of a coincidence when people die on a timetable. When doctors issue a three to six months pass, why aren't the people dying on the second week of the fifth month or the third week of the fourth month? Why does the life seem to run out on the last month the doctor gave them? What if the doctors gave my uncle six months to a year to live? Would he have lived to hear the fireworks on another Independence Day? Are the limitations of life in our body or in our mind? Do we put too much stock in the doctors? Do we allow them to decide our fate right down to the day we pass? If patients had a placebo injection of HOPE perhaps the duration of their time on earth would be more pleasurable and extend beyond three to six months.

I was lost in thoughts of hope for days. Should doctors keep our glasses half full even if we say we can handle the truth? What is their responsibility to us? It's a hard call. Some patients in <u>The Anatomy of Hope</u> outlived their prognoses by years. Would the truth have brought them to expiration sooner? Is hope really the fountain of youth wherein one drink keeps all of the aging evils away? Hope brought me to the computer. Hope made me want to learn more.

When I asked The Bow Tie Bastard the function of the thyroid, he flatly replied, "It's the gas pedal in your car. It makes you go." A cool analogy no doubt, but I needed more. I decided to begin with the basics. Elementary research 101 began in my computer armoire. I opened Webster's New Collegiate Dictionary (1977 Edition) and found the following enlightening information:

> **Thyroid** adj. #1. of relating to or being a large endocrine of craniate vertebrates lying at the base of the neck and producing esp. the hormone thyroxine. #2. The chief cartilage of the larynx

> **Thyroid** noun. #1. Thyroid gland or cartilage; also: a part (of an artery or nerve), associated with either of these.

> **Thyroidectomy:** Surgical removal of the thyroid gland tissue.

I was having a thyroidectomy or removal of the thyroid gland tissue. I much preferred The Bow Tie Bastard's break down of "the gas pedal in my car". Vehicles need <u>gas</u> to <u>run</u>. Would pills have a high enough octane to replace my thyroid? My plus-sized ass hadn't run since the Reagan administration, so I knew I could live without running. But could I still walk without a thyroid? I thought about my energy levels, my weight and my adrenalin. I broke down the word **adrena**line and began thinking about my **adrenal** glands. Years back in college, I gained about eighty pounds in less than three months. To make matters sexier, the hair on my head was falling out and landing on my chin in the form of a beard. My skin texture was changing and I wasn't sleeping. The doctors said that I had an adrenal gland disorder. I think I gave up an entire swimming pool of blood in the Boston blood labs. Test after test, new things were added to my veins. Things like cortisone and cortisol.

During the testing period, I graduated from both college and my health insurance. For years I lived without insurance, overweight, and over worried about my health. I suffered through electrolysis hair removal sessions waiting for a doctor to figure out what was wrong. There wasn't a "Former Skinny Bitch" support club in my town for girls previously known for being "HOT." I lived on fad diets, and wasted gym memberships, with the hope that someday I'd look normal again. Shortly after I walked down the aisle, a little plastic card arrived in the mail. My health insurance was the passport to a diagnosis of Polycystic Ovarian Syndrome. Could my ovaries, adrenal glands, and thyroid have been connected all along?

From there, I started researching cancer and thyroid sites. I spent a lot of time on the American Cancer Society site at www.cancer.org. I loved another site that seemed to be a little more specific to my particular cancer called The Thyroid Cancer Survivors Association, Inc. www.thyca.org. I also love reading the info on checkyourneck.com. My thyroid research brought me to a gorgeous word. BUTTERFLY! -The insect that starts out as a worm and ends up flying high above the land with celebrated color, full of majesty. Butterflies dance carefree, as light as feathers, all over the world. I wanted to be carefree and light again.

As I mentioned before, spring time was my link to sanity. Whenever the cancer was too much, I'd say a prayer asking the Blessed Mother Mary to help me cross the finish line through winter into spring. After the prayer, I'd envision butterflies, dragonflies, birds, daffodils, tulips, lilacs, and grass. I'd set up a daydream picnic, surrounded by warm breezes and the scent of hyacinth with bees buzzing around the buds on the trees. Sometimes, I'd take my fantasy to the ocean. Since it was my reverie, I'd add the elements from my home and yard. I pictured my bed on the shoreline, and placed my lilac trees and heritage roses in the sand. I invited my Carolina Wrens, Sparrows, Chickadees, Nuthatches, and Cardinals to fly along the beach. I added my butterfly loving Heliopsis and Coreopsis flowers to line the ocean, filling my horizon with fluttering fairies in Monarch hues. Some days my whimsy future world was all that could restore my spirits. I recommend having a place filled with future to take your mind when your heart is heavy.

One low afternoon, I pulled my cart over in the grocery store to transcend to that vivacious place. Moments later, I heard a strident

"EXCUSE ME!" from an impatient shopper. Her body actually grazed my arm as she passed. At the risk of becoming aisle nine road kill, I had to snap out of my dream and continue on my not-so-merry way. Those were the days when I wish I had a painted t-shirt. "Walk around me, I have cancer and I'm trying to work it out!" Or "Carrots shouldn't be purchased in a can. I have cancer walk around me."

I feel compelled to add that we all have the occasional impulse to be rude. We have all sat behind the person at the traffic light waiting for them to move. Some of us honk. Some of us yell. Some of us flash the peace sign with only one finger up. I used to be that girl. (The honker, that is.) My sisters used to say that I needed a support group to kick the habit of horn honking. Now, I try to consider what is going on in the world of the person. Whether in the car ahead of me or blocking the produce, everyone has a story. Rather than get upset, I try to remember how I felt during my suffering. I take a deep breath, cut them some slack, and hope they are merely enjoying a lovely daydream.

Back to wondering how I caught thyroid cancer...Here is what I have come up with. Mum took us to the dentist regularly as children. I had x-rays there. A drunk driver hit me when I was eleven years old. I was riding a Shetland pony on a quiet back road in my hometown. The car came out of nowhere and creamed us. I had <u>extensive</u> head and neck x-rays. As an adult, I had my wisdom teeth removed. More x-rays. My husband worked a nuclear power plant for a few years. I did his laundry, touched his clothes, picked him up from work a few times...HELL, I lived with him. Did I pick something up then? As a child, our family friends lived along high-tension wires miles away from a power plant. Whenever we played in the backyard we were feet away from the power lines. I drank well water out of their sink. I showered in their house. Was I exposed then? I grew up in the Cranberry Capital of the World. I remember riding my bike as helicopters sprayed pesticides all over the bogs in the 1970's. I swam in lakes connected to cranberry bogs. I remember watching Gypsy Moth pesticides float down from helicopters in the early 1980's as I played outside. Our family used to rent a cottage on a Cape Cod beach that has recently been labeled a HOT SPOT for cancer. Did I pick something up then?

As a teenager, I visited my father who raised me on an army base weekend after weekend. Military bases used as training grounds contain high levels of radiation. Was I exposed then? In high school, I lived a few houses away from a brass and plating company. Our house was also seated on railroad tracks. That entire section of our town has high reports of cancer and has been linked to amyotrophic lateral sclerosis (ALS), also called Lou Gehrig's disease. Did I catch something back then? As an adult, I talk on my cell phone all day long. I use a microwave. I fly in commercial planes. For years I flew in my biological fathers' plane. I swim at a beach on the Cape near an air force base. I've heard perchlorate (a persistent and problematic pollutant) from the jets can seep into the ground and wash into the ocean. I've heard perchlorate can harm thyroid tissue. Did I pick something up then? I use a computer and I watch TV. I'm sure I've walked barefoot on grass lawns that have been enhanced by chemicals. Most of my friends have granite counter tops. It has been said that they emit radiation. I eat food that contains ingredients I cannot pronounce. For years, I ate meat loaded with anti-biotics and hormones. How did I get this seemingly *ENVIRONMENTAL* cancer? To this day, I have no idea.

I am still intrigued by the idea that something in our country is making us sick.

I met a woman who said, "Oh, thyroid cancer runs in my family. My mom had it, my grandmother had it, my aunt had it and my sister had it." Jokingly I said, "Wow, do you guys live near a power plant or something?" Her entire face changed and she replied, "Yes, they do live near one. *Right* near one. Why does that mean anything?" I assured her that I wasn't an expert on thyroid cancer, and that she should speak to an endocrinologist.

My friend sent a magazine article about the relationship between thyroid disorders and whip lash. There was a section about car accidents and the long-term effects they may have on your thyroid. The story was singing the praises of chiropractic care. According to the article, a neck vertebra out of place can push on the thyroid region causing hypothyroidism. I spoke to a chiropractor friend of mine about this hypothesis, and he agreed. He said the fatigue of hypothyroidism seems to be lifted once the spine is in proper alignment. In the late 1970's, most of our parents didn't take us to see a chiropractor after an injury. I'm sure my neck was out of whack after being hit by a car.

Sometimes I think my thyroid was the weakest link in my body. The cancer to which we are all predisposed, found that weakness and set up shop. Over the past twelve years, my weight has gone up dramatically. I had a facial hair explosion. I was losing hair on my head, my skin and nails were really dry. I was having problems sleeping. Granted, most all of these symptoms fit the profile of P.C.O.S., but they also fit the profile of hypothyroidism. How long had the cause of my body transformation gone undiagnosed?

After reading about the thyroid and thyroid cancer, I began reading about staging. I am embarrassed to admit that I never asked what stage of cancer I was in. I suppose in the back of my mind, I didn't really want to know about **stages**. For a girl who grew up singing her heart out on stage under the lights, suddenly the very word stage seemed unbelievably limiting.

From staging, I moved on to reading about the importance of a second opinion. I'm sure some people love the Bow Tie Bastard. To be fair, I've met a few women who couldn't say enough about him. Incidentally, their scars looked phenomenal. The B.T.B. was not a good match for me. Please shop around until you find what you need. Most often, thyroid cancer is a slow moving cancer. In most cases, this cancer can wait a few weeks for you to find the surgeon who is right for you. Many say papillary thyroid cancer is the *good* cancer. Do not settle for a surgeon just because you are scared. Peace of mind is the best medicine and will significantly impact your recovery.

I understand why Dr. Smith asked me not to go on-line, but I wasn't afraid. My research helped me feel in the loop. I couldn't wait to meet the next surgeon. Nothing in the research scared me. Before my research, I was more fearful of the unknown. That's life. We fear the things most foreign to us.

With the investigation behind me, my next objective was to make the most out of the days leading up to meeting with the new surgeon. You'll never guess what I did during that time. I planned a gala for 250 guests, wrote a eulogy for my own funeral, recorded a CD and scheduled a photo shoot to preserve my perfect, pretty, and unscarred neck. What can I say? Cancer made me a bit manic.

You Gotta Have Friends

O<small>N</small> D<small>ECEMBER</small> 30TH, 2004, <small>MY</small> S<small>TATE</small> Representative friend called me at home. He wanted to set up a meeting to discuss an upcoming project he wanted me to be a part of. I said, "While I have you, I need to let you know that I have thyroid cancer. I'm not really sure what kind of commitment I can make to you this time around." After offering to help me find a surgeon and research the best methods of treatment, he said, "How about I come over tomorrow morning so we can talk."

His visit was a great diversion. The minute we made breakfast plans, I began planning our menu and table setting. I polished my favorite server set and flatware. I washed my beloved vintage set of china tennis plates covered in violets. I cleaned my favorite platters and cake plates, purchased and arranged two-dozen purple roses, ironed my purple napkins, cleaned my water goblets and juice glasses, and then sat down to plan the bill of fare. I prepared two varieties of quiche, butter pound cake with lemon curd and blueberries, coffee cake and bagels with cream cheese, strawberries and whipped cream, assorted cheeses with cracked pepper water crackers, grapes and cold ham, Danish and chocolates. Our beverages were tea, coffee, orange juice with sliced lime, and water with mint leaves. I have to say everything looked *stunning*. It was the best way I could think of to say goodbye to 2004.

As I stood at the table covered in banquet finery, I couldn't help but think I had prepared a festival feast for the Gods. I needed them all to shine good fortune down on me for the upcoming New Year. I'm sure my state rep crony thought the spread was a tribute to his visit. Secretly, I wanted the presentation of my gifts to pay off in 2005. A huge lover of Greek mythology, I was certain somewhere in the skies the spirit of Athena, (Goddess of reason, knowledge, literature and arts) would call on Apollo, (God of music) to discuss protecting my voice. Together they would send a text message to Dionysus, (God of wine and <u>patron of the arts</u>) to ask The Goddess Hera if she would pitch in since she watches over married women! Once they determined whether or not they would help me, they could text message the God Hermes. He is the messenger to all other Gods. No doubt having God's personal email address, he could send him a brief text note saying "Lorna has honored us with the fruits of the land, (Danish has fruit in it!) arranged on King's fine china along with treasures such as *gold* forks, knives and spoons (I really did use my gold set that day) in perfect harmony. Rose oil is permeating the walls. She has served her penance. OH ALMIGHTY LORD, PLEASE FOR THE LOVE OF APHRODITE, CUT HER SOME SLACK IN 2005! If you need to discuss this, I'll be at Starbucks. Peace out, Hermes."

At 9:00AM on New Year's Eve morning, I greeted my state rep friend at the door. I flashed my classic, "I'm doing really well. How are you?" face and we made our way in to the dining room. His mission was to appoint me as the chairperson of an enormous benefit gala celebrating the work he had done on a bill. The bill contained an incentive designed to encourage the Motion Picture Industry to make films in Massachusetts by providing at tax break. Rather than shooting in other less expensive places that resemble New England, the bill would encourage film makers to set up camp in Massachusetts. The goal was to bring millions of dollars to my home state each year though the industry and tourism. Saying yes to his proposal to plan the gala could enable me to work shoulder-to-shoulder with some of the local big wigs. Heavy hitters in the biz including producers, writers, publicists, celebrities and casting agents were to be on the guest list. As he walked me through the job description he said, "Of course, I was going to ask you all of this before I knew you had cancer."

My state rep pal needed a soup-to-nuts leader. From elegant wedding showers, baby showers, birthdays and anniversary parties, I had dabbled in event planning for years. From there, I graduated to coordinating a few weddings for my friends. That led to being the campaign manager for several local political elections. I produced a few local demonstrations for a world-renowned psychic medium. I had produced over sixty plays, musicals, recitals, concerts and film projects. With that experience behind me, I knew that I could handle the task of planning a political gala. I just didn't know if I could handle it with cancer.

This gig was totally different than anything I had ever done. In addition to planning the menu, renting the hall, decorating the hall, selecting centerpieces, creating favors, lining up musicians, assembling a live and silent auction which included finding enticing items to bid on, designing an invitation and tickets, formulating the guest list, creating a keepsake program for all of the guests and contacting all of the press, I had to get in touch with state reps, senators and congressman, both to invite them to be on our host committee and to see if they were available to attend the event. Since this was a benefit to celebrate my friends work for the film industry, I was expected to contact several publicists and agents to encourage celebrity support for the event. I'd need to find high profile auction items, a key-note speaker, and at least four celebrities to sign autographs and meet the guests. I'd need people to work at the event as greeters, auctioneers, box office support and photographers.

I was honored that my state rep friend asked me to spearhead the gala, but I doubted my ability to rise to the occasion. I told him I needed some time to think things over. The event was slated for the first weekend in May 2005. My surgery was most likely going to be in late January or early February. My radioactive iodine treatment would take place early March. I wasn't concerned about the actual surgery slowing me down. I was concerned about my energy level after the hypo-thyroid period.

My friend is a nurse. She had thyroid cancer a year before my diagnosis. She was exhausted for months during her recovery. Several other thyroid cancer patients told me that the hypo-thyroid stage in preparation for the radiation was the bumpiest part of the road. A few of my thyroid cancer colleagues were unable to lift their heads from their pillows to function anytime after 4:00 P.M. each day. One woman told me it felt like she was going through puberty, pregnancy and menopause, as she was slowly being built back up on varying doses of Synthroid after her radioactive iodine. I had no idea what to expect. All I knew was that in my thirty-three years, I had only been really sick once. I got the chicken pox at the age of twenty-seven. I was down for about nine days and moped around for the week following. Other than that, I had never even missed a day of work due to illness.

After vacillating for about an hour, I decided to decline the offer. Two minutes after my state rep friend left my house, my phone rang. It was my friend Vivian calling from Naples, Florida, to wish me a Happy New Year. I heard Vivian's warm, Jackie O sounding voice say, "Hello, my darling. How are you? I've been thinking of you. I heard about your news. I wanted to wish you all good things in the upcoming year."

Vivian is a breast, lung, and brain cancer survivor. I met her on a visit to Naples in October of 2004, a few days before Dr. Smith felt my lump. After only five days with her, I felt like I had known her my entire life. As I drank in her stories about survival and hope, I realized that God spared her life three times so that she could remain on earth to inspire and bring clarity to all that needed healing. She was a land angel. The final day of our visit, I told my friend (her niece) that I was meant to meet her. I knew our connection was going to signify something in my life. It was one of those experiences that you cannot put your finger on but you know happened for a reason.

Vivian went on to say, "How are you *really* doing, Lorna?" To most people, my response is always "I'm fine!" I opted for truth with Vivian. I told her that I was merely hanging in there. "May I give you some advice?" she said. "Try to keep your <u>mind busy</u> with projects or work that isn't ordinary or mundane. Focus on <u>new</u> projects and <u>new</u> work that will keep your mind active and strong. Stimulate your brain with goals for the future. Think <u>down the road</u> and not so much in the now. Try knitting a blanket or something out of the ordinary. This helped me a lot when I was sick. You have to keep your mind active." Her message hit me like a ton of bricks. Talk about timing! My state rep friend had just delivered Vivian's remedy in my lap, and yet I doubted my own strength and was about to concede.

I thanked her for the call and promised to keep her updated on my progress. As soon as I hung up the phone I called on a few of my most creative and available friends. Within an hour they arrived on my doorstep. Thank goodness a majority of my feast was still on the table. Ladies are more agreeable when they have luscious treats in their bellies. Seated around a table of friends and fine food, my opening monologue began with, "I was offered a great opportunity today, but I cannot do it alone. I would love your help. I think we can accomplish a wonderful feat and have a blast together. Your support would allow me to glance on the horizon of my future. It will take me out of the <u>now</u> and give me something to focus on. I'll do as much as I can, but if I begin to fall, I'm going to need to land on you. If it's too much, you'll have to catch me and possibly finish the project without me. I have no idea how my recovery is going to be. What do you think?"

All but fair-weather-friends, my cherubs launched into the mission with open wings. Knowing that I needed this diversion, they were willing to sacrifice a lot of their time and energy to join the crusade. At that point, a notebook came out and we began brainstorming! As we scribbled thoughts and ideas down, my mind went to Vivian. She was so right. Hours had passed with my friends around the dining room table. I hadn't once thought about cancer. Amen!

On New Years Day morning, I wrote down a list of things I wanted to accomplish in 2005. I wanted to go to Italy. I wanted to sort through my old clothes. I wanted to select a ring for my one-year anniversary of wellness. I wanted to book a photo shoot to preserve my body as God made it- free of any scars on my neck. I wanted to schedule a follow up shoot to capture my new image with the scar as part of my acceptance. I wanted to record a CD of my voice to safeguard the sound God gave me. I wanted to organize my pantry. I wanted to bake breads and cookies.

I wanted to build a theatre for my students. I wanted to volunteer my time for a charity. I wanted to lose weight. I wanted to print all of the photos on the memory card of my digital camera. I wanted to buy a convertible antique car, preferably a 1971 Cadillac commemorating the year I was born. I wanted to finish all of the books I was reading. I wanted to see the Grand Canyon. I wanted to buy a long-haired, sable Dachshund puppy and name her Brinsley. I wanted to drive to the beach near my mother's house every day after work in the summer and float on my boogie board for hours. I wanted to mend any relationships in bad standing. I wanted to forgive the people who had hurt me. I wanted to watch five years worth of South Park episodes on DVD with my husband. I wanted to be totally honest with everyone. I wanted to paint the hallway off of my dining room, and cover it with pictures of my friends and family. I wanted to sit on the steps in that hall and get lost in all of the memories. I wanted to mail my grandmother a letter or postcard once a week. I wanted to tell people how much they mean to me. I wanted to finally see STAR WARS, GONE WITH THE WIND, IT'S A WONDERFUL LIFE, and CITIZEN CANE. I wanted to highlight my hair. I wanted to spend time with my family. I wanted to be a better wife. I wanted to be a better sister. I wanted to be a better daughter. I wanted to plant more flowers. I wanted to plant a tree. I wanted to be a better friend. I wanted to take long rides. I wanted to try new restaurants. In 2005, I wanted to **live**.

On January 17, 2005, Massachusetts observed Martin Luther King Day. I had received a lime green invitation in the mail a few days prior that read "Join us for a Celebratory Funeral to set Lorna's Thyroid Free!" (Date, time, place, contact info) "Please bring either a scarf or necklace of yours for Lorna to borrow during her recuperation. This way she will be thinking of us as she wears our borrowed treasures." I'm sure this notion has given you some idea of the diversity of the friends I have in my life! The Ya Ya's as I call them, (inspired from the Divine Secrets of the Ya Ya Sisterhood) are all highly-creative, people. My mum, sisters, uncle, mother-in-law, and Roger also made the invitation list. They, too, fit the silhouette of Ya Ya.

Insomnia showed up uninvited and unannounced the night before the funeral. Around 2:00A.M., I sat at the computer and began writing the eulogy for my thyroid. Four pages later, I had seriously put that gland to rest without any sorrow or regret. Ashes to ashes, dust to dust. As I wrote the eulogy, I couldn't help but wonder why thyroid gland replacement surgery wasn't an option. I mean we donate organs, right? Why not have thyroid gland donors?

The title of my eulogy was "Farewell, Mr. T". Everyone attending the funeral seemed to be reading He's Just Not That into You by Greg Behrendt and Liz Tuccillo. To keep things funny, I tied into the philosophies in their book. I think it's sort of telling that I referred to my thyroid as a MALE for the entire first page of the speech. Let's face it, my thyroid wasn't making me happy, wasn't doing his job, wasn't respecting me, wasn't respecting my body, and ultimately, wanted to control me. I wasn't going to allow it. My dead beat thyroid brought out my inner Donna Summer. I found myself singing her rendition of *I WILL SURVIVE*. I was too much woman for that thyroid. I was too "all that and a bag of chips" to continue living with a dysfunctional man in my house. So the thyroid was being served eviction papers.

The second page of the eulogy moved away from the seemingly Jerry Springer set and became more authentic. It recaptured the exact moment when I found out I had cancer (something I had never shared with any of my friends and co-workers) and how the knowledge of my disease helped me to slow down and appreciate life. The eulogy went on to mention my newfound strength and how my research and questionnaires gave me a sense of empowerment. I wanted my friends to know that we all have choices. We don't have to trail along like lambs to slaughter when we get sick. I thanked the people I love for embracing my quirky ways of dealing with my predicament. I thanked them for being the most remarkable support system a person with or without cancer could ever hope for. I told them not to worry about Mr. T. Jokingly, I told them that I consulted with my famous medium friend. She saw my thyroid crossing over without any problems. Now you really know how nuts I am!

I let my friends know that in my psyche, they'd be cruising with me down the hall of the hospital to bid farewell to my thyroid. Together we'd sit in a big white 1971 (the year I was born) Cadillac Convertible. We'd listen to the radio and laugh in my friendship wagon all the way to the O. R. Every single person in that room (and some who were not able to join us for the funeral) would accompany me in spirit in the backseat of my Caddy until all of the cancer was removed from my body. In their company, I wouldn't be afraid. Drained from working on the presentation, I went off to bed thinking *I cannot believe I just wrote a eulogy for my thyroid? What next, Lorna? What other wacky things will cancer encourage you to do?*

The next day, I dressed for the funeral. I selected a deep red v-neck shirt. My ambition was to pull the power and might off of the red shirt. Let's face it; I also wanted to show off my perfect neck line for the last time in front of a majority of my posse. I wanted a lot of neck cleavage. As I adorned my lips with my intense red lipstick, I thought of Geralyn Lucas, author of "Why I Wore Lipstick to My Mastectomy." In the last line of the after-word she wrote: "Each time I wear lipstick, I am emboldened by the memory of that day: the IV line in my arm, my surgical gown on with my butt hanging out, and my perfectly applied lipstick. I swear I can still taste the hope." –Her use of the word HOPE was seared into my soul the second I read that parting sentence.

Armed with my red v-neck T-shirt, I felt ready to psychologically bury my cancer-ridden thyroid into the ground. When we pulled up to the funeral, I saw the vehicles of so many people I loved. Walking into the funeral was tremendously cathartic. Everything was covered in butterflies. The theme seemed to take over every room in the home. The cake had butterflies on it, the centerpiece of fantastic spring flowers was arranged in a planter with butterflies all over it, and the children in attendance were holding butterfly wands. Butterfly lollipops were all over the tables with butterfly stickers and erasers. The program for the afternoon was garnished with butterflies. There were even butterfly henna tattoos for guests who wanted to get a little **inked**. Music was playing and everyone was smiling. The dining room table, kitchen table and center-island were all covered with my favorite foods and treats. Best of all, no one was looking at me with eyes filled with pity or concern. The vibe in the house was buzzing with love and hope. That was truly the best part about the day.

The funeral service began with my friend welcoming everyone. She is a great writer and her introduction was top notch, filled with humor and heart. She read a really funny poem about my thyroid. When she finished, she turned the floor over to me. I read my piece. Sharing tears and laughter with my friends made the experience liberating. The presentation of gifts was next in order. I received the most amazing souvenirs and keepsakes. Many friends gave me scarves from their personal collections. All of my gifts were marvelous but one was especially fascinating. Hidden under blankets on a sewing bust form, sat a totally glammed-up hospital gown. My friends sewed sexy hot pink boa on the collar and cuffs, and adorned it with a gorgeous hot pink rhinestone butterfly pin. I nearly wet my pants from laughter when I saw that thing. It was a work of art that encapsulated their definition of me. In their eyes I was still funky, glamorous and fun. I was not a cancer patient.

The next part of the celebration was called "The Dance of the Ya Ya's." Most everyone danced in the living room to the song "You Gotta Have Friends" off of one of the Bette Midler CD's. The children were holding my hands and boogying all around me. The moment was magical. I was hugging people (by the way, I was never a hugger) on the dance floor. I floated around as freely as a butterfly. After the song, we feasted on fine food and shared our prayers for 2005. The favors were fine-looking tea cups filled with crushed lavender seed potpourri topiaries and moss. The favors symbolized my future and helped me visualize all of the mornings I have to drink tea. Every sip out of the tea cup would remind me of a time in my life when my friends and family rallied around me to form a seal of love, approval, strength and security. Thoughts of my thyroid funeral still move me to tears.

When I tell people about my thyroid funeral they usually ask, "Did you bury something in the back yard in a shoe box? Was it some new age thing your doctor encouraged you to do as a way of preparing for your surgery?" I always laugh and say, "No, just an insanely like minded group of people celebrating the future of a friend."

Handshakes

I WORE BLACK THE DAY I MET The Bow Tie Bastard. The day I met my new surgeon, I dressed in a baby blue shirt, gray slacks and pearls. I was sick over the thought of not liking him or worse, having him not like me. Although the "C" was encompassing my life, I didn't have a plan C. Plan B (to get a second opinion) was as far as I had gone. I condensed my questionnaire and gave my mother an unobtrusive pad for note taking. I was trying to rev myself up for a new beginning with one of the most experienced surgeons in our country. Why was I so worried? Had I really been that traumatized by The Bow Tie Bastard? How could a physician who never even touched my skin, leave such a scar?

As the artist formally known as "strong and courageous" I questioned where my might had gone? I was the kid who started her own business from scratch at age twenty-four without an ounce of financial backing. Where were my street smarts? I was the girl who told jokes to the men in the House Chamber of the Massachusetts State House moments before I sang for them. I could charm anyone. Where was my confidence? I was the girl who was paid $200.00 per hour on special assignment as a consultant in her field before the age of thirty. I had brains. What was I so afraid of? I was the fighter who had worked three jobs for years, 70-80 hour weeks just to build a resume and reputation in the business. Why did I question my stamina? I was the one who sang in front of sold out crowd of 34,000 people. I had talent. I was the girl who cooked food for anyone who was sick, had lost a loved one, or had a baby. I gave money to people in need. I volunteered. I was a good person. Why did I doubt my worth? <u>Where was I</u>? When had I become a creampuff? Did a five foot, six inch, bow tie wearing man really rob me of my identity?

The day of my diagnosis, my world fell around me. The first step to pasting the sky back up was getting in the car to meet surgeon number two-Dr. Gregory Randolph M.D.

The receptionist at his office was hip, friendly and young. She greeted me with, "Oh, hey there, Lorna. How was the traffic? I have some paperwork for you." Her tone resembled the chitchat of two girlfriends at the local diner having a plate of whole wheat blueberry pancakes. Just then, a nurse called my name. My entourage (Roger and mum) accompanied me into a small office. A nurse joined us and began setting up a very hi-tech looking machine. She attempted to spray something up my nose. "Excuse me," I said. "I'm not here for *that*. I am here to discuss having surgery with Dr. Randolph." With a bewildered look she replied, "I know, <u>this </u>is what we do for<u> that</u>." I respectfully encouraged her to hold off until I had a moment to meet with the doctor.

Just then, surgeon number two entered the room. Extending his hand to me he said, "Hello, I'm Greg." *Did he just say GREG?* "This must be your..." "Husband and mother," I replied. "Hello there," he said, while shaking their hands. Thank you for coming in today." I wanted to say, "Excuse me, did you just <u>thank us</u> for coming in today, **GREG**? Or do I need my hearing checked? I mean, after all, *you* are a surgeon, right? I think you are an E.N.T. as well, so can you check my ears?" (I am smiling right now as I type.) I will never forget what a difference his salutation made. In the theatre we call that <u>making the most of your entrance</u>. I began smirking to my husband. The urge to bust into a Sally Fields impression of "I like him, I *really* like him" was overwhelming!

Dr. GREG Randolph went over my file. As he spoke, I was humming Beethoven's 9th Symphony **ODE TO JOY** in my head. GREG was **the one**. The moment needed underscoring. A few moments later, he drew a sketch to demonstrate the procedure. He put a face on the drawing. I asked, "Is that me?" He replied, "Yes, I'd like to illustrate what I am going to do during the procedure." Then I asked, "Would you mind giving me some eyelashes? I think I'm going to need eyelashes to prepare for what comes next." Within seconds he added long strokes of fabulous mascara-laden eyes to the illustration. In my head, I wrapped my hands around him with a huge hug. *HE HEARD ME. HE IS LISTENING and he is willing to accept my quirkiness.* I wanted to display his artwork on my fridge under a thyroid shaped magnet. He honored my ridiculousness. By my standards, he was perfect! To spin from the movie **Jerry McQuire**, he had me at the handshake, but the eyelashes sealed the deal. He was so thorough and meticulous in his presentation I hardly had any questions. When I asked questions, he responded as if they were the most important questions in the world and he was hearing them for the first time.

His voice was soft, unthreatening, informative, and confident. His eyes were patient and understanding. He communicated with my family as if we were all sitting around living room talking. There was nothing antiseptic in his presentation. He even <u>laughed</u> a few times. The man was <u>real</u>. I was no longer afraid. Testimony to my lack of fear came when he walked over to the machine the nurse had prepped and said, "Now I am going to put a scope down your nose so that I can see what is going on." Normally, the idea of something as long as a snake snaking down my nose would have sent my **freak on** into over-drive. I trusted Greg and that trust allowed me to stay calm. *The Bow Tie Bastard didn't do this. Old school Bow Tie Bastard!*

Dr. Randolph explained the importance of recurrent laryngeal nerve monitoring and how his system would help protect my voice in surgery. In short, he told me that the recurrent laryngeal nerve, which is located near the thyroid gland, supplies motor function to the larynx (voice box) and that damage to this nerve during surgery, can result in a patient losing the ability to speak. Monitoring the nerve continuously during surgery can help avoid damage to the nerve and preserve the patient's voice. Dr. Randolph is responsible for the development and use of recurrent laryngeal nerve (RLN) monitoring during thyroid surgery. He travels the world raising awareness for the benefits of this work.

At the conclusion of our visit he asked if I had any questions. My response shocked me. I couldn't believe the words came out of my mouth, as I replied, "No. I am really looking forward to the surgery. Thank you so much for your time." No doubt my smile was unstoppable, but was I really looking forward to the surgery? I hadn't been that cheery since early October before I knew anything had gone off course in my body. I think I skipped out of his office. The minute I was in the Jeep, I called the B.T.B.'s office. I told his receptionist that I had just left my second opinion meeting and that Greg was a better fit. I apologized for not coming to a decision sooner.

Although I may have deserved it, I wasn't prepared for the spanking I received. She repeated everything I had said to her. "You just had a second opinion? You are <u>canceling</u> your surgery? You are sorry for the delay? Sorry? You **never** should have kept your name in our book if you intended on going elsewhere. These appointments take months to schedule. You held up surgery for another person. I'll be *SURE* to take your name out of our book!" The next thing I heard was a SLAM. That is correct, folks, she hung up on me.

I felt like an ass for bringing her to a boiling point. After all, it wasn't her fault the Bow Tie Bastard behaved so badly. In my defense, the whole surgery/second opinion thing was new to me. I wish doctors distributed protocol packets or etiquette sachets upon the first meeting. I truly had no idea how things worked.

I've always been an aggressive consumer. When it comes to purchasing my vehicles, I spend hours reviewing data and driving around dealerships. Why on earth would I have done less when selecting a surgeon? I had to shop around. Here I am being a real shit~ if the B.T.B. truly wanted me to stay in his book, he may have considered being more kind. If you ever find yourself in my shoes, kindly ask about the office protocol. In the long run it seems best not to burn any bridges.

With only seven days left until my surgery, I mapped out my

immediate goals for implementation. My first call was to the recording studio. I told the owner that I had thyroid cancer and less than a week to get my voice on disc. Just as I was about to explain the severity of my situation he said, "I have thyroid issues myself. I totally understand where you are coming from. I am familiar with the risks associated with this surgery. We'll get you in here right away." My next call was to photography studio. I was following up with an email I sent a few days prior explaining my state of emergency. The owner got on the phone and said "I have had my thyroid removed. We'll take care of you. What day works for you?"

Back-to-back phone calls with back-to-back thyroid issues. Coincidence? Kismet? Or a sad commentary on how many Americans are suffering from thyroid disease as a result of something in the environment making us sick? If the photographer and the man from the recording studio hadn't had thyroid issues, would they have respected the immediacy of my projects? I stopped by my school to select music for the CD. As I read through all of the songs in our library my heart felt hesitant. I thought about the superstitious people who refuse to have a baby shower until the child is born. By preserving my voice on disc was I messing with fate? By preparing myself for the worst, was I setting myself up for the worst? OR was I just being typical me, the efficient and organized girl who shops for Christmas in August on the tax-free day?

I thought about all of the children in my life. I envisioned them growing up hearing stories of how I used to sing the speckled frog song to them. I thought about my mother. An amazing singer in her own right, Lord knows I inherited my voice from her. Naturally, if things went wrong on the table, she'd take comfort knowing her daughters' voice was forever alive on a disc in her care. That brought me to my grandmother Concetta. Her mother, my great grandmother Jovanina Gandolfo, sang Opera in Boston. Without question, she'd want a memento of the voice her mother passed down to me through her daughter.

Lastly, I thought of the children I might have some day. I thought about how vacant bedtime would seem void of lullabies. My mother was the lady of lullabies. As a child I had secretly hoped to follow in her footsteps. Despite my amazing new surgeon, it seemed too smug to assume that my vocal instrument would remain untouched. I decided to approach the CD as an Easter card rather than a plan B if my voice was ruined. I decided to mail the CD's out as thank-you/Easter notes to everyone who helped me during my illness. I found solace in the idea of having a CD at home to remind me of what a blessing it was to be able to sing- even if only for the first thirty-three years of my life. My voice was my exclusive gift from God. I needed to wrap it up for safekeeping.

Ducks in a Row

I AM A 33 ¾ YEAR OLD woman, daughter, granddaughter, wife, sister, auntie, step-mother, godmother, goddaughter, daughter-in-law, friend, niece, cousin, teacher, mentor, actor, singer, entrepreneur, leader, risk-taker, role model, full scholarship conservatory graduate, that just happens to have a sick thyroid. My thyroid has cancer. I do not. This may change me, but I will not allow this to define me.

January 22, 2005
Blizzard of '05
11:06 P.M.

Like so many other nights, I was unable to sleep. The ten o'clock news team had just finished warning us of the first blizzard in 2005. With nearly three feet of snow already on the ground, I had a feeling I'd be in the house for a few days. I decided to get out of bed to begin drafting my CD jacket and insert. The little ditty above became my mantra.

Snow had drifted along the picture window of my dining room, covering the first row of glass panes. Our home was engulfed in fluffy iridescent flakes with drifts up to six feet high on the two acre property. As I sat in the dining room typing away on the computer, I felt fortified. The snow felt like an embrace. My soul seemed blanketed. There was stillness in my core that evening. That stillness became the place that I pulled strength from in the weeks that followed.

In search for a few of my favorite quotes about love, friendship and kindness, I started opening my books. I wanted to express my gratitude on every page of the CD jacket. I selected the following quotes from the following authors.

> Giving is so often thought of in terms of the things we give, but our greatest giving is of our time, and kindness, and even comfort for those who need it. We look on these gifts as unimportant - until we need them.
>
> Joyce Sequichie Hifler

> People are like stained-glass windows. They sparkle and shine when the sun is out, but when the darkness sets in, their true beauty is revealed only if there is a light from within.
>
> Elizabeth Kübler-Ross

> I do not wish to treat my friendships daintily, but with roughest courage. When they are real, they are not glass threads or frost-work, but the solidest thing we know.
>
> Ralph Waldo Emerson

From there, I wrote the introduction. A copy is on my web site. Everything in my life was on the line, so that is what I named the project. It was imperative that I wrote the intro before I knew the outcome of the surgery. I needed the words to be vivid. I didn't want to look back and write how I thought I felt about losing my voice once it was already gone. On the Line was an invigorating interruption from cancer. With the CD jacket saved on file, I tried to rest.

I glanced out at the whimsical wonderland wondering what we'd wake up to find. As I turned off the kitchen light, I noticed the clock read 1:45 A.M. My surgery with The Bow Tie Bastard was scheduled for January 24th, 2005. I never would have made it into the city. My mum says that everything happens for a reason. Clearly, my surgery with The Bow Tie Bastard was never meant to be. I think I was supposed to meet the B.T.B. By meeting him, I knew exactly what I was looking for in Greg, surgeon number two.

Covered in ice and snow, the lilac trees were bowing over pressing against our bedroom windows. In the eight years we had lived in our home, I never recalled seeing the limbs that distressed. The storm was stomping down on us. Talk radio was spewing out statistics regarding the storm. It seemed as though this blizzard had tied or beaten the legendary Blizzard of '78. When I was seven years old, the snowstorm of '78 cancelled school for over a week. I remember my mum pulling us downtown in laundry baskets tied with rope to buy groceries. Now almost 26 years to the day later, the entire state of Massachusetts was covered in white.

It was Tuesday of the blizzard and very few businesses were open. Around 10:00 A.M., I called the man at the recording studio. Much to my surprise he said, "If you can get here, we'll make a CD." With the Jeep in four-wheel drive, I made my way through the snow. The sun was shining down on my town creating the prefect backdrop for a movie about an enchanted kingdom. I envisioned cancer-curing fairies with ivy and holly wreaths in their icicle hair twirling magic wands around me. Each twirl zapped away cancer cells. Covered in white, the world around me looked uncontaminated, disease-free, and pure.

The CD mix-master greeted me at his door with a huge and helpful smile. His studio was spacious and state-of-the-art, not at all like the little phone booth boxes I had formerly recorded in. He loaded all of my music into his system, did a sound check and dove into recording. Every time I finished a song, I knew I was closer to having surgery. With each song digitally placed in safe keeping, I felt as if I were putting my children to bed. The feeling was intimate, tender and loving. Through the power of music, all of the anger and frustration seemed to float out of my body.

On a mission, I refused to take breaks in-between each track. As the hours past, my voice became increasingly fatigued. I'm sure my lack of sleep added to the overall stress of my vocal chords. At one point the sound man asked, "Do you want to finish this another day?" "I don't have another day" I replied. Hearing those words come out of my mouth scared the hell out of me. Would today be the last day I'd sing? Praying that he'd sense my longing to complete the CD I said, "I'm hoping to take the photos tomorrow, I have pre-op on Thursday and I have surgery on Friday. Can we just try to keep going? If it sounds bad, we don't have to use it." He agreed and put up the next song.

If my surgeon ran into a problem, my voice was already salvaged in the computer at the studio. In that single act, the mix-master had rescued my sound and soul at the same time. The rest was in God's hands.

The next day I arrived at the photography studio with a few changes of clothing, cosmetics, some jewelry and a shitty attitude. My energy was near to the ground that day. With total shades of my December disposition, I could hardly get myself out of bed. I resented doing my make-up and hair for the photos of my pre-surgical body. Nothing seemed fair. I was two days away from having an awful scar across my neck.

Feeling sorry for myself, my sorry ass entered the studio with my I still have cancer half smile. I introduced myself to the photographer and changed into my first outfit. As I stood in the dressing room, I glanced in the mirror to touch up my face. The individual reflecting back at me looked *so* tired. As if she hasn't slept in weeks, she looked one hundred years old. She had empty eyes and a fearful brow. She looked helpless. I didn't know her. I couldn't help but wonder if I should photograph someone so foreign to me? Did I really want to preserve a face of so much pain? The image seemed unworthy of holding onto.

I had all of my ducks in a row. I recorded the CD and I had to take the final photos of my perfect neck. Unwilling to steer off of my path, I closed my eyes, took a deep breath and walked into the studio area. My mind was all over the place with a crazy stream of consciousness. *THIS IS PART OF IT, LORNA, ALL OF THIS, THE GOOD -THE BAD -THE UGLY-THIS IS IT! THIS IS THE FACE OF CANCER!*

AS PAINFUL AS IT IS, YOU'LL WANT TO REMEMBER THIS. THIS IS PART OF WHO YOU ARE, WHERE YOU ARE GOING, AND WHERE YOU HAVE BEEN. YOU CAN DO THIS, LORNA! I sat on a stool and spoke to the photographers about what I needed them to save on film. They seemed confident that they could find my beauty and my soul, cancer and all.

As the camera lights started to flash around me, I felt like I was going through a tunnel. I saw my husband taking my hand underwater in Key West, Florida. He held on tightly, allowing me to snorkel against the current. I saw my nieces and nephews on their very first birthdays in the hospital. Their eyes looking up at me, as if to say, "I made it, Auntie. Let us begin our adventure." I saw the essence of my mom's natural true beauty. Lying next to me on the beach, her skin glistening in the sun, she was carefree and stunning! I saw my sister Elizabeth's face when we boarded the plane as children on our way to Disney. I saw my sister Tahlia's eyes light up when I handed her a Sweet 16 birthday card with the key to my old beat up car taped inside. I saw my grandfather's expression every time my husband and I brought him a surprise lobster with a stick of butter. I saw my grandmothers' expression when I asked her to be my Confirmation sponsor. I saw my stepson Brent's glow every time he returned from a fishing trip with my husband. I saw my childhood father Scott singing "Daddy's little baby loves short bread, short bread" to me when I was little. I saw all of my friends with all of their children sitting around a long dinning room table, smiling and laughing. I saw myself floating in the waters of Mexico, weightless and without cancer. All of the moments that marked my heart were in my mind's eye.

I experienced a tender transition in my life. I wasn't saying goodbye to my past, I was safeguarding it. The photographs were the preservation of the time between the *old* and *new* me. With the mere click and snap of the camera, I was able to unite the phases of my life through art.

"Okay Lorna, we are going to set up a different backdrop. Why don't you put on your red shirt?" As soon as I felt the freshly ironed shirt fall over my breasts, the authority of the scarlet fabric called for immediate attention. My melancholy mood seemed to subside. I felt stronger and more prepared to finish the session. Color really does feed the soul. I do not recommend wearing black, navy or brown when you are sick. My best days were spent in cranberry, red, pink, purple, baby blue, lime green or creamy shades of clothing.

Later that afternoon, I got a call from my friend Jennifer. In 1978 she approached me after my spontaneous "Up on the Housetop" solo on top of a table at recess. Apparently my performance left her convinced we were destined to be great friends. Our kinship began around the age of seven and has remained intact ever since. Some twenty plus years later, she is an anchorwoman in New Hampshire. "Hey, it's me," Jen said in her familiar *I'm not on the air* voice. "The girls want to know if you are up for meeting us for some dinner tomorrow night. We'd love to see you."

"Sure. Email me the details and I'll see you there," I replied in my *I still have cancer* voice. The girls she was referring to were some of my gal-pals from the Middleboro High School Class of 1989. They were all married with small children, and successful careers. Every outing with them ended in side-splitting laughter. I literally craved a good dose of some of my oldest friends in the world. Just before leaving, I kissed my husband goodbye and made my way for the door. As I turned my body, my glove slipped from the knob on our three-and-a-half-inch thick front door. I somehow ended up slamming my finger in the jam. The door felt as if it closed on my finger at ninety miles an hour. I fell to the ground with a galaxy of stars all around me. My finger was throbbing!

Roger helped me over to the hearth room and asked me to move my finger. Naturally, I refused. It was swelling and the ache had spread all the way up my arm. I remember whimpering, "What is wrong with me? I keep doing dumb ass things. Why can't I get it together? Who slams their finger in their own door?" Ever composed and full of wisdom, Roger handed me an ice pack. After he calmed me down, I was able to bend my now purple and puffy finger. Totally drained and defeated, I said, "I'm not going. I'll call Jen."

"I'll drive you to see your friends" he said. "You shouldn't cancel. They want to see you and you were looking forward to it. Come on, let's go." At that point, the dam in my tear ducts gave way and tears flooded my outfit. "What is wrong with me?" I screamed! "I hung up my phone in a cup of coffee. I just slammed my finger in the door. I cannot remember anything. I cannot stay focused. I can't sleep. <u>What is happening to me?</u> I JUST WANT MY LIFE BACK! Will things ever be the same? This isn't fair. It's been **WAY TOO LONG**! I'VE BEEN WALKING AROUND WITH CANCER SINCE DECEMBER 15th! I want my life back!"

One of the best things about my husband is that he doesn't try putting a band aid on anything. Once you are diagnosed with cancer you realize the powerful in that amenity. His words of truth began with, "Lorna, this is going to suck for a while. But you are *so close* to getting through the hardest part. Things may never be the same. But you have to allow yourself to do crazy, out of the ordinary things right now. You have to cut yourself some slack. You need sleep, Babe. Most of this is happening because you haven't been sleeping. Your body is tired. <u>You are running on empty.</u> The good news is your finger isn't broken. As for your cell phone...we replaced it. Those things aren't important. They aren't worth getting so worked up over. Let it go." He was right. We both needed sleep.

Like so many times over the past few months, I stuffed my emotions into my designer hand bag, and continued on course.

One-by-one I greeted my old school friends at the table. One friend started asking me cancer questions right away. At one point during the meal, I left the conversation. My mind drifted back over twenty-five years. I saw all of us at Jen's house in our p.j.'s. Her father made us scrambled eggs while we discussed the hottest new jeans and fashion. We all wanted leather sneakers with a colored product symbol on the sides. I longed for the pink emblem. The night before, we had curled our hair with an iron. It was the eve of one of our ski trips. We decided to fall asleep at 1:00 A.M. rather than 3:00 A.M. because, after all, we needed our rest. So much had happened since those days in the early 1980's!

I was the oldest in the group, which made me the first one to get a license. I remember sitting around the high school cafeteria table showing my friends the photo on my new passport to freedom. Now, I was the first one to have cancer, sitting around the dinner table showing my friends where my incision was going to be made. When asked if they would repeat puberty, most people say "NOT ON YOUR LIFE!" But at that moment, I'd have given everything to be back at Jen's, curling our hair talking about fashion and boys.

After dinner, my friends said goodbye in the parking lot. Jen was the last to say goodnight. She walked me to the Jeep and paused as if to say, "You know I love you, girlfriend!" But instead "I'll be thinking of you" and "You'll be FINE" came out of her mouth. I didn't need to hear the "I love you," I saw it all over her face. I saw love on all of their faces that night. Jen was more involved with the daily grind of my illness. She called or emailed constantly from December 15th to the final hour on the eve of my surgery. She had become one of my earthly guardian angels.

As I undressed that night I realized I hadn't had sex with my husband in days. Hell, weeks even. Sex was the last thing on my mind. The last thing he intended to do was pursue me for sex. He pretty much followed my lead those weeks leading up to my surgery-and I appreciated that. He probably needed to feel close with me then more than ever. The *knocking boots* phase of my recovery was most likely weeks away. I didn't see myself having sex the night before my surgery; so that moment was my last chance to be alone with my man. I have to say having sex was a good call. I recommend a friendly frolic to anyone who is really stressed out. As we began to make love, I became increasingly aware of how I felt. For me, it was the last time I'd be romantically intimate in my birth body. I wondered how he felt. My husband was connecting with his entire wife-the girl he met in 1985-in one piece, unscarred and whole.

I couldn't help but wonder if he felt like he was kissing cancer or fooling around with a sick person. I didn't bother to ask. I took comfort in having him near me. My only regret was that I didn't intimately reach out to him sooner. Emotionally, I was all over him in the form of crying, yelling, bitching, or talking. A little less loathing and a little more loving on my part should have been in order; but I couldn't turn back the cancer clock. All I could do was pray my husband understood and forgave me for how dreadfully I behaved the weeks before my surgery.

The next day we headed into Boston for hours of pre-op. Just in case you are taking notes, once again I had a dismal disposition. Whenever I had to do something cancer-related my behavior was abysmal. The ironic thing is that I wasn't a spoiled or bratty kid growing up. Don't ask me how I learned to be such a monster of an adult when the cancer came. I never expected to be so unattractive and mean.

The city was still a mess from the blizzard. As we sat in traffic, the fact that I had cancer made my blood boil! *When will I get to the acceptance point?* I thought as I waited for the cars to move. *When does all of this become easy?* Finally, we arrived at the hospital. I signed in and took a seat. The first phase of the pre-op was seeing Dr. Randolph. While I waited, I noticed a woman rummaging through the magazines on a table next to me. It was clear she didn't find anything that interested her. I introduced myself to her and extended my personal stash of reading materials from my bag. Much obliged, she selected one of the magazines and took a seat across from me. Moments later in the sweetest Irish accent imaginable, she said, "What are you here for, Honey?" I told her that I had thyroid cancer. "I do, too" she exclaimed. "Oh, what a pair we are. You are so young to be sick." *Yeah, no shit*, I thought to myself.

"I'm Mary" she said, and went on to explain that years back she had half of her diseased thyroid removed with another surgeon. The cancer returned. "I'm getting rid of all of it this time" she said. She had quite a wit about her. Before long both of us had escaped our medical reality and were cracking jokes and shaking up the waiting room with laughter. We exchanged information, and vowed to be the support system if either one of us needed a friendly voice over the weeks ahead.

Next, I headed down to the Radiology Lab for a CT scan. I had to remove all jewelry, and hairpins from my body. My slacks had a zipper, but that didn't seem to be an issue. Fully clothed, I positioned myself on a long table. The room was freezing. I remember wishing I had worn socks. There was a large donut (which seemed to be six feet round) encompassing the table. The tech explained how the table was going to move under the donut and how important it was not to move while the unit took pictures. My favorite part of the walk through was when the tech said, "This will be over in less than ten minutes." As for claustrophobia, I didn't have a problem at all. In the first chapter of this book I shared my horrific full body scan incident with you. The CT scan was stress free. I didn't feel trapped or closed in. In addition to enjoying the ten-minute respite, I took great comfort in knowing the scan results would help Dr. Randolph design a plan for my surgery.

From Radiology, I made my way to the lab. After confirming that I wasn't pregnant, I had a consultation with an anesthesiologist. We discussed a lot of my allergies, measured my weight, (always so much fun) and covered rules for the morning of surgery. I could hardly believe I'd be back in Boston less than twenty-four hours later to exorcise my thyroid. The January 28, 2005, surgical date had finally arrived. I anticipated a certain readiness to rush in grounding me for my operation. To date, no such surge occurred. I couldn't help but wonder if I'd ever feel ready to embark on my new thyroid-free life.

That night I prayed to God in search of a calm mind for surgery. *Patience Lorna,* I kept repeating to myself *it's all about patience…in time all of this will be behind you…and you will be on your way to feeling like YOU again…* Thing is- I knew I was lying to myself. How on earth would or could I feel like "ME" again in the absence of the very gland that makes people feel like themselves? *Baby steps girlfriend…you must not clutter your mind with the complexities of cancer every waking moment of every day…for now you must simply suffice it to say, "This too shall pass."*

Untouchable

THE NIGHT BEFORE MY SURGERY MY cell phone rang. "Lorna, its Greg Randolph. Look, I've been thinking- after looking in the book at tomorrows surgeries- I'm not sure we should go forward with the 3:00 P.M. Friday surgery. The case before you is very involved. We may run very late. There is a possibility you may not get in until after 5:00 P.M. That would be an entire day without food or water. With respect to your case, I'd like to see you on Wednesday, February 2nd. You'd arrive at 6:00 A.M. as the first surgery of the day. Does that work for you?" Stunned and in shock, I had no idea what to say. This is what I came out with, "Whatever you think is best. I need you to be well rested and on your toes. If morning is better, let's do it. I'll see you Wednesday then?" I still cannot believe I said that to him.

Some would translate this news as six more days of freedom. All I heard was six more days of cancer. I agreed with the decision to move my case, but worried about my ability to hold out one more week. I had reserved little batches of my sanity. Each day, I'd uncover the lid to my private stockpile of reason, and ration it out accordingly. I had only measured enough to get me through the morning of the surgery. I wasn't sure that I had ample ingredients left to double the batch. What would happen if the cancer-starved cupboards of my brain were left bare? Could I make it through six more days? Would I go insane? That night I prayed to Mary for the strength to cross the finish line. I was trying to find the silver lining. I was handed an additional week to come to terms with my cancer. I tried to rest knowing my fate was in God's hands.

Two days later, a group of us went to a restaurant in an old church in the center of Sandwich. We dressed in our finest frocks in preparation for an evening of escapism, fine food, and laughter. A man was playing a grand piano near the bar and singing old Broadway standards. The acoustics were incredible. After a killer meal, and a bottle of champagne that cost more than a monthly car payment on my first vehicle, my friends asked me to sing a song. There was an underlining urgency in everyone's voice. They were saying, "Come on Lorna, sing a song," and I was hearing "Lorna, sing tonight because in four days you are having surgery and you may never sing again."

Most people don't understand how many factors go into spontaneous performing. There is always the question of whether or not the person at the piano has sheet music you are familiar with, if their arrangement is in the proper key, and lastly, and how well the pianist is at following a singers' lead. With respect to how dreamy and artsy the idea of joining a stranger at a piano in an old church on Cape Cod seems, I knew singing could also be a disaster.

Once I finally got up the courage to risk sounding like a Moron at my new favorite dining establishment, the pianist rejected the idea of having a soloist join him on the stage. I knew what measures my friends would take in order to get me up there. *This is going to turn into WAR!* I thought knowing they wouldn't stand for the refusal. *Put on your seatbelts folks, it's gonna be a long ride!"* "May I see the owner?" was the next sentence I heard from our table. *Oh Jesus, let's not play the cancer card here. It's house policy that customers don't sing, that is what the waiter quoted from the pianist. Let's just go with policy.* The next thing I heard was, "She is a professional singer. She is a graduate of the Boston Conservatory. She is having surgery this week because she has **thyroid cancer**. We would all like to hear one song. Is that too much to ask?" At that point, the manager was table side, "We would <u>love</u> to have her sing a song. And, for the record, we have had other customers sing. I'm sorry you were discouraged by your waiter. I'll talk to the pianist for you."

My eyes were starring at the table the entire time.

Within minutes, I was at the piano looking through the sheet music. "Thank you," I said to the pianist. "I'm having surgery on Wednesday and well, I'm out with some friends, and -it would make the evening really special *for them* if I sang a song. Artist to artist, I'm so sorry to put you out." Luckily enough, the pianist was very compassionate and said, "Wow, thyroid cancer can be a bitch for singers. God love 'ya, I'll be prayin' for 'ya. Let's find a song."

As a male singer, very little of his music was in the proper key for my voice. My options were to sing really high (like a man robbed of his family jewels), to sing a song A Capella (without the piano), or to walk back to the table in defeat. I decided to sing A Capella. Just then, the pianist found <u>All I Ask Of You</u> from Phantom of the Opera. The duet was written for a male and female singer. I had performed the piece at weddings years back. I was reluctant to make my Cape Cod debut with such a rusty song. Before I could say yes or no, he was playing the introduction. *Here it goes, Lorna, the moment of truth! Stand up straight and get those notes out!* The performance was averagely sweet. The crowd was very forgiving and the high ceilings made it impossible to sound bad. "Sing another one," the pianist said. I selected one of my old college standards <u>The Nearness of You.</u> I performed the piece almost daily on the Spirit of Boston cruise ship.

Our friend sang that song for us at our wedding. As we danced beneath the early June moon with ninety-eight of our closest friends and family, I whispered the lyrics in my husbands' ear. Not since our wedding had the song touched my heart as it did that night on Cape Cod. The simple lyric told the story of my illness. All I needed in the face of cancer was the nearness of loved ones. Without them, I would have gone mad.

With my head held high above the cancer in my neck, I walked off of the stage. It was a perfect evening. At the end of the night Roger made a toast. "To: Whatever happens." Our friends repeated "To Whatever Happens" and clanked glasses. Then Roger went on to say, "And to my wife…my love: I love you now, I love you always, no matter what. In sickness and in health, I love you always." Thank goodness for the dinner at the Belfry Inn. My high spirits served as a shock absorber for what was about to ensue.

Has it ever rained in your bedroom? I don't mean outside through a window, I mean has rain ever dumped through the ceiling on your bed? The morning after my fabulous dinner with friends, a rare wave of heat hit my corner of Massachusetts. The sun rapidly melted the blizzard remains on our roof. Russet water seeped through our ceilings all over our brand new king sized duvet and bedding. I am serious about bedding. I spend a small fortune to make our bed a haven of fluffy clouds. The white clouds were drenched with polluted watery mud. My heart began to disintegrate. I had five-gallon buckets, pots, and pans under the leaks. Towels covered the floor. Trash bags were wrapped around the posts of our bed.

With butter cream walls, stark white molding and wainscoting, and a mahogany bedroom set adorned with crisp linen cut work bedding, I have always adored our bedroom. As the water spoiled my beloved retreat (the room I'd so desperately need when I returned from the hospital) I found it increasingly more difficult to exhale! Fighting back the tears, I heard my sister's fiancé and Roger shoveling snow off of the roof above.

As I stripped my bed, I felt like I was being stripped of everything I loved. It was as if every comfort and solace in my life was being taken away. Just then my sister Tal entered Mother Nature's crime scene in the bedroom. "This is going to take me **hours** to put back together again!" I barked. "This is *not* how I wanted to spend this time." "We can fix this, Lorna," she said. "It won't take long. It's going to be okay." ***NOTHING IS OKAY*** was screaming through the walls of my psyche. Wasn't there enough upheaval in my life over the past two months? Did I really need more heartache?

About an hour later, Roger discovered the non-verbal, hot mess I had become. "Lorna, I'll repaint the ceilings, I promise." Before I share my abusive response with you, I have to disclose Roger's profession. Roger is a union painter. He works in Boston six days a week, beautifying offices and buildings. My house has paint chipping away from the clapboard. My back hallway sports the sheet rock he put up nearly nine years ago sans any signs of Benjamin Moore. Being the nice guy that he is, my mother's house has been painted, nearly all of my friends houses have been painted, my sister's houses have been painted, friends <u>of our friends</u> houses have been painted, and the parents of our friend's houses have been painted. Usually his fee for friends is the cost of supplies, a lobster dinner, or my all time favorite; a fixed speeding ticket.

I listened to the leaking water fall from the ceiling into the paint buckets of broken promises. Every drop reminded me of how often my needs came second. I unleashed every outstanding I.O.U. Roger had ever issued. With the venom of a cobra I said, "You won't repaint the ceiling! I just know you won't! Don't make promises you cannot keep. I don't want to hear it. If you DO repaint the ceiling it will only be because I have CANCER. My cancer cannot cure your apathy for me or our home! Square up on all of the other things you promised me nearly a decade ago. Maybe then you'll be able to make some *new* pledges to me. For now, I don't want to hear any promises. <u>Everything</u> is <u>literally</u> falling down around me, Roger. <u>You cannot fix my cancer by painting our ceiling</u>."

I always had a biting tongue. Cancer had made it a piercing tongue. It was raining in Roger's world, too. I lost sight of that quite a bit as I came down the homestretch of my illness. They say we always hurt the ones we love. I had a super-sized can of *whoop* ass at my hip from diagnosis through recovery. As embarrassing as this is for me, I have decided to recount the events highlighting my behavior the week of the surgery. I want to help patients who may be flying off the handle at their spouses. I'm not a therapist. (I'd love to play one on T.V.) I'm not authorized to say whether or not this type of abuse during a time of crisis is normal.

Rather than hitting redial on all of the long-standing issues in our marriage, I wish I shared my fear of cancer. I urge everyone reading this book to think before yelling. Remember the underlining issue; <u>the real truth of the matter</u> is that we, as cancer patients, are **scared**. Fear can kick up horrible panic. Misdirected anger was a huge side effect of my cancer. I recommend trying to vocalize this fear to the people you love. If you don't want to burden or frighten them, I recommend talking to someone else (perhaps a therapist or friend) about your concerns.

If my surgery with Greg had been on Friday as originally planned, I would have come home to the water wreckage. My husband was planning to stay at a hotel near the hospital over the weekend. Without any warning, we would have returned to an incredible mess. By then, the mattress would have been ruined. I preserved hundreds of dollars worth of bedding by not being in the hospital. (Imagine trying to clean that muddle days after surgery!) I sat in the old wooden Windsor chair at the foot of our bed trying to embrace the silver lining. The sun was setting. Amidst the buckets of water there was an August-in-winter glow. The late sun illuminated an antique photo of Mary and baby Jesus above my bed. I tried to pull strength from Mary, but like my mattress, I remained stripped bare. *This too shall pass. Remember to breathe.*

Other than my uncle dying of cancer in 2002, I was having a pretty damn good run. I was in my ninth year of a very successful business. We had enough money to take vacations each year, eat out with friends, and buy just about whatever we longed for. Everyone in my family and circle of friends seemed happy and healthy, in great marriages, with healthy children. Even stretching as far back as my college years, things were relatively easy. I went to school on an enormous scholarship and loved my studies. LIFE WAS GOOD. **Really good**! Too good, I guess. It was becoming more difficult to accept the misfortune of having cancer in my thirties.

My childhood was a little tricky. We moved around a lot. I was the new kid in school quite a few times. My parents were divorced. My father who raised me drank. That is to say, I hardly knew him sober. He was also a Vietnam vet still serving in the Army. I found out about my biological father (and his decision not to stick around while my mother was carrying me) when I was around eleven-years-old. My dad who raised me was stationed in Germany when I realized he wasn't my blood father. I met my biological father (who is a self-made successful businessman) when I was twenty.

The time between eleven and twenty years old fostered underlining feelings of abandonment. I lived my life as a very untrusting girl. Despite the fact that another man stepped in, married my mother, gave me his name, and loved me as his own, my sense of paternal detachment (and all of the lies surrounding my identity) was always just below the surface.

My mother's second husband was a substance abuser (alcohol and drugs) with a violent temper. Many nights were spent in fear. As a young girl, I remember our home being sprayed with mace as police tried to ground the chemically enraged monster sized man in order to restrain him from hurting the officers, himself, and my mother. I'll never forget the sound of our front door being kicked in years later as he entered the house in a cocaine craze, swinging a baseball bat around in the darkness of my mother's bedroom. His fit of rage was in violation of the restraining order my mother had secured. I remember going to high school the next day, electing not to share my experience with my friends; full well knowing some of their families would read about my situation in the police log.

I remember being a few years younger and fleeing from my step-father at the break of dawn after watching all of our belongings piled into a truck. I remember sitting quietly next to my pregnant mother on a bus headed to Florida. I remember returning on a plane to reconcile the madness in Massachusetts a few weeks after we left. I remember hearing dinner plates smash up against walls, leaving pasta and sauce dripping down to the floor. The sauce resembled my mother's impending bloodshed. Nearly every moment spent in the house with that ticking bomb of a man was a moment spent in fear. I remember a heart-pounding panic every time he started to yell; his voice is so vivid that even today, the thought of it can take my breath away. This abuse took place in the early 1980's when recreational drug use seemed to be everywhere.

In addition to alcoholism, drug abuse, physical abuse, and verbal abuse, my step-father was a different race than the rest of my family. My hometown was a white working class town. Out of the three hundred and ten students in my graduating class, only a handful of students were not white. I was living with a Cape Verdean man. For outsiders looking in, my step-father was <u>black</u>.

After several stays at local rehabs (and I'm guessing a lot of soul searching) he cleaned up his life. Although the relationship ended in divorce, he seems to be leading a better life now. I am proud to say that I can sit with him at family gatherings with forgiveness. We have shared many laughs since the years filled with tears. He is the father of my baby sister and grandfather to my sweet nephews. My adult spirit has moved on, but trace pieces of my child heart remain unhealed.

You can *imagine* how dissimilar it was to have a bi-racial sister growing up in a small town. You can *imagine* how I worried about her identity struggles and whether or not she'd find her way in a predominantly white suburban area. You can *imagine* how extraordinary it was to have a *black* abusive step-father in an age when no one openly talked about unhealthy and dysfunctional households. But unless you've actually *lived* that life, you have no idea how intricate the circumstances can be, especially when you are a teenager coming of age and life is one complicated mess.

You may wonder what any of this has to do with having cancer. Although my dysfunctional childhood seemed like the end of the world back then, I wouldn't have changed a thing. My extraordinary childhood set the foundation for the resilient, over-achieving, ass kickin' firecracker of a woman I am today. Not many women are self-employed in business at twenty-four years old while holding down three other part time jobs. Knock on wood, I have never missed a payroll cycle or made a mistake that I didn't learn from. No matter how tough things got, my 1970's school of emotional hard knocks gave me the stamina to roll with life's blows. I graduated at the top of my class with a PH. D. in SURVIVAL SKILLS.

As an adult, I basked in the abundance of my blessings. I considered the hard years and challenges of my childhood to be my time served. I closed the chapter on the eleven-year-old girl headed for a life ridden with unhappiness and self doubt. I pardoned my biological father for not raising me and with baby healing steps, welcomed him in my life. I forgave my step-father for all of the nights I spent in fear. I exonerated every person who hurt me and began living my life with a healing and loving heart.

So, for some reason I assumed that if I worked really hard at being a good person nothing bad would fall in my lap. With all of my might, I dedicated my life to my family, friends, marriage and career. I forgave those who trespassed against me. I lived an honest life. I went out on a limb to unconditionally love myself and took the time to love my neighbors. I brought comfort to people in need. I expected all of the good stuff I put in the universe to fortify me from awful shit like cancer. There aren't any bumper stickers which read "Cancer Happens **Even If** You Had A Bitch of A Childhood." As arrogant as this seems, I considered myself untouchable from cancer because I had already done my time in hell as a kid.

Don't get me wrong, I knew my <u>time served</u> fortress wouldn't shield me from losing the people I love. I knew death was a natural part of the natural circle of life. I didn't expect my time served fortress to protect me from the throbbing agony I felt as an American after September 11th. I knew ghastly things were going to happen in the world around me. I just never fathomed myself with cancer at thirty-three years old. Nor did I ever imagine my friend burying her young son. Those seemingly unspeakable, impossible, unnatural, and inconceivable episodes occurred within nine months. My wave of nasty luck confirmed that there wasn't a mote vast enough to prevent the enemy from banging down the door to my time served castle of security. I seemed to have been caught by the Hall Monitor of Life without my time served pass. The punishment was a detention hall filled with reality, struggle, bullshit, cancer, and pain. With the arrogance of a teenager, and the naivety of a child, the veracity of just how truly **touchable** I was, came as an unsolicited revelation.

As I wrote in my CD jacket, <u>Cancer doesn't discriminate.</u> At that moment, sitting quietly alone in my bedroom, three days before my surgery, looking up at a brown and yellow soppy stained ceiling, I couldn't help but wonder why I was being administered another dose of challenge. Why was I chosen to bear the scarlet letter **C** on my chest? I had never killed anyone. I had never cheated on my husband. (I thought about it after my diagnosis as a way to break the "only the good die young" theory.) I had never broken the law. I had never stolen anything. (Well, I took a pack of gum in 5th grade after the dare of a friend. We were on our way to CCD of all places.) I had never bought or sold drugs. I had never smoked a cigarette, never drank and got behind the wheel, never stayed out late without calling home, and never intentionally hurt anyone. I never lived the life of a person who should be inflicted or punished with disease.

I didn't deserve to have a scar on my neck for all time. I didn't deserve to worry about losing my voice and career. I didn't deserve to have to poison my body with radioactive matter to ward off returning cells in my body. I didn't deserve to live my life dependant on a prescription bottle with the word <u>Synthroid</u> on it to determine my mood, body temperature, skin quality, hair quality, emotions, metabolism, heart rate, libido, and overall wellness. I didn't deserve to spend the duration of my life worrying if the wickedness of cancer would set up shop again in my body.

I have to admit an overwhelming sense of *why do I bother to be a good person* came over me. *Why bother* is an indifferent and sucky place to be. Regrettably, I rented a room at *why bother* and nested there for a few days. Notwithstanding my love for my husband, for days I blocked him out. I completely stopped cooking dinners, picking up the house, offering him tea and toast in bed, asking how his day was, doing his laundry, and getting the mail from outside. Whenever anyone called the house for him, I asked if they'd call back and leave a message in his mailbox. Our daily checking in cell calls were placed on hold. For a woman who behaved much like a doting wife of the 1950's, my time in *why bother* invoked quite a change.

Why bother spa was running a special two night stay. Since I checked in late Sunday night (after it rained in my room) I could stay through Tuesday (the eve of my surgery) at no additional charge. *Why bother* was quiet, not too hot, not too cold, and void of all energy zapping responsibility and accountability. Even my mother had fallen victim to the amenities of *why bother*. I confided in her less and less, as each hour pointed to packing my bags for Boston.

It was February 1st, 2005, my nephew Tyler's ninth birthday and the eve of my surgery. It was also check out time at the *why bother spa*. As we sat at the local burger and iced cream joint having his celebratory treat, my eyes kept floating over to the enormous clock in the lobby. I only had a few more hours to get ready for the hospital. I asked my mother what I needed to pack. She rambled a few items like a toothbrush and slippers. Just then another random wave of anger crashed over me. I became pissed off about having to pack. I clammed up again allowing all of my fear and frustration to stew in the pressure cooker my head had become. It seemed impossible to laugh. Impossible to joke. Impossible to breathe. Concentrating on what menu item to order required as much focus as a college entrance exam. Certain I had run out of my rations of sanity, I felt like I was going to snap. Unfit for public consumption, I needed to get home. *Why am I so angry?* I thought, trying to lift my mood. *You have cancer idiot!* echoed back at me.

As I sat there hating the entire medical world for not curing cancer, I tried to remember the last time I had truly laughed. I hadn't even smiled since Mother Nature decided to kick my ass by dumping her piss and shit all over my bedroom! *When will this get easier? When will having cancer become part of my routine?*

I kissed my nephew goodbye and told my mom I'd see her in the morning. As I walked through the door of my house, I felt trapped. The eleventh hour (as we say in the biz) had finally arrived. It was time to pack for the biggest production of my life. Time to plan. Time to gather all of my things. Time to write my "incase I don't wake up" note to my mother and husband. Time to say goodnight to all of my family and friends who called to wish me luck. Time to sound *ready* on the phone. Time to break the ice with my husband after two days at the *why bother resort and spa*. Time to sign the D.N.R. (do not resuscitate form) I had copied weeks before. Time to make peace with what was happening to me. Time to surrender to God.

In less than five minutes, I threw my hospital bag together. I took all of the toiletries out of my carry on bag and threw them in my bag along with, a nightgown, a sweat suit, underwear, slippers, a robe, magazines, my rosary beads, a scapula from my Gram, holy water from Italy, my eye glasses, hair pins, my brush, my comb, my cell phone charger and my favorite sugar free chocolates. (I was watching carbs at the time. To think I had cancer, but still felt the need to watch my carbs! How ridiculous?)

Roger asked what I wanted for dinner. I told him that I had just eaten with my nephew. From that point on, he seemed to hover over me. Whatever room I escaped to, he was sure to follow. As to not set free the rage within me I tried walking away from him. The last thing I wanted to do was explode all over him. He had tolerated my cruelty with the patience of a saint. He didn't deserve another bashing. After all of our years together, you'd think that he would have heeded my physical warning. Without any words, my body language was shouting "Stay away!" He followed me back into the kitchen, and sat in a chair while I rummaged for something in our cabinets. After two days of not talking he said, "Babe, I would do this for you if I could. I want you to know that I'd give **anything** to do this for you…to spare you of this… to have the surgery for you. I wish it could be me doing this tomorrow and not you."

His words felt like enflamed matches hitting my body. As if my soul were made of lighter fluid the conversation in our kitchen began to ignite. In a burning response I said, "How ironic that you wish this was happening to you tomorrow? I couldn't agree with you more! I'm guessing you feel that way because you know in your heart that it _should be you_ tomorrow. You have somehow fallen under life's radar. You must be feeling guilty about that. YOU have pushed life's envelope **countless times,** and yet somehow I am the one packing a hospital bag. You and I both know that you having cancer makes a hell of a lot more sense! YOU smoke, YOU drink, YOU drive on the highway absolutely exhausted after double shifts with less than two hours of sleep from a hangover the night before. YOU live life on the edge! I PLAY BY **ALL** OF THE RULES! I do not deserve to have cancer! I don't deserve this! It *SHOULD* be you!"

My diabolical behavior made me detest everything about myself. He didn't deserve to be drawn and quartered in our kitchen. I didn't warrant his forgiveness. Although on some level I meant every word I threw at him, it wasn't the right time for confessions of that nature. Shortly after my totalitarian tantrum, I made eye contact with him. The pain and helplessness that looked back at me will forever be engraved in my mind. Was I trying to make him feel as bad as I did? Am I truly capable of that type of torment? Earlier in the book I mentioned how I didn't need anyone to jump in the foxhole with me. Was I kidding myself? Did I want him to experience the carnivorous clutches of cancer?

After a quick replay of each stabbing sentence I shouted, I stood before him and wept. "I am **so sorry**. I FEEL LIKE I AM LOSING MY MIND, ROGER!" I was sobbing and repeating *DAMN IT! THIS IS SUPPOSED TO BE THE **GOOD** CANCER? GOD DAMN YOU CANCER!*

The disease had reduced me to the slightest justification of a human being. Just then, the phone rang. It was Jennifer. She had been remarkable throughout my entire journey and deserved to hear my voice for what may be the last recognizable time. As I tried to pull myself together, Roger briefed her on my break down. "Hey man," she said. "What's going on?" "Just a little fucking cancer!" I said through tears. I am pretty sure if was the first time she ever heard me cry. "Lorna, I was waiting for this. I was a little worried that you hadn't let all of **this** out. The jokes stop here, okay? THIS SUCKS, Lorna, but you are SO CLOSE to the end of this part. CRY, be mad, go nuts...but know how close you are to putting this behind you. Come on, you can do this. Tell me what's going on. What are 'ya thinking? What's on your mind?"

I remember how relaxed and calming her words sounded. I think her voice actually lowered my blood pressure. I calmly replied, "I think it's unfair. Don't ask me why, but after waiting over six weeks for this day to come, I don't think I'm ready. I haven't accepted it yet. Now I'm out of time and that pisses me off! AND I just told my husband that HE deserves cancer. That's what I'm thinking! That is *really* what I'm thinking." I heard Jen laughing about my spousal slam-fest kitchen cancer mosh pit. She assured me that Roger would recover from my outburst. Her laughter thawed the iceberg souvenirs I had been carrying around from the *why bother spa*. I began to melt back into myself. We laughed for a few more minutes until in her ever-young, spirited voice she said, "You **are** going to be okay, girl. I'll see you tomorrow when you wake up, my friend. Get some rest. God Speed!"

Roger and I had a snack in the same room I had torn his guts out in moments earlier. He held my hands across the table, and without any words, I knew he had forgiven me. Opting not to talk about our fight he said, "Why don't you take a hot shower and go to bed." On my way to the bathroom, I placed a final call to my mother just to make sure she was okay. Our conversation positioned positive and healing thoughts in my mind. As the piping hot water pounded on my frantic frame, I murmured a prayer petitioning God to help put my mind in order. *Make my mind right, Lord. I'm going a little crazy here-please get my mind right. Don't let cancer take my thyroid and my sanity.*

Minutes later, covered in lavender oil and warmly tucked in the linen clouds of our bed, I felt shockingly calm. I'm not sure if God had answered my plea, or if I, at long last accepted what was happening to me. Perhaps I was just too exhausted to fight any longer. One thing was certain- it was the last time I had to fall asleep with a thyroid full of the cancer.

The Little People

On *Thyroidectomy Eve* I took in about six hours of uninterrupted slumber. The alarm went off around 4:00 A.M. For the first time in a long time, I wasn't in a foul mood. Although relieved by how clear my head felt, I couldn't help but wonder how symbolic that clarity was? Did this mean I was finally ready? Oddly enough, I related to all of my friends who had become mothers that morning. It was as if my water had broken. I was on my way to push out a malignant tumor, in turn giving birth to a new life. I knew that by sun down the pain would be worth it.

Shortly after I dressed, mum arrived. It was pitch black outside, yet all of us acted as if it were a normal, sunny morning at a functional hour. We loaded the car and headed into Boston. My peaceful groove scared me. *Is this passive aggression? Is my hostility hiding behind the 5:00 A.M. clouds in the sky? Is the animal within me going to break out with the morning sun?* I psycho analyzed everything that morning. I wanted to remember those emotions for the rest of my life. God willing, February 2, 2005, was the day Dr. Randolph was going to take the cancer away-forever.

Four days away from my thirty-fourth birthday, it was my **re-birth day**. I was going to wake up reborn in a new cancer free body with a fresh new start to a cancer-free life.

In the elevator of the hospital, I met a woman named Amy. Turns out, we were all headed to the same department. She worked the registration desk. As I filled out my paperwork, I remembered that Mary (the woman from Ireland who I met during pre-op) and I were having surgery on the same day. We spoke earlier in the week and toyed with the idea of trying to be roommates. I ran that by Amy. She enthusiastically offered to look in to it. Originally I had requested a private room. Once it was clear that was most likely not going to happen, I stressed how much I'd prefer to shack up with Mary rather than a total stranger.

The groundhog had just seen his shadow. There was a close-up of his little furry face on the TV in the waiting area. I connected with the tiny creature on the screen and imagined him speaking to me through his miniature black eyes. I heard him say, *Lorna, I took care of 'ya. You have several more weeks of winter to hibernate and get well. Don't you worry, Missy, when you are ready, spring will be waitin' for ya. Break a leg in there today!* I actually thanked the groundhog and chuckled at how utterly screwed up my life had become. I was conversing in my head to groundhogs. What next?

My name was called and I went into an office to speak to a nurse. I answered a ton of questions in my calm Zen-like voice. Frankly, it was a tone I had never heard come out of my own body. I was impressed by how together I sounded. At one point the woman said, "I have to say, you have an amazing attitude about all of this! It's not often that we see people so prepared. It's like you aren't even nervous. *ARE* you nervous?" "Not really," I said as casually as if we were in a new restaurant trying to decide what to order. "Well good for you!" she said. "I can tell you are going to do just fine. Dr. Randolph is an amazing surgeon."

From there, she asked me more specific questions about my allergies. I told her that I had been patch-tested years back and was pretty faithful to a weekly allergy shot routine. When asked about latex allergies my first response was, "I don't think so." From there I proceeded to tell her about every skin reaction I had ever encountered. She asked me to change out of my clothes and into the gown. I thought it was odd that I had to remove all of my clothing. I felt so hypocritical: I gladly strip off every stitch of clothing to have massages but had an attitude about getting naked for surgery.

As I stood all alone, totally nude in the glaringly fluorescent cubical, I took one last glance at my untouched body. I lovingly and acceptingly smiled at all of the imperfections on my frame. My *less than* America's Next Top Model legs, belly, and breasts looked back at me with confidence and strength. I pulled my hair aside and took one last look at my beautiful neck. The same neck my family blew raspberries on when I was a child to make me laugh. The same neck that rested perfectly on pillows while my mother read bed-time stories. The same neck I put my gold cross necklace around when I received first communion. The same neck that I tied a scarf around to disguise the hickey my boyfriend gave me in ninth grade. The same neck that wore the pearl necklace my biological father gave me the day I graduated from college. The same neck my nieces and nephews fell asleep and nestled upon as babies. The same neck my husband nibbled on in the kitchen as he peaked over my shoulder to see what I was I preparing for dinner. The same neck I drenched in sunscreen on beaches all over the map moments before drinking in the glorious beams of heat. The same neck I wrapped in woolen scarves during the cold crisp winter. The same neck I stretched and massaged before singing the National Anthem at Fenway Park. The same neck my husband kissed when we made love. I wanted to burn the impression of my perfect, happy neck in every corner of my memory.

Until that moment, I had mourned the potential loss of my career but had neglected to truly mourn my anatomy. That glance in the mirror was the last time I'd see the neckline I was born with. *I have so little time to take all of this in…I have so little time to say goodbye to this part of me…* As I stared at my neck in the reflection I thought *If only I could save this perfect naked neck.*

I had read about the occasional permanent numbness some thyroid cancer survivors experience after surgery all around their incision. A few girls I chatted with on-line said that even years after the operation, they lacked sensation in that area. That in mind, I placed my hand on the front of my throat. Below my finger tips I felt my heart beating. I closed my eyes and envisioned my pulse as a Native American drum beat. I envisioned that beat soaring through the skies, summonsing all of the medicine men in the land to gather around me.

My maternal grandmother is Sicilian. My maternal grandfather is Penobscot Indian. As a child, I was named Pockshula (meaning wildflower) at a ceremony. My paternal grandmother was Cherokee. Roger's grandmother was Mohawk. I prayed to the spirits of each tribe and asked them to watch over me. *You are a warrior, Lorna! You have Native blood in your veins. You were named Pakshula. Like the wildflowers, you require very little to thrive and grow. Walk out of this room and begin your new life. Today is the celebration of your re-birth. You are standing in the middle of a fire circle in your honor. Today we celebrate your worth. Go get your new life. Below your fingers is merely flesh. Only the flesh of your neck will be altered, but your spirit and soul will continue to soar. Your native spirits will guide you to health.*

My next stop was a quick goodbye to Roger and mum. As the nurse walked me to the waiting area, I concentrated on not crying. *DO NOT CRY! IF YOU CRY NOW YOU WILL NOT STOP, AND THEY WILL HAVE TO SEDATE YOU! YOU ARE A WARRIOR! LET THEM SEE YOU TALL AND STRONG! YOU ARE A THREE HUNDRED-YEAR-OLD OAK TREE!* I smiled at my mum and looked directly in to my husbands eyes, as if to say, "I'll see ya' in a few." "We'll be right here waiting for you. I love you!" mum said, as she beamed her classic award-winning smile.

The nurse brought me to a surgical holding area. There were several patients on portable beds waiting to be seen. A man introduced himself. His knew from his nametag that he was Italian. "I am going to be operating the nerve monitoring system today. I heard you are a singer. We'll take good care of you." Just then the anesthesiologist walked over to me. He, too, had an Italian name. I remember the nerve monitoring man saying, "Oh, you have the big guns in here today. He is the Chief of the department." My mind drifted back to my maternal great-grandmother Jovanina Gandolfo. She came here from Sicily when she was a teenager. Her husband (my great-grandfather) owned a successful olive oil and produce company in the North End of Boston. Throughout my childhood I remember her clapping and singing lyrics like "Yeah, Yeah, Yeah, no Pasta Fuzole tonight" in Italian. Although she never performed an aria in front of us, my great grandmother sang opera in the city as a young woman. It was without question that from heaven she had sent me a team of paisano's to watch over me.

"I want to talk about your allergies" the anesthesiologist said." Notice when I scratch your arm the type of reaction you have? (My arm had a visible white line on it.) We are going to do this a little differently than planned. It's going to take us a bit longer, but I want to make sure you are okay." Before long, we were chatting about genres of music, the Red Sox and my work at the casting company. "I'm going to give you a little something to calm you down" he said as he injected my arm. I wanted to be in clear mind all the way up to "COUNT BACKWARDS", and I was hoping the injection wouldn't compromise my clarity. Honest to goodness, even before that shot, I was not afraid. I had totally surrendered that night before and was ready to move forward with my life.

I have to confess rather strange things went through my mind during those moments waiting to go in to the O.R. *I haven't kissed another man in years! If I die today, Roger will have been the only man I have kissed in an eternity. I wonder what it would have been like to kiss another man? Maybe if I kissed more men, I wouldn't have contracted cancer. Should I kiss this anesthesiologist? Bad things happen to good people. Why the hell have I been **so good**? I'm going to start drinking coffee when I wake up. I used to LOVE coffee. Why did I stop drinking it? Why was I on a mission to be so good? Look where it got me. I haven't had white sugar in over a year... what have I been trying to prove? I'm going to be bad when I wake up. One bad ass girl who eats sugar, and drinks caffeine, and KISSES random men with my coffee breath!*

A nurse interrupted my delusion and placed motion sickness discs behind each of my ears. I had requested them at pre-op. My nurse friend recommended them to take the edge off of the post-surgical nausea. "You are the singer, right?" she asked. "Oh, I love to sing. I always wanted to act and do plays." "It's not too late," I told the nurse. "I work at a casting company and they are always looking for new faces. You should take a few classes. You can do extra work to get your feet wet."

I heard my voice talking but my body felt like it was drifting on my boogie board in a sea of divine warm water. I was completely unattached to the words coming out of my mouth. From there, I brought in my Catholic peeps and began praying to Mary. *Hail Mary full of grace the Lord is with thee...blessed...is the...fruit...*Another nurse said, "Dr. Randolph will be ready in a few minutes and we'll get started. You are going to do great." I stopped her and asked, "Is it okay that I have my contacts in? I have no idea where my glasses are." "We're going to have to take your contacts out, Lorna. When you wake up you can put your glasses on." She said. I must have become a touch more sluggish from the injection. I remember wanting to stress to her how difficult it would be for me to see without my glasses. I tried telling her that I'd need the glasses the minute I woke up; but the words didn't come out properly.

I remember thinking about things that hadn't crossed my mind in years. *I wish I could find my cell phone. I need to call my mother. I have to let her know how sorry I am for not having her give me away at my wedding. What was I thinking? Maybe we'll renew our vows and I'll have her give me away. That was a stupid mistake... No regrets...just wellness...yes, wellness... that is what I'm going to focus on...wellness...being well. Hail Mary full of grace...*

Somewhere between the Hail Mary's and the Our Father's, a woman's voice said, "I'm going to wheel you into the room now." As she was talking to me, Dr. Randolph appeared and said, "Good morning, Lorna. We are all set. Everything is going to be just fine. You are going to do great!" I remember smiling back at him. I don't even know if I responded to his affirmation. Suddenly I was under really bright lights. In the distance I heard people talking about the singer and how I had offered one of the women extra work at the casting company. In my drunken defense I tried to say, "I meant that. It's never too late to try something new."To which Dr. Randolph jokingly replied, "Great, she is trying to take my staff away from me." To the nurse he said, "You'd be a wonderful actress. We just may have a problem fitting your head in the door when you return to work here after a day on the set."

I remember being fiercely impressed by how cool he was around his colleagues. Everyone was kidding around and speaking to one another with a casual, humorous repartee. My surgeon was the big cheese in the room and yet he seemed to encourage a freestyle farewell for each patient as they went under. The team created an immensely positive energy in the room, making my final coherent moments with cancer amazingly cool. I am very certain my final moments with The Bow Tie Bastard would have been much different.

Just then, I said a quick prayer thanking God for Dr. Randolph. I sincerely could not have asked for a better surgeon to help me bid adieu to the past fifty days of grief, fret, perplexity, sleeplessness, disease, and despondency. My incredulous cancer was about to meet his match! At Dr. Randolph's request, I allowed myself to descend into the deepest dormancy enabling him to conquer the battle between good and evil in my body. I don't recall any fear. Before I closed my eyes, I looked up at a ceiling filled with bright white light. The realist in me knew the intensity of the illumination was to assist the staff. The spiritualist in me knew the brilliance of the beams was to remind me that God was in the room shining his protective love down on me. And finally, my surgeon asked me to count down. *And so it begins…*

I woke up to a woman's voice saying, "Hello. I'm going to need you to take full deep breaths as often as you can. You are doing fine. It's over. Okay, full deep breaths. You are in recovery. I need you to breathe." I requested a drink. "We'll start you off with a few ice chips. You have to work on your breathing okay?" Believe it or not, I was aware of how shallow my breaths were. I didn't feel my diaphragm moving at all. To be very clear, I didn't feel anything move and that gave me the creeps. As I sucked on the ice, I felt really dizzy and disoriented. I kept trying to focus my eyes on the woman talking to me. I remember being frustrated over not being able to clear my vision.

"What is on my legs?" I asked. They were hot and I felt like I had ski pants on. "Boots to prevent clotting during the surgery" the nurse said, while reminding me that I needed to take larger breaths. "Can you please remove them? I am **really hot**." Hot may have been euphemism for claustrophobic, but I wanted out of the restraints. "Let's focus on your breathing and then we'll take them off."

As several more blurry images passed by the end of my bed, I remembered my concern about my glasses. I panicked when I realized that they hadn't found my set of eyes. Anyone who wears contacts or glasses knows how awful it is to go without them. "May I have my glasses?" I asked. "Oh you need glasses? I'm not sure we know where they are. They may already be up in your room with your things." With growing aggravation I said, "Well, I had them at registration. When they took my bags, they took my glasses. Please, find my bags or find my husband. He will find my glasses! I will vomit if I continue to open my eyes without my glasses."

From that point on, I opted to keep my eyes closed to avoid the nausea that was brewing from my blurred vision. "May I have more ice?" I asked. No one answered me. When I opened my eyes, I realized no one was standing near me. Unable to project my voice above a whisper, I waved my fingers for what seemed like an eternity. A new female voice said, "Yes, can I help you?" I asked her if I could have a drink. She told me it was too soon to have a drink and that I had to stick with the ice for a while. "Focus on your breathing," she said as she left. *Focus, what a funny word choice…I cannot <u>see</u> but she wants me to <u>focus.</u>*

After a while, my glasses were placed on my face. Once that small fire was put out, I became fixated on getting the boots off of my legs. The heat on my legs began at my groin and stretched down to my toes. I have always hated the feeling of clothing on my skin underneath blankets. Sleeping in p.j. pants is something I never do. "May I sit up?" I asked the nurse at a desk directly in front of my bed. "We'll get you up in just a bit. You really need to take deeper breaths. I'll get you some more ice."

"Where is my family?" I asked as she made her way over to me. "Once you are breathing better you can go up to your room." I was **so** relieved to hear those words. Up until that point, I thought I was *in* my room. I feel silly admitting this, but I thought I was going to spend the next two days in a room with six other beds, a nurse station, phones ringing, and bright lights. My legs continued to burn under the boots.

I filled my entire mouth with ice. I stored the freezing cold chips in my cheeks in hope of extinguishing the piping-hot smolder I felt in my legs. "That's too much ice! You need to slow down," a nurse said in a disapproving voice.

I was incredibly agitated in the holding area. I expected to wake up and see my mum on my right side and Rog on my left side. In the movies people always wake up with their loved ones at their side. I woke up to a nurse who seemed to have gotten lost on the way to the maternity ward. "BREATHE" was about all she ever said. I had no idea if I had done well in the surgery. I had no idea if Dr. Randolph got all of the cancer. I had no idea how long I had been under. I had no idea what time it was or where my family was. All I knew was that I wanted out of there. In an attempt to speed up the transition to my room, I tried my best to expand my diaphragmatic region. By placing my hands under my rib cage, I took in a long breath through my nose and exhaled through my mouth. I repeated this several times until I felt my hand moving up and down. I tried to envision the breath starting at my toes then whirling up around my head stretching the entire length of my frame.

A few minutes later, an encouraging voice told me I was ready to go to my room. As we wheeled through the halls and onto an elevator, I remember feeling normal. I kept quizzing myself to test my brainpower. *One plus one is two. Two plus two is four. Four plus four is eight. Today is Feb 2nd, 2005. I am in Boston. My name is Lorna Jayne Brunelle. George W. Bush is our President.* My mind was sharp. I didn't even hesitate when answering my own questions. I wasn't in any pain at all. *Talk about a good cancer, I feel like I can go home today. This truly is the good cancer.* "Here we are," the nurse said as she wheeled the portable bed right next to one of the beds in the room.

I had the window seat. The entire wall on my left was comprised of glass windows overlooking the beautiful city of Boston. Thrilled to have something fabulous to look at, I smiled and let out a huge sigh of relief. Although anything would have been better than the holding area, I didn't expect to have a five-star view. "Is my family here?" I asked. "We'll call them up shortly. We just need to get you settled," the nurse replied. On the count of three, I was shuffled from my O.R. bunk to the bed in my top-of-the hub suite.

Anxious to put my contacts in and freshen up, I continued to send "I'm fine" signals to the nurse. As I fixed the sheet on my bed I realized my leg boots had been removed. Confused and worried about not remembering the moment my lower extremities were set free, I began to panic. *Okay, girl, you must be floating in and out of consciousness. Perhaps you are taking little cat naps along the way. After all, you must be under the influence of some type of drug. DO NOT WORRY. This is to be expected. Baby steps. Good news, the restraints are off and your legs have been liberated! Stay calm.*

Before long I heard mum's voice in the hall. She entered the room with my grandmother Concetta and Rog. "You look wonderful, Honey!" my gram said with a touch of shock in her voice. "No really, Lorna, you look *amazing*," mum said. My husband walked over to kiss me and said, "You look beautiful. I missed you, Babe." My husband began reading a few notes from Dr. Randolph about the surgery. "It looks good" and "she did great." Shortly after, my biological father, his wife and their son (my half-brother) walked into the room. You'd think having spent years on stage performing for people I'd be used to having an audience staring at me. That day, it was extremely odd to have a crowd at the foot of my bed making small talk and looking at me. The entire situation was just a little too surreal for me.

Mum began chatting about a book she was reading. One of the chapters was about Cuttyhunk, a section of the Elizabeth Islands off of Buzzard's Bay. Her words became blurry in my head. I must have closed my eyes for a moment and drifted away. As I dozed, she told the crowd about a school for lepers on one of the islands. Several residents reported seeing an apparition of a lady in a white dress. They also saw several little people running around the island.

I asked my husband to call my team at school to report how the surgery went. Reenie answered the phone. As I mentioned before, she is a breast cancer survivor. Eager to hear her voice and to know how work was going, I took the phone for a few minutes. "Reenie, it's OVER. I feel <u>amazing!</u> I can totally expand my lungs. I am taking in the biggest breaths ever. I feel fantastic. I feel better than I have in months!" Little did I know it's common to feel marvelous immediately following surgery. "Work is fine, Lorna." She said through tears. When I asked her why she was crying, she said, "I'm just really happy to hear that you are okay <u>and</u> your **voice** sounds _exactly_ the same. That must be a good sign. Take care. I'll talk to you tomorrow."

After several more "you look greats" and "if you need anything, let me knows" "I'll see you tomorrow's" and "I love you's", most of my company departed. My husband left to locate some food for me. My room was empty, but I was in the company of a phenomenal sunset. Pain and cancer-free, I took in the brilliance of the golden glow over Boston. Feeling like a champion, I closed my eyes for a short rest. _You must always remember today, for it's the beginning of the rest of your life._ _Happy **New Life**, Lorna Jayne **Cancer Gone** Brunelle._

I spent most of the first evening starring at the skyline. Normally a stomach sleeper, I found it near impossible to rest sitting upright. I longed for sleep but couldn't gather up more than the occasional catnap. Every few hours, a nurse from Italy came in to give me a dose of pain meds. Other than having my wisdom teeth removed my freshman year in college, I don't ever recall being on pain meds. I was hesitant a few of the times she visited with the little paper cup filled with _Dr. Feel Good_ tablets. I wasn't in pain and didn't really see the point in taking the drugs.

A former thyroid cancer patient warned me about one of the uncomfortable side effects of pain relief. -Constipation. I wanted to avoid that at all costs! Years back, my husband took me to Mexico for my thirtieth birthday. Afraid to drink the water, I backed off of anything that wasn't bottled, resulting in less than half of my regular water intake during our visit. That mixed with an all-inclusive package, adding the occasional frozen banana daiquiri and rice and cheese on every plate in sight, led to one hell of a back up in bowel world. After **nine** days, I gave birth to a kiwi! There isn't anything sexy about having your husband give you an enema on the Mayan Riviera of the Yucatan Peninsula. I never want to revisit that type of closeness with my man. I was apprehensive about popping poop stoppin' pain killers every four hours.

Regardless of my plea to skip a dose here and there, the nurse convinced me to stay on my preventative course of treatment. "You don't want to be in pain, Miss. This will help you down the road." *Easy for you to say!* I thought each time she said that. *Chances are you've never passed something the size of squirrel's head out of your back door.* "If you are going to recommend that I take every dose of these pills, I'm going to need my pitcher of water filled throughout the evening. I cannot afford to have a *situation* in bathroom land. I need to keep my system hydrated. Would you mind helping me with that?" I asked, while I pondered how nasty it would be to engage the sutures of my incision in a wrestling match on the toilet between my neck and my bottom. In appreciation of my fear of another barbaric bathroom saga, the nurse agreed to keep the water coming.

Without any hours of slumber I watched the sun come up. It was February 3, 2005, and my first cancer-free sunrise in months. Rounds began at the crack of dawn. A team of eager young-ins walked in with the vigor of a Macy's Day Parade band. I was expecting a delicate method of introduction in dim lighting with a quiet 6:15 A.M. vocal tone. Much to my surprise, the band flipped on the blinding overhead lights and marched into the room with clipboards in hand. The conductor asked, "How are you today? Did you get sleep?" "Not so much on the sleep end, but lots on the rest," I replied.

"Any tingling in your lips, fingers or toes?" the conductor asked. (A classic sign of calcium levels dropping) "No, I'm feeling pretty good. Just a little tired," I said. Soon after the band marched out of our room and down the hall, I got out of the bed to dress for the day. It was an outrageous chore to wheel my portable IV line into the bathroom while carrying my toothbrush, other toiletries and the portable shower kit the nurse had delivered to us. I was hooked up to dozens of wires. As I tried to wash up, I noticed a disc under my breast connected to a wire leading to my walk-man type pack in the pocket of my hospital gown. I got chills as I faintly remembered the nurse hooking me up to all of that once we made it to my room. It was yet another foggy moment that entailed a stranger poking around my private parts. Clearly the disc was UNDER my breast. The last time someone other than my husband went to second base with me, I'm pretty sure a complimentary dinner or movie preceded or followed. This time however, nothing that eventful had taken place.

God bless the nurses who lift boobs all day. I quickly realized that I was going to have to let go of my privacy hang-ups and just accept that strangers had touched me in outlandishly unordinary places for <u>thyroid</u> surgery. The upper region of my crotch and area under my right breast was no longer sacred husband territory. In that moment, I'm pretty sure I became a full-fledged grown up. Suddenly it was no longer acceptable to behave like an eight grader when talking about boobs and crotches. The professional staff had to place the boots on my upper leg to prevent clotting in surgery, and the professional staff had to place a disc under my breast in order to monitor my vitals from the nurse station down the hall. There was nothing silly about it! Once I convinced myself of that, I thanked my lucky stars that I was knocked out or semi-conscious for both violations.

I felt like a million dollars once I brushed my teeth, washed my face and combed my hair. The smell of my eye and face cream reminded me of my normal daily routine. I became a smidgen homesick. I was eager to dump my hospital gown and slip into something a little more dryer sheet scented. Little by little, I was becoming more aware of a tickle that had developed in my throat earlier that morning. When I took a deep breath, I could hear a fluid like sound causing a rumbling in my chest. Much like a car trying to start up, the noise seemed to climb up my chest and land in my throat, then fall back down again as I breathed. Afraid to cough, I kept drinking water and sucking on cough drops. Knock on wood I never get colds, so I pretty much ignored the sensation in my chest assuming it was some delayed expulsion of the anesthesia.

Shortly after rounds, Dr. Randolph stopped by my room. As he recounted my procedure I was fascinated by what he shared. Apparently, I have a frayed nerve that looks like a tree. He had read about oddly shaped nerves, but hadn't seen one until he worked on my neck. He referred to it as "unique anatomy." "It took a little longer to accomplish what we had to do, but it was very interesting," he said, with a little spark in his eye. Then he asked me to sing a few scales. My bed-side serenade was reminiscent of a monster in heat. He didn't look one bit alarmed. "My speaking voice sounds exactly the same. Why is my singing voice so awful?" I asked. "It takes a little time" he said in an encouraging voice. "I expect a beautiful recovery. I'll come by again later on."

Within an hour of Dr. Randolph's visit, his Fellow stopped by to remove my stitches. Dr. Chris was a very hip, young English fellow that was miles away from home. Although he appeared extremely young, his charm was old-world. "How do we do this?" I asked as he made his way over to my bed. "Well, normally, I tie your sutures to a string, then I tie the string around the door, then I slam the door really fast and they all fly out! OR I could very gently cut each suture and ever so carefully remove each little piece with virtually no pain or discomfort. Which would you prefer?" *Good looks, charm and a sense of humor. YOU GO, BOY! You'll go very far in your career. BRAVO.* "I have been coughing a lot. Is it okay for you to remove the sutures even though I have been tugging at them all night?"

"I can leave them in a little longer. Here's the bonus – by doing this, your incision will look like a Frankenstein scar for the rest of your life. You'll be able to see all of the little dots on the top and bottom of the line in the middle. Shall we wait? It's up to you?" I realize that his words may come across as sarcastic on paper, but in real life he was wicked (there's a Boston slang for 'ya) funny. As he quietly worked his away around my incision, I contemplated asking him why he chose a life in medicine. It was obvious he could have been a politician, lawyer or even an actor. As a happily married woman who works at a casting company, this fellow had a great face for film. He was hospital eye candy in a Dr. McHot kind of way.

Just as he proposed, I didn't experience any discomfort while he freed my incision of sutures. The handsome Fellow smirked and said, "Have a nice day, girls. I'll see you later on," then walked out of the room. What is it about smart, handsome and talented men calling women *girls* that makes us melt? Making sick people feel that special is an art. Both the Fellow and Dr. Randolph could write a book on it.

Throughout day friends and family came to visit. My state rep friend greeted me with the same shocked salutation. "You look and SOUND great!" His visit raised the energy in the room and before long everyone was deep in conversation. While my visitors were talking, something caught my eye on the left side of the room. The cover of one of my books appeared to have an enormous black spider on it. I was shocked that no one else seemed to notice the museum caliber insect. It was something straight out of the Smithsonian or an arachnophobia flick. Totally ignoring the conversation in the room, I glared at the spider waiting for it to move. I turned away for a few minutes, reengaged in the topic of discussion and then turned back to the book.

An overwhelming sense of relief came over me when the cover of the book resumed its normal appearance. -A woman's legs in black stockings, with a seam up the back, in incredibly high black heels. For any Candace Bushnell fans out there, (the creator of Sex and the City) it was the cover of her <u>TRADING UP</u> novel. I opted not to share my inaccuracy with anyone in the room.

While my friends continued to converse, I noticed a flash of color race by the end of the bed. The rush of color hardly cleared the top of my blankets. I tried to refocus my eyes, words, and brain back on the dialogue in the room. Just as I began to say a sentence, a tiny little person ran by my bed. Worst of all, he had quite a nasty expression on his face. He wore a small red hat and was dressed like a gnome. Amazed that no one in the room was paying much attention to my 36" visiting troll, I chalked him up to a hallucination. *He's not really there, Lorna! It must be the drugs! He's not really there!* As I continued to tell myself to ignore what I was seeing, several other pissed-off little trolls ran around my room. Each one wore a different colored cap and peaked at me around the corners of the bed. Each troll had a ridiculously disapproving face. *What have I done to offend you? Take that look off of your faces! Get out of here!* I demanded as they continued to mock me in front of my guests.

Oh my gosh, now I'm talking to my hallucinations. Lorna, you have to say something to your husband or mother, they'll get a nurse and stop this madness. But if you tell them now, your state rep will think you are insane. You are the chairperson of his upcoming gala, you cannot confess to seeing little people in his presence! Just ignore the trolls and they will go away! The little people seemed to enjoy my confidential turmoil. Their faces continued to squish

105

up as if to say, "Screw you sistah, we ain't leavin'!" *Okay, so, if I have to see troll/gnomes in my room, why can't they be happy? Where are the trolls that frolic, sing, and play? How come I got stuck with the pissed off trolls?* At that point, I had a village of angry little trolls scooting about my room. I closed my eyes and began repeating my quiz. *One plus one is two, two plus two is four, four plus four is eight, George W. Bush is our President. I am almost 34 years old. Hail Mary full of grace...*Finally, the uninvited pests disappeared. Without a flinch, I tried to resume my presence in the room. I couldn't get over my delirium and was convinced it was time to get off the drugs. Some systems just do not respond well to meds. My body processed the pain meds like a batch of 1960's mushrooms. (FYI: I have only ever "done" culinary mushrooms!)

I controlled the visions by refusing all pain meds from that point on. My friend Nellie hallucinated on pain meds, too. So if you ever find yourself in the hospital having a bad trip, remember that you are not going crazy. It's just the drugs talkin'. My mother told me about the chapter she shared with everyone in my hospital room. While I dosed off, she spoke about recorded sightings of little people running around the island of Cuttyhunk. Clearly my subconscious picked up on her story and my mind, under the influence of drugs, ran a sprint with the information.

I didn't share my troll tales until I returned home from the hospital. I advise you to tell someone you are hallucinating as it is happening. Having cancer is hard. No one needs pissed off trolls making life more difficult.

Unhappy Birthday

$\mathcal{R}$OGER FILLED MY WATER PITCHER BEFORE he kissed me goodnight and headed off to the hotel. Thanks to all of my visitors (excluding the trolls) the day passed by rather quickly. While I was in the bathroom washing up for bed, I had an uncontrollable fit of coughing. I rolled a towel up and placed it on my incision. The pressure of the towel kept my incision in place as I coughed. I could feel a ton of phlegm-like stuff trying to exit my body. The only other time I had experienced that sensation was back in high school when I contracted walking pneumonia. *You haven't been sick in almost twenty years! This must be a reaction to the anesthesia. Your lungs are wondering what the heck was pumped into them yesterday. Try to calm down and take deep breaths!* My cough would not subside. At one point I saw stars around my eyes. *Am I going to pass out in the bathroom of this hospital from a cough? Oh God, please give me a break! I have to get back to my bed to call a nurse.*

When the nurse arrived I tried to explain exactly what I was feeling. "When is the last time you had pill?" she asked. While I was trying to figure out what that had to do with coughing and mucous, I told her that I wasn't going to be taking anymore drugs as they were upsetting my body. "I'll get you an over the counter pill then," she said, as she left the room. I swallowed the pills and tried to sleep.

A large full moon shined into my room. Although the light was exquisitely peaceful, I could not sleep. I had been up well over thirty-three hours and I craved rest. The rumble in my chest was getting worse. I tried to stay very still and took the smallest breaths imaginable. I had to go to the bathroom. As I walked, I felt the rumble in my chest jump around and try to make its way to the top of my body. *Shit! It's happening again!* I rolled up the towel again, pressed it against my neck and tried to expel some of the junk in my body. Small amounts of yellow goo flew out of my mouth.

Before long, I was barking out stuff into the sink at full volume. So much mucous was surfacing at once I found it hard to catch my breath. I literally felt like I was drowning. I panicked (which made things worse) and tried to suppress the attack. *What in Gods name is happening? Where is all of this mucous coming from? Why can't I catch my breath? Please, Lord, make this stop!* Against my restraint, more phlegm forced its way out of my body through another fit of coughing, yakking and choking. *I have to call for help. I cannot get any breath! I'm going to pass out.* I made my way back to the bed to call a nurse. (Don't ask me why I didn't press the button in the bathroom.) During my trip to the bed, it became nearly impossible to breathe. *I can't breathe! I can't breathe! I can't breathe!* ***I'm drowning.***

With the weight of two trucks on my chest, I pushed the nurse button and waited, gasping for pockets of air through a sea of fluid in the back of my throat. I was certain that at any moment, I was going to pass out. Just then my concentration on my breathing was interrupted by a glorious unworldly presence in the room. I felt certain that someone was standing at the foot of my bed. I'm not sure if it was my guardian angel, or Rose's son Sean, but as the nurse came in to assess me, I knew someone else was in the room watching over me. The nurse called for an E.R. doctor. Within minutes a very kind man was in the room. He listened to my lungs and asked me a few questions. "She seems to be having an asthma attack. Set her up on a Nebulizer." "This will help you breathe. You should feel a lot better in a few minutes. <u>Try to relax, Lorna</u>."

My heart was pounding. I was hot, clammy and desperately wanted to see my husband. The nurse hooked up a cool little container with a pipe. Before long a steamy flow of medicine was coming out. "Take deep breaths," she said, as she taught me how to maneuver the devise. My lungs felt like Old Man Winter had blown a huge blast of life into them.

Finally able to breathe I began to calm down. In fear of another troll altercation I refused the offer of a sleeping pill. The force at the foot of my bed stayed with me while I relaxed enough to shut my eyes for a few minutes. As I lay on the bed utterly drained and defeated by my body, I wondered if I was at the beginning of a long, hard recovery. My spirit was zapped. I felt so fantastic the day before. No one warned me about how quickly things would change. That night, I thought about my good friend and her participation in a menopause study at a famous hospital in Boston. After years of debilitating night sweats and hot flashes she agreed to be part of a study that involved her taking a new medication to cure menopausal symptoms. She signed a waiver stating that a percentage of the participants were going to be issued placebo pills rather than the miracle menopausal pill. Shortly after she began taking the pills, she felt amazing. Her hot flashes were gone, her night sweats had stopped, and she was sleeping through the night. Finally after suffering through menopause, she was living a happy, normal, and healthy life.

I was with her in Boston the day the doctors told her she was being dismissed from the study because she had been issued placebo pills. The news was both devastating and extraordinary. In that moment I realized the power of our beautiful minds. My friend had temporarily cured herself with her mind. The placebo pills were her ticket to a new life. Once the pills were gone, her symptoms returned. I couldn't help but relate her situation to my cancer. Did I have the power to cure my cancer with my mind? Did I make a mistake? Should I have skipped the surgery and searched for a more holistic approach to shrinking my tumor? Was my mind strong enough to cure my illness? Unlikely since I couldn't even fight back against the trolls.

My incident in the hospital was the most terrifying moment of my life. I have a whole new respect for people who suffer with intense asthma. The irony is that I truly believed I was going to die (in a hospital of all places) surrounded by professionals who prevent people from failing every day. Unfortunately, that evening was not the last of my horrible nights. My good cancer was proving to be much more cumbersome than I had imagined.

As the sun peaked over the Boston skyline, a parade of doctors marched in and flicked on the blearing lights for another round of rounds. Once again, the conductor asked us a few questions, and continued on his route. I continued coughing up junk the following morning. It was nearly forty-eight hours and the occasional cat nap was all I had to show for sleep. Going to the bathroom to brush my teeth seemed like an Olympic event. *You'll sleep when you get home, Lorna. You just need to be home in your own bed. You have to stay positive. Chin up, Girl.* My daily affirmations were becoming less and less convincing. My body felt like someone had taken a stick and whipped it for months.

My total stay at the hospital was from 6:00 A.M. on Wednesday, to 1:30 P.M. on Friday. I have heard of other hospitals releasing patients the day after thyroid cancer surgery. I was extremely grateful for the extra day. As eager as I was to be in my own bed, I couldn't imagine dealing with an asthma attack at my home. I was discharged with a warning about dropped calcium levels. If I felt any tingling around the mouth, finger tips or toes, I needed to hit the local emergency room for evaluation. If calcium drops, the person often needs an injection. I have to confess, the warning about calcium levels freaked me out. I had been experiencing tingling on the right side of my face all afternoon. Lord knows, they took blood out of me during my entire stay. Obviously, my levels were fine. I kept telling myself the sensation was a sign that things were healing.

The ride back home was intense. I felt every bump in the road. *Maybe I should have accepted a few pain meds for this trip,* I thought as my husband tried his best to avoid the potholes on the beaten New England highways. The ride in the car was the inauguration of my latest post-op delight – crying. I cried in the car but had no idea what I was crying about. Once we got home, my husband set up little comfort stations in the house. I had blankets and pillows in the living room, hearth room, and bedroom. My nests for rest were cozy, but my state of blues lingered. I assumed all of the hormonal rebalancing would come during the hypothyroid stage leading up to the radioactive iodine radiation. It never occurred to me that I'd feel the loss of my thyroid days after the surgery.

Roger made me some lunch. Although my neck felt like I had a 2X4 nailed to the back of it, I could chew and swallow most foods. I was just too tired to eat. *If only I could sleep until spring! Wake me up when this is over...*A few hours later, I went to the bathroom and discovered that I had my period. As you may recall, the pre-op doctors asked me to stop all of my meds. I completely disregarded what would happen if I stopped taking my daily dose of a mild birth control pill, used as hormone treatment for Poly Cystic Ovarian Syndrome. Without that routine med in my system, my body assumed it was time to menstruate. Suddenly, the suspicious tears in the car made sense. Don't get me wrong, I understood that my thyroid had been yanked from my body. I understood that I was no longer producing any natural thyroid hormone. I knew to expect highs and lows in the mood department. I just didn't understand why the crash happened as soon as we pulled out of the hospital.

I tried to watch a little TV but I wanted to crawl out of my own skin. I couldn't get comfortable anywhere in my house. Throughout my time in the hospital, I longed to feel my flannel sheets on my body. Little did I know how hard it was going to be to lie down on my bed. I had to prop every pillow under my back all the way up my spine in order to prevent my head from nodding off to one side as I napped. After hours of trying to rest in my bed, I retired to one of the leather recliners in the hearth room. My mother-in-law gave me a "C" shaped pillow (how appropriate) to rest my neck in. That pillow allowed me to doze off without waking up to the startling discomfort of my neck bobbing down.

I also found it very difficult to look to the right or left. It was impossible to bend over. In spite of all of the time I spent pre-surgery selecting recovery reading material, I found it impossible to hold a book (hard or soft cover) long enough to read a page. I didn't seem to have the strength to support a magazine either. The tension from my hands seemed to travel up my arms and settle in to my neck. I tried to sit at the table to read. After a few minutes my neck hurt from bending down to see the pages. In short, reading was out of the question. I contemplated taking half of a Percocet in order to relax, read, sleep, or get out of my body. The memory of the trolls was too vivid.

I won't try to sugar coat this-I was in a lot of pain. I felt a constant pulse in my neck. Still hacking up yellow junk from my lungs, my incision endured quite a work out. After one of my most impressive bathroom episodes (complete with seeing stars around my head after coughing for about ten minutes) Rog called my surgeon. Dr. Randolph called in a prescription for a liquid suppressant with a **kick.** The potent fluid reduced the cough, but made my <u>no sleep for three days</u> head and <u>no solid food</u> belly, feel dizzy. I felt like I was on an amusement park ride. In desperate need of grounding my equilibrium, I closed my eyes and tried to relax. *Room spins…are you kidding me?*

Again, one side of my face was numb. In addition to which, my toes **and** fingers felt numb. *Oh my goodness, my calcium must be dropping. Or is the codeine making me feel tingly? What do I do?"* I explained my sensation to Rog. Ever the drama queen, I reminded him that my nurse friend had thyroid cancer and developed Bells Palsy during her recovery. "Do you think I have Bells?" I asked in complete panic! "I'm going to call again," he said with an, "I have **no idea** what to say" look on his face. Under Dr. Randolph's advice, we drove back to Boston for assessment.

BIG SURPRISE- my calcium levels were fine. They were more than fine actually, they were PERFECT! Bewildered by the tingles in my body I asked the E.R. doctor why I felt so numb. The E.R. doctor replied, "Miss, I think you need sleep. The combination of meds in the hospital and cough medicine may have upset you. You seem to have a bad track record with pain meds. It's a tough situation. You are most likely not sleeping because you are coughing and are in pain, but the medicine to treat the cough seems to be upsetting you. I can tell you that this does <u>not appear to be Bells</u>." While he spoke I noticed a scar on his throat. "Did you have thyroid cancer?" I asked. "This is from a tracheotomy," he said, neglecting to share the nature of his scar. He went on to say, "The most important thing I can offer you is that your calcium levels are fantastic. You are going to be fine. Try to get some rest."

I cried all the way home. *My face is still numb. No one believes me. My fingers were numb a few hours ago. My toes were numb, too. I keep choking on junk that is flying out of my body. I cannot sleep. I'd rather have my old contaminated thyroid than deal with this. Cancer and all—I want my old thyroid.* It is true folks; I really wanted my cancerous thyroid back. How messed up is that? How lazy and *non-warrior* is that? The clock in the Jeep reported a few minutes after midnight. It was February 5. My birthday was one day away.

"I cannot take much more of this!" I said loudly. From the backseat I heard mum say, "Lorna, we are only given what we can take. You just need some rest." She meant that God only dishes out what he knows we can withstand. At that moment God was on my shit list and I didn't want to be reminded of the way in which he works with his children. I simply didn't have the stamina for Gods' lessons that night.

Within forty minutes, I was upright in the recliner and trying to sleep. My lower back was screaming from days of an upright sitting position. My breathing was shallow. *I will only allow myself the tiniest of breaths. I do not want to start coughing again. I am too exhausted for a fit of coughing. I will sit here as still as a snake and survive on the smallest quantities of air.* Whenever I'd nod off to sleep, I'd feel my body falling off of a cliff. Everything around me was black and I was plunging downward like a jet about to crash. "I'm going to die!" I said as I woke up gasping for air. "You are not going to die, Lorna." Roger said from the recliner on the other side of the room. I'm right here. I'm listening to you breathe. TRUST me, if you stop breathing, I'll be right here. Besides, babe, breathing is an involuntary action. Even if you pass out, you will continue breathing. Try to go to sleep." "But when I try to sleep, I feel myself slipping away. I'm dying. Then I catch myself and I come back." I said realizing from his face that he either didn't get me, or felt really bad for me.

As I type this chapter of my journey I take great pause reflecting on how vile that time was. I hadn't slept in **four** days. I had three hard core pain meds in my bloodstream. I wasn't eating balanced and frequent meals. I had a full blown asthma attack under my belt and was passing great amounts of phlegm from my lungs. Let's not forget my body was also experiencing a furious and unexpected period because I stopped taking my meds before the surgery. In short, I was a damn mess. To top it all off, I thought I was going to die in my sleep. Does life get any scarier than that?

The next day I confided in my friend Rose. Turns out she, too, had the same fear of dying after surgery. She knew exactly what I was talking about. That night, she and Jane came to my house at bed time. They are both certified Reiki masters and have worked with various methods of eastern healing modalities for years. Rose is also a certified hypnotherapist. As I sat in the recliner, both girls worked on healing me from head to toe through energy work. They administered Reiki, massaged my hands and feet, and tuned up my spirit. While they worked on me, they recited affirmations of healing wrapped up in white light, love, and protection. Jane tried to teach me a way to meditate in order to fall asleep. "Hear that clock in your bedroom, Lorna? That is your heart beat. Like the clock, NO MATTER WHAT, your heart will not stop ticking. You have to let go, now. You have to sleep. YOU WILL NOT DIE. You will be fine. Your body just needs to rest."

While Jane spoke, Rose wrote a letter to my subconscious that read: *I am divinely protected. I am safe. I slept when I was at my worst and nothing happened. So I am even safer to sleep now! My angels will watch over me as I sleep. I am safe. This is going to pass. I am going to ground myself by sending my tree trunk down to the earth and keeping myself rooted to the earth. I am safe! I have to remember that when I feel my craziest, it is my hormones! Just my hormones and my body trying to heal. I WIN!"* The letter had a smiley face with luscious eyelashes drawn on it. "We are going to put this near your bed, Lorna," Rose said. "Lorna, I have been there. I know how you are feeling. Trust me; you will not die if you sleep. Trust me. Your energy was a little scattered and low, but we have worked all of that out.

You are rebalanced and ready for sleep. In a few more days all of those drugs will be out of your system."

Those who don't believe in the power of hands on healing would think we were a pack of crazy kooks. (Incidentally the proper definition for KOOK is somebody whose behavior is considered eccentric.) Call it what you will, but I slept pretty well that night. Meaning, rather than eight minutes of a cat nap, I had about three hours of uninterrupted sleep. The healing soiree my mid- wives of wellness threw me worked. Beyond the healing festival in my hearth room, I took great comfort in knowing that someone else experienced the same fear I had.

If the E.R. doctor had said, "Miss, it's normal to feel tingling on your face…you've just had surgery. Things are bound to tingle here and there." Or if he said, "You are coughing up junk from the anesthesia. Many people have reported the same behavior. It's nothing to worry about and should pass in a few days," I'm pretty sure I would have felt a little better. The business of, "I have no idea what you are talking about" and "I have never heard of anyone reporting a tingling face before," worried me. I was certain my post-op symptoms were exclusive and that was bothersome. The numbness and tingling went up the right side of my neck, traveled to the back of my neck and continued on up to my face. I thought my neck was going to swell up (internally) and close off the airway to my lungs. That scared the hell out of me.

My only other thyroid cancer friend (who is a nurse) had Bells Palsy post-op. She had numbness on her face and then she had Bells? Where did that leave me? Naturally, I assumed I was developing Bells. It seems like a silly assumption now as I look back, but I'll say it again folks, I was a first timer. I strictly went off of what I heard. As Reenie says it's all in presentation. I need the doctors of the world to understand and respect that we, as the patients, come to them petrified, exhausted and completely at their mercy. When a doctor says, "I have never heard of such a thing", we as patients translate that into a most terrifying prognosis.

Sorry to be a pain in the ass about this matter, but I've since spoken to **several** thyroid cancer survivors, and most of them have experienced tingling and numbness from the neck up on to their face post-op, that was <u>not related</u> to dropped calcium levels. So what is that about? Was I the only one whining to an E.R. doctor my first day out of the hospital? Does everyone else in America keep anything foreign feeling in their body under wraps in the hope that it will go away? Why are we afraid to communicate with our physicians?

The next day I tried to stay on top of my sadness. My fits of crying were sucking the life out of my body. I remember feeling like the character Bridget Jones as I made daily mental diary entries. *Thyroid cancer recovery* **DAY THREE**: *Number of times I cried today~four. Number of times I wanted to die today~one. Number of times I coughed up disgusting internal matter in the sink today~three. Number of phone calls I refused today~seven. Number of times I missed my old cancer- ridden thyroid today~countless.*

Day after day, I'd wake up hoping to have a wonderful day. Little by little it would deteriorate into a pile of shit. Then with my spirits squelched into the hardwood floors, I'd walk by a delivery or card. Friends had sent me flower, tea, spa and chocolate dipped fruit baskets. The sites, smells, and sentiment were testimony of the people who loved me. I've always been one of those girls who love their birthday. This was much more than that. This was an overwhelming sea of support in my home. People ranging from acquaintance to life long friends were routing for me. Their confidence encouraged me to believe that I <u>would</u> recover. The cards with hand written words of encouragement reminded me that I wasn't alone in my fight. Each day that support persuaded me to pick up the pieces of my new broken life and try to glue them together.

Later that afternoon my entire family was at a birthday party for my nephew. My absence added guilt to my resume of misery. I was sitting at the dining room table crying (for about the third time) feeling bad for myself because I was missing the birthday party. For years, my nephew would say, "What kind of cake are we going to have this year, Auntie?" Together, we'd brainstorm ideas for the perfect creation. One of my favorites was a cake with a construction site on it inspired by a hit TV show for children. We crushed graham crackers to make piles of sand and loaded the beds of little dump trucks with the cookie dust.

My friend Bob, a builder in real life, portrayed the famous cartoon character and led all of the children in a bird house building project during the party.

This was the first year I not only didn't make his cake, but it was the first year I missed his celebration. Those thoughts led to a series of sobbing which led to an encore of how I was ruining my husbands' life by being sick with cancer. It was high tea at my pity party when suddenly I looked up at the flowers all around me in the room. They looked like a brigade on the front line ready to kick my ass. The phrase *Flower Power* had never made more of a statement.

We are the Army of Beauty! Our soldiers are roses, tulips, lilies, daisies, freesia, delphinium, irises, and sweet pea. We have come to fight your constant urge to ignore the beauty and blessings around you. Work it out, sistah, because although we look pretty we have a lot of potency and power. We will not tolerate your disrespect much longer. Open your eyes! We will only be stunning for a few more days. So wake up and enjoy our splendor! You have to learn how to rest. Be still with us for a few more days, Lorna. We are here to help you mend. You are missing your nephew's birthday but he will have another birthday. This…this is your time to find your way back to wellness. We will be your winter garden of hope and glory. Right here in your home, we will remind you of the hot summer disease free days to come.

The Petal Platoon spoke with great gusto and shook me out of my pessimism. Another example of how out-of-the ordinary my life had become- It didn't even seem odd that I was taking advice from blossoms and foliage.

For anyone whose budget is not conducive to sending bulging bouquets to a friend after surgery, please know that all of the cards and emails I received bestowed deep sentiment to my heart. Those written words continued to comfort me long after the flowers dried up. My breast cancer surviving friend Reenie sent me a card every week for about ten weeks. Her dedication was remarkable. Weeks after my cancer was the top story within my circle of friends, a pretty envelope was delivered to my home reminding me that someone out there was still thinking of me. I highly recommend this practice of correspondence to anyone who wants to cheer up a friend in pain.

On that same theme, I also recommend spacing out your deliveries and correspondence. If you know some one in your family or circle is sending flowers to your loved one the first week they come home, opt to send your notes, emails and flowers the second or third week. Special treats arriving to the home over a period of time makes for an unbelievably distinct series of pick-me-ups for the patient! Doctors say thyroid cancer recovery takes about 2-4 weeks, but your hormones are out of whack long after your incision begins to heal. I found that depending on the size of the tumor, how much the surgeon is able to remove in surgery and whether or not the cancer was contained or had spread into the lymph nodes, many thyroid cancer patients have to go through radioactive iodine radiation treatments. The radiation extends the recovery time.

I plan to address all of this later in the book, but in order to prepare my body for the radioactive iodine treatment I had to become totally hypothyroid. That preparation caused a constant state of emotional mayhem. WEEKS after I was back in make-up, driving around town doing errands, my body remained in pandemonium. From the outside looking in, I was to quote my friends a "fast healer" who was "doing very well." Inside, I felt like I was losing my mind. So to wrap up my point on this matter, if you know someone who is sick, please send them notes of encouragement even <u>after</u> they look better. I can almost guarantee their healing journey has just begun.

Another unproductive day had passed. Roger and I tucked ourselves into the leather recliners. As usual, I sat upright in the chair for hours dozing off for a few moments here and there. I was mind-bogglingly (is that a word?) frustrated. There is an old Chinese proverb that reads, "You can buy blood but cannot buy life, you can buy sex but cannot buy love, you can buy a position, but cannot buy respect, you can buy a house but cannot buy a home, <u>you can buy a bed but cannot buy sleep.</u>" At that moment I deemed the proverb as incorrect. If it weren't for the trolls, I could buy a prescription for a pill to make me sleep!

The morning of my birthday the sun was brightly shining on the cold February ground. I desperately wanted to wash my hair. My neck and back were throbbing. It had been five days since my head felt hot water beating down on it. I couldn't think of a lavish gift finer than a good hair washin'. Through the years I have celebrated my birthday in warm places, seated in the best restaurants, on beds at the most decadent spas on the east coast, and around tables in houses with friends and family eating lobster until my belly popped out of my pants. But on that day, all I wanted to do was wash my hair. I paused with yet another reminder of my personal evolution. *This cancer really could change my life for the better. The smallest pleasures are once again **sacred** in my life. I used to pride myself in always stopping to smell the roses, never truly appreciating the luxury of the less obvious wonders around me like being able to wash my own hair. This little blessing will be the start of a better day and attitude.*

Every morning since my return home from the hospital, like clockwork, around 10:00 A.M., I unlocked my front door to see my mum's face smiling back at me through the glass. She did our laundry, picked up the house, answered my phone, returned my calls, opened my mail, helped write out my thank-you cards, cooked food and kept me company. This enabled my husband to have a few cancer-recovery-free hours a day. Roger could and would have done all of this for me. I am certain that he needed a break from camp cancer. I really wanted my mum around. Truth, when you are feeling low there is *nothing like* having your mum prepare homemade tapioca pudding or pastina with butter, basil, and chicken.

This day in my recovery was slightly different. It was my 34th birthday.

As soon as I saw her face I started crying. "Happy Birthday!" sounded like a major oxymoron and felt like a smack in the face. As my mum tried to console me, I decided that washing my hair would have been too much for me that day. After the not so invigorating wash up, I put on what had become my cancer uniform. My white linen nightgown, my hot pink cardigan, my hot pink slippers and a purple and pink scarf tied around my neck. The scarf was not for fashion; it kept my neck warm. In my amazingly drafty, old farm house there was a science to staying warm. In honor of my birthday, I brushed my hair and put on earrings. Pre-surgery, I promised myself I'd never sit around in my nightgown. It was only day four since the operation and

I never imagined how fatiguing it would be to dress. Walking around in p.j.'s for days was just one of many instances where my preconceived notions about my life and behavior after surgery were way off the mark. Reminder: I was recovering without pain meds. I know recovery is a little easier for people who can stomach the pain killers.

I could hear guests in the living room. Before leaving the bathroom I glanced in the mirror and thought *not too bad, Lorna. Happy 34th Birthday, girl.* Totally worn out with a flag pole for a neck, my main focus was to make it through the day without crying. That goal consumed all of my basic energy. Before I knew it, I was dizzy and needed to melt into the loveseat. My husband came in and said, "Lorna, I think you are doing too much today. You really should try to take a nap." He was right, I was beat. Rather than admit it, around 3:00 P.M., I attempted to dress in real clothes. It was Super Bowl Sunday and the New England Patriots were playing their 2nd consecutive Super Bowl. I wanted to get out of the house.

As I assembled an outfit for my sister Elizabeth's annual Super Bowl party, I tried to give myself a little pep talk. *You can do this Lorna. You can put on these clothes and go to Liz's house and be with your family. It's been four days, it's time to get out of the house.* My neck could not tolerate the weight of my bra holding up my double D chest. I opted to layer my shirts as to not advertise my 1960's braless declaration. As I placed my jogging suit jacket over my t-shirt, I smirked a bit at another big change. I would normally never leave the house without a bra. Yet there I was, preparing to watch the Super Bowl at my sister's house without an ounce of make-up on, my boobs flying free and oh, yes, nothing prepared on a dish to take with me. I wasn't bearing a plate of brownies or a bowl of guacamole and chips. For the first time in my life, putting on clothes was about all that I could take on that day.

The walk to the driveway felt like I was in slow motion. As I pulled myself up in to the Jeep, my neck was swearing! Near to my sister's door, I could hear the sounds of all four grandchildren running around. Everyone was talking and laughing. The sound of the children is why I got dressed. I needed that noise. I wish everyone owned CD's of their family to play during those moments when the silence of illness is too much to take. As we walked in, all of the kids yelled "Happy Birthday, Auntie Lorna!" None of them stared at me as if I was sick. My niece Paige asked to see my incision so I removed my scarf to show her. "Oh, that's not a big deal," she said as if to say, "I thought it was going to be a gaping hole in your neck with blood dripping out of it." I expected to have an unhappy birthday, but the children in my life made it impossible.

Forgetting that I couldn't really chew crunchy foods, I made a plate of the game food I'd normally eat. The homemade salsa with tortilla chips, chicken wings, veggies, and dip required too much chewing to get down. I opted to eat minced up ziti and sauce. Shortly after we ate, my family brought a candle lit birthday cake into the dining room. As they sang "Happy Birthday", I marveled my sister Liz's monotone key of the song. I took pleasure in remembering that some things in my life were the same despite how much had changed since my diagnosis.

The chaos of Super Bowl XXXIX Sunday was perfect. My loud ethnic family bellowing over the screeches and sounds of the kids playing as the guys debated the outcome of the game seemed like heaven to me. After years of growing up longing for a quiet, upper-middle-class suburban family life, I wouldn't have changed a thing. Boobs freely hanging out in a chair in the living room of my sister's house without any make up on, surrounded by the people who knew me better than anyone else in the world- I cherished things just as they were.

The Pats brought it home again on February 6, 2005. At the end of the day, their victory was the least important part my celebration.

The Wonder of Words

IF THE PATS CAN WIN TWO Super Bowls in a row, I can sleep in my own bed. Roger helped me build a tower of pillows to create a very elevated position. No matter how hard I tried, the pain was too intense to rest in any stance other than sitting upright. I **so wanted** to sleep in my own bed the night of my birthday. Extremely discouraged by my lack of success, I became increasingly more ghastly by the minute. "When will I be able to sleep in this bed?" I snapped at my husband. "I'm so **over** sleeping in that chair. I never expected this portion of the recovery. No one mentioned how hard it would be to lay flat on my back. They all must assume patients take the pain pills?"

Assuring me that within a few days I'd be in the big bed, Roger said, "I'm sleeping in a chair, too, Babe. I'm doing everything I can to support you. I think you have to be patient." *Be a patient cancer patient… a patient patient is just too much to ask…*"You are right, I'll be in the bed soon," I said making a mental note to back off of the violin playing. Every day seemed to have a string quartet serenading my sentences. I was certain everyone around me could hear the underscore.

The next three days were spent trying to cope with the constant spells of sorrow and dizziness, the ever changing body temperatures ranging from Arctic cold to Arizona hot, the unyielding ache in my neck and head, and my conscious awareness of upsetting the people around me. No one liked to see me cry as most often the tears were provoked by no apparent reason. Whenever I drank a hot beverage or ate a steaming dish of food, the tingling sensation would return and migrate all over my neck and face. Refusing to drive back into the hospital, I walked over to my bottle of calcium. I found horse-pill-size tablets impossible to swallow after thyroid surgery. I spliced calcium gel tablets open with a knife, squeezed the insides onto a spoon and squirting a lemon wedge over the chalk-like goo to help push it down.

Ignoring the pins and needles I encountered, I became confident the sensations were merely part of the healing process. In addition to continually coughing up sludge from my lungs, I had developed a new pass time. Clawing at my skin. For hours, I was digging at a nasty rash that looked like chicken pox all over my legs. My body disliked the sulfa in the antibiotic. I had hive type welts all over my legs, arms, and stomach. Needless to say, the aggravated fire-engine-red bumps on my body doubled both physically and mentally as the cherries on top of my stress. I hit a major breaking point and wanted to strip off my skin. I dug at my flesh for weeks making the situation on my skin unbearable.

I ended up on a different antibiotic to clear up the damage I had done by scratching and infecting so many of the welts on my body. To help prevent you from embedding your finger nails into your tissue for weeks, I recommend that you visit the webmd.com site to read up on this topic. My friend had twins almost a year before my surgery. She was put on antibiotics after the c-section. She had the same exact rash or hives that I had. I used to watch her rake her legs with her fingers while I'd hold one of the babies. I called on her a lot during my hive-infested hibernation, as I knew she'd be able to empathize with me over how radically uncomfortable life was. I've since spoken to people who said some pain meds upset their skin and caused them to itch for days on end.

Eight days after my operation I was scheduled for a follow-up visit with my surgeon. For the first time since my surgery, I got completely dressed and felt like a human being again. I wore my winter white slacks, a black v-neck sweater, and my cream, gold, black and cranberry designer scarf. My husband helped me put my bra on, (not at all as sexy as it sounds) and helped me tie my hair back in a low pony tail. Even with the dull ache in my neck, I lifted my arms to put on my make-up. With each stroke of the mascara, I felt a little more like my old self.

Once I finished applying my lipstick, I stepped back and looked at myself thinking, *you know what, Lorna, with this scarf on, no one would ever know you were eight days out of surgery. Today you are no longer a sick person. You are a girl going into Boston for lunch with her husband and mother.* As I stood in front of the closet contemplating what shoes to put on, I glared at my black patent leather heels for a long while. *Are you really ready for heels today? Why on earth would you even want to wear heels today, Lorna? Flats are IN. Go for comfort. It's only been eight days– you don't need height to be an ass kickin' hero.* I slipped my feet into my flats without the slightest air of fashion defeat.

My husband walked in the bedroom and said, "Wow, you look great, Babe." It was nice to hear that he appreciated my effort. Mum greeted me with the same reaction. It was as if she had her daughter back. "You look **good**. Are you having a good day? Did you sleep last night?" she asked, assuming sleep would have been the only way I could have pulled off a real outfit and make-up. "No, I didn't get a lot of sleep. I couldn't go into Boston in my pajamas, so I got dressed." I said with a touch of <u>can you believe I look normal again?</u> in my voice.

As we headed down the corridor to Dr. Randolph's room, it occurred to me that on my last visit I was a woman with cancer. I marveled at how much had changed in such a short amount of time. My surgeon entered the room. As always, he addressed mum and Rog with warmth. Then he said, "Okay Lorna, so you have been experiencing some tingling and such in your face. Is that still going on?" I answered yes. "Well, your calcium levels look beautiful. So that is great news. I know you were having some difficulty sleeping and some fear about falling asleep. How is that going?" As I began to explain how I felt, he gently said, "Lorna, if you want to address your fears, I think we should talk about that. But you need to know that you are not going to die if you fall asleep. You are doing beautifully. Really, Lorna, it's only been what? Eight days or so? You are doing remarkably well. I suspect a wonderful recovery with great results." Again, his voice soothed my worried heart. In time, I knew I'd be okay.

On the way to the car, my husband suggested that we go out for lunch. "Sure," I said, "Lord knows I shouldn't waste this black lace bra on a hospital visit. Let's eat." By the time we were seated, my neck, shoulders, and head were so stiff I could hardly move. I was praying for the extra-strength over the counter pain meds to kick in. In the past, whenever I felt a little sluggish, a bright lipstick and a great pair of earrings would raise my spirits within minutes. That day however, there wasn't enough lipstick or bling in the world to infuse the energy I needed to last six hours in real clothes. I missed my cancer uniform of comfort. I no longer cared how un-sexy I looked.

That night I decided that <u>no matter what</u> I was going to sleep in my bed. I figured what the hell? I had on make-up, a real outfit and a bra. It was the perfect day to resume the life of a grown up who sleeps in a big bed. I loaded up on the over the counter pain meds and situated myself on a mountain of pillows. My neck felt stiff but my lower back felt amazing. For days my sacrum had carried the pressure of my body sitting upright in the chair. It was time to reward my lower back by getting in the bed. I have to admit, it was not at all comfortable but I was determined to overcome that obstacle.

Several hours later, I woke up in a panic. Hysterically disoriented, I yelled, "I'm falling!" to my husband. "I feel like I'm soaring down into darkness. I'm going to die!" "You are not going to die, Babe. You had a dream. I'll get you some water. Just sit up for a bit," Roger said. When he made it back to the bedroom, I was sobbing. "I just want to sleep in my own damn bed, <u>through the night,</u> without interruption. I wish I had never gone through with the surgery. They said it was a slow moving cancer, I should have just kept my old thyroid." Rather than argue with me, Roger allowed me to vent about how unimpressed I was with my decision to rid my body of disease. He stroked the hair and tried to get me back to sleep. I remember thinking *I should be rubbing his head.*

He is going through just as much shit as I am. Oh God, please speed up this recovery... I've had enough.

The next morning I dressed in a sweat suit and garnished my face with a little concealor under my eyes and some lip gloss. *This is as good as it's going to get today,* I said to myself as I made my way in to the kitchen. *I am going to have a normal day, no crying, no anger...I'm just going to enjoy this day. I may call the office to find out how work is going. Who knows? I may even email a friend.* I swallowed a vitamin E capsule (to help the scar heal) and squirted the insides of a calcium tablet onto a spoon. As I chased the nasty chalky goo down my throat with lemon juice, I finalized the pep talk with myself by saying, *and most of all, I'm not going to be curt with Roger or mum. I'm going to think before I speak and stop this madness. It's been nine days. It's high time to get back on track.* Determined to prove to myself that I was back on track, I invited my husband into the bedroom for a little private time. Was I in the mood to have sex? -What do you think? Wanting sex or not wanting sex was not the issue: I wanted to cross the act of having sex off of my mental recovery check list of "WAYS TO KNOW YOU ARE BACK IN THE GAME OF LIFE." Remember, I am an actor, so I'd like to think I was very convincing that morning.

The decision to have sex wasn't for or about my husband. I wanted to convince myself that <u>*I*</u> was back to "normal". It was refreshing not to think about cancer, hives, crying or pain during the time we spent in the bedroom that morning. Sure, after the fact, my neck wasn't thrilled with my frolic between the sheets. But my mind felt triumphant and my soul felt a few steps closer to being whole again. That momentary euphoria shocked me because I was never a woman who defined her worth, womanhood or femininity by sex. Everyone has those overloaded pockets of time wherein sex falls secondary to sleep? Nine days after surgery, sex was something I needed in order to feel full functioning.

Shortly after, I had a visit from my friend Jane. As she passed through the dining room she noticed two enormous scrap books on the table. "What is this?" she asked. "Mum and Paige have entered all of my cards, emails, notes, and photographs into these books for me. Look through them. You won't believe how cool they are." I said as she turned the pages. While taking in all of the cut-out butterflies flying around emails of inspiration, advice, and humor mixed with pictures from my thyroid funeral and all of the cards people sent me, she said, "Lorna, this book is an episode on OPRAH. Do you realize what this is? This is a testament of all of the people who love you and the power of their healing words, friendship, and support. You have strangers from the community who have sent you phenomenal emails. This is a rare and amazing documentation of your worth and value. You need to treasure this."

Aware of the impact the wonder of words made on me, I was somewhat surprised that Jane had the same reaction. The books were bursting at the seams; each one stuffed about three inches off of the binder. The cover of each book had a little tree on the horizon with a long, windy country road rolling over hills on a plain. The atmosphere above the road and grass was filled with white clouds with an inquisitive sapphire blue sky peaking through. It was as if my present self was the clouds and my future self was the sparkling sky waiting to shine through. In simple type just to the left of the scene on the scrapbook the following words were printed: Around each bend in life's path, new memories are made.

Many of the notes and cards were spring themed covered with spring tulips, daffodils, butterflies and gardens in bloom. The books were another example of my way of coping with and paying tribute to my cancer. For me, saving all of my letters and cards was an ordinary way to sort out my disease. For Jane, the method of healing was *extra*ordinary. Apparently not everyone chronicles their cancer as I had. I confess the thyroid funeral may have been a little off the map, but the scrapbooking just felt right. I cherish the contents on each page just as I did when I was sick. I posted many of the notes on my web site. By sharing the powerful letters, I hope to inspire readers to reach out to those in pain through pen. The power of the pen is not to be taken lightly. I read and re-read many of those notes, day after day, throughout my recovery. Their strength fueled my soul.

No matter how hard I tried, I could not get comfortable in the bed. I longed to lie flat on my stomach and sleep with my head turned to the right on my favorite pillow. I couldn't have what I wanted, and that pissed me off. With the body language of a three-year-old child pitching a tantrum, I grabbed the remote control and turned on the TV. It was around 12:30 A.M. On the screen I saw a clean cut handsome young man standing in front of a full orchestra. At the top of the piece the entire frame was filled with the man's face. He sang boldly, as if to say, "Hey, Lorna, hear my voice and be well. Before long you will be feeling good." Here are the <u>Feeling Good</u> lyrics written by Anthony Newley and Leslie Bricusse.

"Feeling Good"

Birds flying high
You know how I feel
Sun in the sky
You know how I feel
Breeze driftin' on by
You know how I feel
It's a new dawn
It's a new day
It's a new life
For me
And I'm feeling good

At this point in the song I was totally pulled in. The orchestra was playing a bad-ass bass line rhythm while the amazing entertainer held me on his every word.

Fish in the sea
You know how I feel
River running free
You know how I feel
Blossom on a tree
You know how I feel
It's a new dawn

It's a new day
It's a new life
For me
And I'm feeling good

Dragonfly out in the sun you know what I mean, don't you know
Butterflies all havin' fun you know what I mean
Sleep in peace when day is done
That's what I mean
And this old world is a new world
And a bold world
For me

By the top of the next verse, the handsome man on the screen was wailing and the band was full throttle, playing a strip-tease type current. I felt like I was shredding my body of pain, sleeplessness and worry, as his voice pounded a new mantra of healing into my cranium.

Stars when you shine
You know how I feel
Scent of the pine
You know how I feel
Oh freedom is mine
And I know how I feel
It's a new dawn
It's a new day. It's a new life…For me…and I'm feeling good.

The last note of the song whirled through my bedroom like a mini tornado of encouragement, wellness, and truth. Just then I heard the late night talk show host say, "Michael Buble' everyone!" I got out of bed and made my way to the kitchen, repeating *Michael Buble', Michael Buble'*. The next day I woke up and saw my scribble on a piece of paper. I explained to my friend Reenie how the song had touched me. She immediately offered to pick up the CD. By the end of the day I emailed my entire address book encouraging my friends to run out and buy it.

In bold purple ink on the computer screen I typed, "This song will rejuvenate your spirit and lift your soul! The message reminds us that we have the ability to restart our lives at any point" The overall impact of the piece gave my inner compass a sense of direction. Having been in spiritual limbo for nearly two weeks, the lyrics to the song grounded me and helped me focus on positive thoughts.

It is evident that words got me through those first few hard days of my recovery. The hand written words that were mailed, the typed words sent over the internet, the words spoken on my answering machine, the words mum and husband said to me each time I melted down, the words Michael Buble' sang during my hour of desperation, the words I wrote in my journal which have since become this book, the words I prayed God would hear… all of those words mark my journey.

Words, the power and wonder of words, were more effective in my recovery than any of the troll hallucinating pain killers I was discharged with. I challenge everyone dealing with cancer to write down their thoughts. From sickness to wellness, record your feelings. Today, I use those words as a gauge for where I have come from, where I've been, and where I'm going. Those words are the core of who I am.

Words documenting my most vulnerable days tattooed on the blueprint of my soul. No matter how tempting the desire to erase all of the pain may be, as cancer survivors we cannot wipe away what we've been through. To ignore that time in our lives is to give back the trophy we've earned for putting up the fight. Our inner strength shouldn't ever be expunged. Whether in pen ink, pencil lead or charcoal, type writer ribbon, crayon wax, marker fluid, eye liner, lipstick, or computer cartridge; your encounter with cancer needs to be saved in print for future hours of proclamation. Those words are the trophy from your championship.

Helplessly Hypo

DR. SMITH CALLED TO WALK ME through the preparation for my radioactive iodine radiation. Step one was to become void of any synthetic thyroid levels in my body in order for the radiation to do its' job. Step two was to go on the radioactive iodine diet that had to be stringently obeyed or the radiation wouldn't work. The final step was to swallow the little purple pill and go into quarantine for a week. For anyone unfamiliar with the term and effects of hypothyroidism, please refer to the thyca.org site. Before hanging up the phone, Dr. Smith said, "You are going to feel crummy, Lorna. I will call to check in on you. Try to keep your spirits up."

Life without thyroid pills was becoming very unpleasant. I was slipping into the world of hypothyroidism. I felt like I was a slug living in a turtle's body. For a visual of what hypothyroidism feels like, I encourage you to Google search photos of the ancient sphagnum bog people of Northern Europe. Thousands of years after death, perfectly preserved human bodies are found bearing a striking resemblance to how each individual appeared when they were alive. In every photo, the cadavers seem frozen in time, stiff and cold. Each time someone asked how I was feeling back then, I wanted to say, "Sphagnum bog girl". Doubting the effectiveness of my description (my history geek club has very few members) I opted to say, "Hypo is Hell." While hypo I was freezing cold and my muscles felt **bog girl** stiff. Most days I longed for the Tin Man's oil can. I literally felt like I needed a lube job to make chores like folding laundry less taxing on my body.

Up until my hypo days, my body never ran cold. I found it impossible to adjust to the new temperature. I have to elaborate on this because I found it to be most shocking of all of the side effects. After my thyroid was removed, I used to take my p.j.'s, slippers and robe into the bathroom each night before my shower. After turning the water up to the hottest setting, I'd try to move my joints around under the heat. Once the shower was over, I'd jump out, cover my entire body in lavender oil (my skin was <u>unbelievably</u> dry) and brush my teeth so the oil could soak in. I'd layer up to lock the temperature and hydration in my body.

This was such a change for me. For years (pre-cancer) I'd take a shower and walk around naked until my body cooled down enough to dress. While hypo, from the bathroom I'd scurry to my bed and nest beneath four layers of bedding to lock in the heat. I even placed a blanket up against the headboard in back of my pillows to wrap my hands under to keep stay warm. After a few weeks deeper in to my hypo hell, my warming ritual occurred in the morning *and* at night. I needed the heat to start and end my day. While in the house, I'd wear scarves, sweaters, slippers over my socks and a bathrobe to stay warm.

Before I had cancer, I despised socks! But that bitter arctic cold was unlike any other feeling my body had experienced regarding extreme elements. Several bitchy mood swings were sparked by my lack of ability to stay warm. I tried to apply the sense memory skills I learned in acting to improve the situation. *Lorna, you are at Chitzinitza in Mexico. It's 102 degrees and Roger has climbed to the top without you because the sun is so searing you are afraid you'll pass out. You are sitting on a rock looking out at the temple wishing you were in the ocean. This is the hottest your body has ever been in your life. Breathe in the heat, breathe out the cold…breathe in the heat, breathe out the cold…*Much to my despair, the meditation didn't stick.

I remained chilled to the bone for weeks. I'm talking jaw-chattering cold, folks. It's true, at times my jaw actually chattered. With so many wonderful symptoms of hypothyroidism, I hardly know what to share with you next! (Sarcasm no doubt noted.) Let's see, my finger nails were brittle and breaking, my arms, legs, belly and scalp felt like someone had allowed five hundred mosquitoes to bite every square inch of them, leaving behind a desiccated itch that was impossible to hydrate or mend; my emotions were off the hook (as my students say) crying for hours then sitting totally still for days, and my sex drive was as dry as my skin. My muscles were stiff. As far as being limber goes, pre-surgery, audiences of students and staff at school were often awestruck by my ability to kick my feet way above my head. Students would put sticky notes on the walls and challenge me to kick inches above each paper. No matter how plus-sized my ass had become, I was without question, limber. All of my flexibility went away when I was hypo.

In short hypothyroidism was the nastiest time of my life. I pray to God I will never ever, ever have to relive it. I remember waking up and thinking, *I feel okay. I'm going to clean the house and get a jump start on a pile of laundry* only to fade away half way in to the wash cycle of the machine. Remember, the hypothyroid stage is weeks after your surgery. By then your entire support system of friends and family has resumed their normal lives. My husband was back to work with nightly meetings. My mum was stopping by less and less throughout the week. Other than having a woman come in to help me clean every other Monday (God bless Nancy) the housework was all mine.

Desperately reaching for the piss and vinegar of a kitten, I'd gather up all of the clothes and made my way to the laundry room. By the time I'd start the machine, I'd have to sit in a chair to rest. After several minutes in "time out", I'd make my way to the bedroom to assemble the bed. For weeks, I never made it to the decorative pillow stage of bed making. I'd have to take a break after the sheets, comforters and duvet. I could never do a group of three things. Laundry, bed making and showering, all easy tasks, seemed like triathlon feats once lumped together.

As much as I wanted to get out of the house, I dreaded the trips out with friends. The walk from my house to their cars felt like I was running the Boston Marathon. Pulling my body up from a low riding car felt like I was climbing Mt. Washington. Conserving my energy for conversation, shopping, eating lunch, and getting in and out of vehicles became more and more impossible. I resorted to hanging out with dear friends who understood the importance and power of silence.

My friend Rose used to take me for drives by the ocean and on all of the back roads of Massachusetts with very little mention of trivial things. I soaked that time in as if it were an energy drink. During that hypo phase, my husband and I spent most nights quietly sitting around the house. From the outside things appeared to be normal. On the inside I felt lost. Every day during my hypothyroid descent I felt out of body and empty. I have been really drunk only once in my life. I equate my hypo state to an extreme hangover after a weekend long drinking binge. Every part of my body hurt. There was a constant dull ache in my legs, arms and head. My mind felt like it had taken exams over and over again. I felt as if someone had placed a shawl around my brain. My eyes were looking through a thin veil which prevented my sharp and quick thoughts from escaping out of.

My loss of memory and my lack of ability to focus scared the hell out of me. I was certain I was suffering long-term effects of the anesthesia or a stroke even, until Dr. Smith (my endo) told me that the stress of cancer and hypothyroidism was most likely the culprit. For the longest time (by that I mean months) I'd go to write a word beginning with the letter F and the number 5 would end up on the page. Example: <u>Dear Buzz and Ellie, Thank you so much 5or visiting with me last week. I'm looking 5orward to getting out and seeing all of the daffodils in your yard. 5onldy, Lorna</u>. As I proofed read each note, I'd stop in horror each time I saw the ink on the page. *What in God's name is happening to me? I must be going crazy! Something is wrong. It's as if I've had a head trauma.* In addition to substituting letters for numbers, I was incorrectly identifying every day objects in my life. My mind would say *Roger, can you pass me the pepper* while my voice said *Roger, can you pass me the sink.* The most terrifying turning point was when I looked at my signature on a letter. I had skipped the N in Lorna and the N in Brunelle. Come to find out,

I had skipped that N in all of my signatures on all of the notes I had written that day. My name read Lora Bruelle.

Mum wrote all of my thank-you notes immediately following my surgery. I didn't start writing my name a lot until I was in the land of hypo. I cannot report whether or not my cognitive mistakes were happening immediately following the surgery or during the hypo phase. During my hypo-stage, and the summer months that followed, I misspelled and misused words every day. I became very insecure about speaking in public. As for note writing, unless I had a proofer, I didn't write. During that time I saw an old friend in the grocery store. I found myself explaining that I had cancer and surgery as a buffer, in case strange words were thrown into our conversation. It is so frustrating when the brain doesn't communicate with the hands or voice. I used all of my might to force my brain to write or speak the proper words. I'll be honest, it was exhausting! My pen literally used to stop cold on the paper and pause until I pushed it to write the N.

I shared the fear of having lost my mind with my friend Reenie. As a breast cancer survivor, I felt comfortable running the odd dark depths of my recovery by her. Looking directly into my worried eyes, she said "Lorna stop and think about it-what does the letter F sound like? Say it...FFFFFFFFF. Okay now say the number 5...FFFFFive. Hear how similar they are? Now about you skipping the letter N in your name... Your brain has to slow down to write the letter N. Maybe your brain is still running too quickly. I did this, too, when I was recovering. Guess what, sometimes I still do this. I think we, as cancer people, have too much on our minds. Some things get jumbled up. It gets better."

Hearing her relate to my issues eased my mind for about three seconds- until I wondered why we shared the same post-op problems with words and penmanship. Reenie wasn't hypothyroid after her breast cancer surgery. I was attributing all of my mistakes to being hypo. Does some part of our brain take a vacation during high stress seasons in our body? Are we (as cancer patients) suffering some form of post traumatic stress syndrome? After having worked as a consultant/teacher in a state facility with severally disabled children (most suffering from massive head trauma and or birth defects) I am familiar with the unusual flow of consciousness that streams out of the mouths of people with brain swelling, trauma or injuries. I was brought in on grant funding to sing with the children to stimulate their minds through sound and music. I used music as a form of therapy during my recovery. My other therapy was typing. I know typing in my journal every day helped to stimulate both sides of my brain.

So just to recap…if you have thyroid cancer and you need to prepare your body for the radioactive iodine radiation you must become totally hypothyroid. In my experience, hypothyroidism was worse than my surgery. Please remember that everyone is different and no two recoveries are the same. In my case, my libido was off having an affair on some tropical island. I was left at home with an icy empty shell of a body. I experienced arctic body temperatures, dry skin, hair and nails; lots of crying, hair loss, aching muscles, the inability to concentrate, weight gain, and a constant fog for weeks. Prior to my diagnosis and surgery, I had lost 37 lbs. I took me almost a year to take that weight off. When you are hypo the scale will <u>not</u> move. While hypo, I gained back all of the weight I lost. Life gets better, but it takes time. Try to stay positive.

The next part of this chapter will prepare you for the radioactive iodine diet. Thyroid cancer patients begin the diet the weeks leading up to their radiation. The diet is <u>very strict</u>. It must be followed in order to have successful results. Your doctor will give you a list of the foods you can eat. Visit <u>www.thyca.org</u> for a fantastic list of facts and recipes to help you prepare for this diet. Purchasing all of the food before you begin the diet is an absolute must. Mum helped by taking small day trips with me to places like Trader Joes, Whole Foods, and the local farmers markets for supplies.

If you ever find yourself on this meal plan, please prepare an extra amount of time in the store. You are going to read <u>every word</u> on <u>every label</u> in the shop. I remember looking at my watch. Over an hour had passed and I wasn't finished crossing the items off of my list. I spoke with the butcher, the baker, and the candle stick maker. (Okay, there wasn't a candle stick maker, but I'm in the mood to rhyme.) Seriously, I spoke to the baker, who told me I couldn't buy any of the bread in the store. My banter with the butcher was a lot more promising as he assured me that all of his meats were accessible. (Wow, that reads rather X-rated as I type it.) *Oh butcher boy... Is that a sausage in your pants or are you just happy to see me?* ~Forgive me.

I bought non-iodized kosher salt, fresh herbs, organic fruits and vegetables, old fashioned slow-cooking oatmeal and some gorgeous cuts of steak and pork. All of the meats were prepared without any hormones, antibiotics or dyes. Bleached tea bags are not permitted on the diet. Natural and whole food stores sell tea in non-bleached bags. You can also use loose-leaf tea.

For breakfast, I prepared oatmeal, (again this has to be the old fashioned oats, sold in the round canister) with organic peaches and unsalted butter. You may be wondering why I used organic fruits and veggies. Not all diet hand-outs suggest buying organic. My doctor and I discussed cleansing my body of all food-related pesticides, chemicals, antibiotics, hormones and dyes. For weeks, I ate clean. Even helplessly hypo, I looked forward to cooking new meals. At the beginning of the diet, I reserved one full day to prepare all of the food. For the duration of the diet, I merely had to scoop food out of containers and reheat it on the stove. I used a week's worth of energy that one day in the kitchen but it was a fabulous diversion!

On the subject of energy, for an extra punch of protein, some mornings I added a broiled side of steak or a grilled pork chop. I drank filtered water, loose-leaf decaf tea or sliced fresh ginger in hot water. For lunch, I had salads filled with organic greens and drizzled with homemade dressings made of olive oil, lime or orange juice, fresh grated ginger and a little sugar. I used pure or raw sugar cane. Most often I added sliced steak to the salad. To flavor the grilled meat, I covered the sirloin in a sauté mixture of olive oil, garlic, peppers and onions. My salads varied each day. I added avocado, roasted beets, tomatoes, cucumbers, grilled eggplant, spinach, broccoli, sweet potatoes, grilled summer squash and radishes. Always trying to entertain my palette, I scooped various side dishes out of the premade containers and blended them together.

For dinner, I made grilled fresh pork chops with sautéed peaches, mashed sweet potatoes, with non-iodized salt and unsalted butter. (You are even welcome to add two marshmallows to the potatoes!) I added grilled spears of summer squash and zucchini. I seasoned the veggies with the zest of limes and chopped fresh basil. A few times, I garnished the grilled pork with a chilled roasted red beet salsa with mango, peaches, oranges and red onion. Some nights I made steak with grilled eggplant and tomatoes (seasoned with garlic and black pepper) and a side of olive oil pan-fried cabbage. One night I had fresh turkey breast (from the butcher) baked with green peppers and onions, served with brown basmati rice and a few scoops of homemade guacamole packed with cilantro. I was advised not to have chicken on the diet as many food makers inject broths containing iodized salt into the meat. To be safe, <u>be sure to see a butcher</u> for fresh turkey, pork, or chicken.

My most favorite dinner was on the fifth night. After rereading my shopping list, I realized I could have <u>pasta</u>. Mum and I returned to Trader Joes and purchased plain macaroni, fresh basil, tomatoes and scallions. After boiling the pasta, I added it to a sauté of basil, scallions, tomatoes, olive oil and garlic. Can I just say amazing? As a variation on the theme, I added pork and steak to the pasta paradise throughout the final week. One rainy afternoon I was craving hot soup. I boiled Chinese cabbage, tomatoes, onions, carrots, string beans, and summer squash in a pot for hours with fresh fennel, parsley and non-iodized salt and pepper. YUM!

My father's wife Jane called offering to make homemade bread with all of the ingredients off of the list. She arrived with two lavish loaves of love still warm from the stove. I, in high hypo, was sincerely moved by her culinary intuition. How did she know I was craving bread for my soup? The duration of my relationship with the bread consisted of several scrumptious ways to garnish it! Whether plain or jazzed up with unsalted butter, honey, sliced strawberries lightly sprinkled with sugar, tomatoes, basil or olive oil; those little slices of heaven added a heap of happiness to the meaning of hypo! If anyone in your circle is a baker, place your order now for low-iodine homemade bread.

For dessert or mid-eve snacks, I had fruit salad. I mixed blueberries, strawberries, grapes, mango, peaches and granny smith apples with the juice of lemons, oranges, limes and a little sugar. For mid-day treats, I dipped sugar snap peas and sliced cucumber in guacamole made from avocados, cilantro, lime juice, red onions, non-iodized salt and black pepper. I never felt like I was depriving myself of the traditional salty snacks I leaned toward during my hypo phase.

Prior to starting the radioactive iodine diet, I was eating SLEEVES of crackers per day. As the Synthriod wore off, my yearning for salt pressed on. Like most of the women in the world, once a month I craved a perfect bowl of popcorn chased by a few pieces of dark chocolate. When I had a thyroid, the premenstrual dance called "Sweet Meets Salty" went back into the wings for 28 days as I resumed my normal eating habits. Aside from P.M.S., pre-cancer, the only time I ever considered the importance of a salty cracker was when I glanced into a colander of freshly washed scallops and thought; *shall I bake or broil them?* Ever since my surgeon pitched my thyroid to the curb and my endo drained my body of Synthroid, all I wanted to eat was salt.

I remember calling my Jewish endo and catholically confessing, "I am eating salty crackers by the dozen...as in...at one sitting. I think about salty crackers all day." To which he said, "It's normal for your body to crave salt during this time." I went on to say, "You don't understand. I never even liked crackers before. I was more of a fruit and cheese girl. I usually skip the whole cracker part of the platter, ya know? When will I stop buying bulk boxes of sodium and carbs at Costco?" "Be patient, Mrs. Brunelle," he said. "This is all temporary. I say go with whatever your body needs, within reason, that is. If your body wants crackers, eat crackers."

From there I emailed my friend Lucy in L.A. "I cannot stop eating salty crackers and my ass is expanding as I type this note to you. HELP! Hypo-ly yours, Lorna." She wrote back, "Lorna, give your ass a break. Give your body what it needs right now. Just go with it. You're recovering from some nasty stuff girl...crackers with salt- not so bad. There are worse things to eat." I took comfort in hearing the female spin on my extra marital affair with my new man Ritz.

I love to cook so for me, the low iodine diet wasn't that bad. I approached the diet as a culinary challenge; a two-week long recipe if you will. Quality food doesn't come cheap. My special diet groceries cost more than my monthly Jeep payment. Please plan ahead for the total at the check out.

On the days when I was tired of slugging around the house, I went out eat. Please note that I knew the owner of the restaurant and was friendly with the managers, cooks <u>and</u> wait staff. There was a level of trust, and I knew they wouldn't harm my progress with the treatment by fibbing about the ingredients in each menu item. I stuck to ordering salads with lime juice and a piece of broiled steak. If you can trust the establishment you are going to, make sure you say that you don't want <u>anything</u> added to your meat. Make it clear that garlic salt, onion salt, celery salt, season salt and other flavors are forbidden on the diet. You should also ask them to scrape the grill or broiler before cooking your food.

With very few days left on the diet, Dr. Smith called to confirm the timeline for my treatment. On March 15, I was in the book for a scan at hospital. March 17, I was slated to return to the hospital for the radioactive iodine treatment followed by 5-7 days of quarantine. On March 20, I was allowed to begin taking my delicious brand name T4 hormone replacement pill-SYNTHROID! Can I get an Amen? As a recovery incentive, Jen and my friend Heather planned an April trip to Key West. Dr. Smith assured me his "chunky dose" (his words) of T4 would have me flying high in time for our trip.

In the midst of everything, my friend called to let me know her grandmother passed away. Peacefully, while watching her favorite TV show in her napping chair, she went. Her grandmother was a fan of the little concerts I gave at the local senior center. Always in the front row she maintained perfect attendance at my shows. Her dedication to my voice is why I paused when my friend asked me to sing at the funeral. My first phone call was to my surgeon. "Is it too soon to sing?" I asked. "Not at all." he replied. My next phone call was to a friend who sings locally. "Would you mind singing a funeral mass with me? I don't know if I am ready?" "I'd be happy to sing." She replied. After selecting the music for the service, I tried rehearsing at home. My tone was there, but my confidence was on hiatus. The muscles around my incision were tight. Everything felt taut and angry. Rather than surrender to the discomfort, I called my massage therapist.

For about an hour, the therapist stretched my neck and restored my range of motion. With subtle resistance exercises, she gently placed my head in her hands and asked me to resist her movement. She held my head in her right hand and tried to move my skull to the left of the bed. At that point I would gently press my head into the palm of her hand as if to resist the leftward movement. We did that on each side for a while until I felt my neck regaining its' mobility. My neck, shoulders, and throat felt amazing. While I was on the table she cross fibered my incision with little pinching movements to break up the scar tissue. I started doing that every day at home to prevent a thick rope-like feeling under my skin. With my pointer finger and my thumb, I moved across the scar with up and down pinches. I was also using a silicone scar gel my surgeon recommended.

After the massage, I felt like a million bucks! If you have the financial means to get a massage once a month or once every two weeks after your surgery, I strongly recommend it. I waited a month for my first rub, but stayed in the book for treatments from that point on. If you cannot afford to see a massage therapist, try stretching your neck every day to keep those muscles moving. I can attest to the benefits of range of motion. Stretching will enable you to parallel-park your vehicle a lot sooner! For those of you who do not parallel-park, trust me, the mere feat of pulling out of your driveway and turning your head east to west is made easier by stretching.

The afternoon of the wake, I tried to pace myself. It was my first big day in the life of the *Old Lorna* living in *Lorna's New Body*. I needed to conserve my energy. In my old life, the world with a thyroid, I could stop by several functions and still have the energy to meet up with friends for dinner at 8:00 P.M. In my new life, washing and folding a load of laundry (and I literally mean ONE load of laundry) was just too much to take on in an afternoon. On this day, I had to attend a wake, a memorial mass, and my school's annual fundraiser. Hypo and all, I had to endure three events in a row *and* wake up in time to sing at an early morning funeral. I took a shower and propped myself up on the sofa. *Just take it slowly, Lorna. Go at your own pace. Just breathe and take your time. If you don't make it to all of the events, everyone will understand. It's only been one month.*

The night before the wake I went to bed with a head full of over gelled wet hair. The following morning, my curls were letting their freak flag fly. Although flat ironing was all the rage, there was no way in hell I had the energy to flatten six million sections of my hair. I embraced my early 80's heavy metal band hair. As I placed my earrings on in the mirror a little voice said, *"Hey Lorna, 1980 just called. Every rock band would like their hair back!"* Ignoring my obtrusive fashion commentary, I made my way to the parking lot. "You look **really** nice," my husband said. What can I say? He fell in love with me the summer of `87!

The day was bitterly cold. I put on my long black velvet jacket with faux mink collar and cuffs. As my private way of protesting winter, I accessorized my outfit with a lime green silk scarf. It was my way of reminding everyone that spring was lurking in the distance.

The immediate smell of funeral home mixed with flowers hit me as I walked into the parlor. My mind raced back to the smell of the flowers in the church back in August as I sang the funeral for my friend's father. That was the first time I felt something funny in my voice. While walking over to the casket, I remembered all of the times my friend arrived early at my concerts to get a good seat. As I stood before her casket, I wished her well and told her how honored I was to sing at her going away party. I assured her that she was welcome to sit in the front row whenever she wanted to drop by one of my gigs. While making my way through the receiving line, a guy looked at my jacket and said, "I hope that isn't real!" Ever the activist, this person was referring to the faux mink cuffs and collar. For a split second I wanted to pop him. He had some nerve pressing his political views on me in the <u>receiving line</u> <u>of a wake</u> while I was recovering from cancer.

Just then my anger changed to delight. I relished in the fact that he was treating me like a normal person, and not a sick person. So many people were asking how I was feeling with their sad *she has cancer* eyes, yet he was prepared to pick a fight with me over fake fur. Pre-cancer, I would have pitched a smart mouthed comment back at his inquiry about my jacket. There I stood in post-cancer glory, glowing in the idea of being treated without kid (imitation leather) cancer gloves.

From the funeral home, I walked across the street to my church for Sean's mass. *I don't think I have the energy to get through this night* I thought to myself as I took my seat. Then my eyes went to my friend Rose. A tower of strength, she walked into the church with her husband and daughter. *If she can make it through this night and all other nights without her son, you can certainly make it through a few more hypothyroid hours. Don't ever doubt your strength again, Lorna.*

From the memorial mass, we journeyed to the theatre to watch my students perform in our fundraiser. I was thrilled to see the staff and students. After a few minutes at the show my body whimpered *I'm done...I need my bed...*"Let's go home," Rog said. Much to my surprise, I agreed. The funeral was less than twelve hours away.

The morning of the funeral, I warmed up my voice in the shower, and stretched all of my neck muscles under the hot water. After a few scales, I began to doubt my ability to do the music justice. My voice was tired and my body was <u>beat</u>. Cancer or no cancer, whenever I am fatigued my voice is weak. I had never battled performance anxiety, yet there I was dreading the hour-long stretch of music at the church. *What if I need to sit down? What if I forget where we are in the mass? What if I sound like shit? What if I start to cry?* As a funeral singer, you cannot ever cry during your performance. Even as Sean's mass (when there wasn't a dry eye in the church) I didn't cry. As the singer, you have to transcend into a place that blocks the flood gates until you get home. The beauty of the music and its' power to ease the grieving family is lost if the singer is blubbering through each piece. Being hypo placed a whole new spin on the term blubber. I wasn't safe in my own hypo body. I reached out to my old friend for guidance.

Friend, here you are again, in the front row for a concert...only this time, I could use some assistance. I know you are here...you wouldn't miss your own party...if you could show me a sign that I am ready to sing for you, I'd really appreciate it. As I ran through the first few pieces with the pianist I was thrilled over how decent my voice sounded and felt. Still questioning my stamina, my singer friend joined me in case I needed to bow out of a piece. Shortly after our rehearsal, the guests began to enter the church. *This is it, no matter what happens, at least I tried.* Just like old times, I made my way through the mass without any difficulty. With only two pieces left, in the middle of a song, my singer friend had a coughing fit. Unable to suppress the tickle in her throat, she walked away from the music stand for a drink of water. I continued without her.

I couldn't help but wonder if the fit of coughing was a heavenly sign letting me know I was ready to fly solo again. Triumphant and elated, I tried to control my joy! *I can sing! I can really still sing!* My notes weren't yet powerhouse notes soaring up to the rafters…but they were <u>my notes.</u> I still had my voice to nurture, rehabilitate, and foster. I wanted to do back flips down the aisle of the church all the way to Boston to hug my surgeon!

Rest well in heaven, my friend. Thank you for proving that I can still sing… Amen.

I may have been hopelessly hypo, but my voice was unharmed.

Dirty Bombshell

WITH MY RADIATION ONLY A FEW days away, I began to question my decision to go through with it. I expressed my fear to Dr. Smith. "I am on the fence about this 1-131 radioactive iodine therapy." I said. "The term nuclear medicine scares the hell out of me. I mean, the pill I am going to swallow…it is poison, right? Do I HAVE to do this?" With a little disdain in his voice he said, "Mrs. Brunelle, this isn't Russia seventy years ago. I cannot make you do anything you don't want to do. But in my professional opinion, this is the best course of action for you. After all, one lymph node came back positive in your path report." My heart sank. *Oh yes, the damn positive lymph node in the path report! Couldn't we just forget about that little bugger?*

At risk of pissing him off, I decided to cross the line with my doctor. "If you don't mind, may I ask if you have any children?" Very perplexed, he responded by saying, "Yes, Mrs. Brunelle, I have children." "Can you pretend that I am your child? Say, God forbid, that I am your child with thyroid cancer. How would you explain the necessity of this treatment without scaring me?" After careful consideration he said, "Well, I'd say…Picture a sticker in the shape of a butterfly. Now let's place that sticker on a pane of glass, a window." As he pointed to the window next to the stool he was sitting on, he said, "Now let's peel the sticker off of the glass. What do you see? -A sticky residue, right? Well, that sticker is your thyroid. The pane of glass is all of your nerves and tissue. By removing the entire sticker in surgery, we can damage your nerves which could damage your voice, along with leaving some cancer behind in that tissue. So we remove what we can. The <u>sticky residue</u> left on the window is left-over cancer cells that we cannot remove in surgery. Those cells left untreated can grow and the cancer can return. The radioactive iodine radiation therapy is the Windex that wipes the sticky residue or left- over cells, away. <u>That</u> is why you need this treatment."

Convinced that he had missed his calling in performance art, I was mesmerized by his improv skills. "Okay, I guess I'll do it." I said. "And remember," he said, "We did have that positive lymph node." Although he wasn't trying to hurt me, the second mention of my lymph node made my veins freeze. "I <u>just said</u> I'd do it!" I strongly repeated. "I just needed to hear you break it down for me. It's just a weird concept this *NUCLEAR* medicine. It's hard to wrap my brain around poisoning myself to stay healthy." Too tired and too hypo to challenge him any longer, I thanked him for his expertise. His "Poison -It's More Than Just a Rock Band" speech helped. The last thing he said in the meeting was, "Try to avoid going on line. Ask me if you have any questions."

Constantly resisting the temptation to research the dangers associated with having radioactive iodine radiation, I closed the doors to the computer armoire. I tried to focus on more crucial things like making it through an hour without having to sit in a chair or rest my head on something. I was officially moving around in another time zone. The highest stage of being hypo was the most surreal time of my life. I literally remember holding in my urine on the loveseat of my living room because I was too tired to get up and go to the bathroom. It felt as if my body was lounging in Massachusetts and the bathroom was in Texas. While hypo, it is even difficult to squeeze the toothpaste out of the tube. I had to cut the end of the tube so I could place my toothbrush in the paste from the bottom. The same went with my shampoo and conditioner. Most hypo days, it was impossible to get the product out of the bottles.

Refusing to let the cancer or the treatment for cancer get me down, I pressed on. I jumped into any car that pulled in to my driveway to take me on a day trip. I was <u>helplessly</u> hypo preparing to become a radioactive human dirty bomb. I don't think the people in my life saw me that way -helpless, that is. Not seeming helpless ate up a lot of my sparse energy. That façade resulted in terrible spirals of exhaustion, verbal abuse to my spouse, and fits of crying. Other than poking around the kitchen at turtle speed, very few things brought me joy during that time. I couldn't write without mixing up the words, my skin and hair was dry and cracking, my memory was deplorable, mid-sentence I'd forget what I was talking about, my moods were low, my house was cluttered, my nerves were shot and yet somehow, I continued to chant, *This too shall pass, Lorna. You have to stay strong. You have to stay positive. You have to stay alert. You have to stay hopeful. You have to S...t...a...y... s-t-a-y...a...w...a...k...stay awake!*

For days I awoke to the whispers of the following lines from Shakespeare's <u>The Merchant of Venice</u> in my head. I hadn't been familiar with the text in about fifteen years. My hypo state must have recalled and dusted off the things tucked away in the storage chests of my minds' attack. Ironic, don't you think? My primary memory skills were shot to hell, but there I was quoting Antonio line by line with the recollection of an elephant.

SCENE I. Venice. A street.
Enter ANTONIO, SALARINO, and SALANIO

ANTONIO
In sooth, I know not why I am so sad:
It wearies me; you say it wearies you;
But how I caught it, found it, or came by it,
What stuff 'tis made of, whereof it is born,
I am to learn;
And such a want-wit sadness makes of me,
That I have much ado to know myself.

In sooth, I didn't know why I was so sad. I mean aside from the obvious: having cancer, being dragged off of my meds, taking poisonous radiation, and neglecting to have enough energy to shower and dress within the same time frame, I truly was stumped by my overwhelming *constant* sadness. One would think my brain would have accepted the transition and made the best of it. I was miserable. My sadness worried me. -A lot.

I awoke on March 15 with a troubled mind. My unhappiness escalated on the commute to Boston to meet my radiation team. In an attempt to lift my spirits I tried to reflect on the times in my life when I was incandescently happy. I closed my eyes and thought about the birth of each of my nieces and nephews. I tried to channel the joy the mere expressions on their tiny little faces brought me. I thought about the first time I saw the daffodils, tulips, and crocuses from my very own garden dart up the spring after mum and I planted them amidst the autumn foliage. I tried to allow my body to become as weightless as it was the first time I snorkeled in the company of aquatic companions, in rainbow color, swimming beside me. *Drink in all of your happy thoughts, Lorna. You are going to need them during your quarantine.*

For nearly 20 years, I had put a positive spin on March 15. A Shakespeare fan, I wanted to defuse the potential negative energy nestled in the Ides of March. It was, after all, the day Caesar was murdered. As I said in the beginning of this book, Caesar was on my mind quite a lot that morning. Would Caesar have knowingly poisoned his body with radioactive iodine 1-131? 1-131 is the same stuff that harmed so many people in the Chernobyl region.

The enormity of the hospital in which my scan was scheduled annoyed the hell out of me. When hopelessly hypo the sheer size of a building can spark a tizzy of "I'm too tired for this" entitlement. Roger inquired about the location of the Nuc Med department. Winded from the amount of walking, I looked at Roger and snapped, "I need a registration card before going to Nuclear Medicine! I'm so tired of this whole "register downstairs" thing. In **e-v-e-r-y** hospital we go to, I have to "register downstairs". Why can't *they* email **me** a card? Why can't *they* email the paper work? Better yet, why can't I fill this entire form out on-line?! Why isn't this ever E-A-S-Y?" Rog didn't answer. That meant he, too, was aggravated. I knew I was the cause of his agitation.

Allow me to bitch a moment... For my surgery, I went to one large city hospital. For my endo appointments, I parked in an entirely different hospital. For my scans and nuclear medicine treatments, (which were scheduled through my endo's office) I was at a different hospital. I had the privilege of being part of a new-fangled and foreign team of experts trying to make me well in yet another monstrosity of a hospital building. How many hospitals does it take to cure cancer? Three! -Just another day in camp cancer recovery paradise.

I signed in "downstairs" and waiting for another plastic hospital card. This card was a fetching shade of cranberry. This card paid homage to my hometown, the Cranberry Capital of the World. While weaving through the maze-like hall structure, I snarled at how ironic my life had become. I had plastic hospital cards bulging out of the section of my wallet formally upstaged by credit cards. The passports of a sick person, ranging in size and color, resembled credit cards, but lacked the fun I once had with my friends Visa, Master, and Am Ex.

After about eleven minutes of walking around the hospital in search of our wing, I began having a temper tantrum. With hypo rigid aching muscles and horrible hypo leg cramps, I barked, "This hospital is enormous! I'm exhausted! I <u>hate</u> this place!" I was too proud to ask for a wheelchair. After several more half circles around corners and sprints down long Olympic track-like corridors, I saw a little hand-made sign that read, "NUCLEAR MEDICINE". Below the words sat a hand-sketched photo of Mickey Mouse. As I walked by the sign I thought *what's with the Mickey Mouse sketch? Do cancer patients consider **this** to be the happiest place on earth? Welcome to the Disneyland of disease control.*

After signing in, I took my seat in a chair. As you may recall from the first chapter of this book, my afternoon in the nuclear medicine department was one of the worst medical experiences of my life. I did walk away with a better understanding of how to succeed in a shitty situation. I can sum it up in one word: **COMMUNICATION.**

Remember how I was strapped down on to the scanning table? Remember the street drummers I heard smashing around in my brain?

Remember how the tech agreed to put me in feet first rather than head first, unrestrained? Remember how the tech extended the option of walking around in between scans? Well, **none** of those accommodations would have been offered if it weren't for me saying, "STOP, I'm scared as hell, and I need you to help me make this better." Once I verbalized those emotions, the tech worked with me. In a flash he went from my enemy to my knight in shining armor. So although my first full body scan was traumatic, it was also liberating.

I'm not saying the tech was a bad man. I'm not saying he didn't do his job properly. I'm very certain he did exactly what he was <u>trained to do</u>. I'm saying that from the person who trained my tech, all the way up to the person on the top of the totem pole of the medical tutorial world- must be sure the training for everyone who works in a hospital includes empathy. From the surgeon holding a brain in their hands, to the custodian mopping the floor in the hallway, each staff member of an infirmary must possess and exemplify the respect, understanding, and attention each patient merits.

I understood why I needed the radioactive iodine. I understood why I needed before and after photos to mark the effectiveness of the treatment. I understood why it was crucial for the patient to remain perfectly still on the scanning table for forty-five minutes worth of photos. I just didn't understand why all of those photos had to be taken at once, while my arms and legs were tied down. Once I knew I had options, I felt at ease. If you walk away from this book with nothing more than a better understanding of the rights you have as a patient, then I've done my job.

After my Ides of March freak show in the scanning room, I came home and crashed. Using my bed side as a railing, I hoisted myself into the bed. As always, during my hypo hell, I was glacial cold. I placed my hands and arms under the blanket at my headboard, and pulled the duvet up to my chin. The only flesh exposed to the elements was my nose and eyes. The crying fest in the scan room at the hospital depleted my final energy reserve.

I got out of bed on March 16th, 2005, hoping for a better day. My cleaning lady, (domestic assistant, or whatever we are calling the saviors who help us when we are hypo, or too busy to clean) had just cleaned our entire house. The only clutter left behind was in my mind. One day away from poisoning my body, I found it impossible to clear my head. It was also impossible to nap. We had a chimney service at our home. The constant traffic in and out of the house prevented me from trying to catch a cat nap.

With my quarantine only twenty-four hours away, I wanted to get out as much as I could. The only thing holding me back was my lack of energy. My hypo ass had officially been kicked, and by all intents and purposes, I was already in lock down. One may say my scattered mind was a blessing. Who needs days of clarity to ponder the fact that their body is going to become a toxic hazard. A human dirty bomb posing danger to the people they love.

I was petrified of swallowing the pill. There was never a point in which my exhaustion extinguished my fear. Doctors say a woman should not conceive within twelve months of the treatment. One is safe to assume that trace amounts of poison can remain in the body for up to a year. Dr. Smith gave me a prescription for an anti-nausea to prevent vomiting after I ingest the pill. The vomit is radioactive and harmful to anyone who cleans up the mess. The pill he prescribed is used for chemo patients to prevent nausea. Does that place radioactive iodine and chemo in the same toxic league? Patients don't lose hair with radioactive iodine… but they aren't quarantined with chemo. With so many unknowns, one thing is for sure…both treatments are poisonous.

I was more afraid of the treatment than I was of the surgery. My fear escalated when someone dropped the ball. Allow me to explain. On March 15th, after all of my scans were completed, I was supposed to meet with a team to discuss my radiation. Granted, Dr. Smith filled me in on a few things like the importance of massaging my face after the treatment and sucking on lozenges to prevent salivary gland dysfunction. At the end of our meeting he said, "Don't worry, Lorna, they will go over <u>all of this</u> with you in detail next Tuesday." After my scan, someone in a white coat (but not a doctor) called for "my team." After waiting <u>over an hour</u>, the man in the white coat returned and said, "They are going to call you at home and explain everything to you. They are hours backed up right now." Assuming it was standard procedure to receive a call at home, I left.

Around 4:00 P.M. <u>the next day</u>, I realized that once again, I had to take my medical care into my own hands. "Hello, my name is Lorna Brunelle. I was in there yesterday for some pre-radioactive iodine radiation treatment scans. I'm having a radioactive iodine treatment **tomorrow.** Someone was supposed to come down and explain the protocol to me yesterday but they were too busy or backed up. I've waited all morning for a phone call. Can someone fill me in on what I am to expect? I mean is this HAZMAT suit time? What do I need to do? Can I eat before I come in? I'm unsure about the quarantine procedure. Can you fax or email me the info?"

After a long "Pinter Pause" as we say in my biz (taken from the Harold Pinter style of writing) an agitated female voice said, "**No one** came to see you yesterday? What do you mean they were backed up? <u>There is no such thing</u>. You <u>needed</u> to see the person who goes over the info with you. Someone from Nuclear Medicine makes the call and **immediately** we send someone to speak to the patient." In a bold voice I responded by saying, "Look, I know I'm hypo and my mind isn't very sharp but I waited around. The call was made. <u>No one came</u>. I was SENT HOME."

In a disapproving tone the woman said, "Well that NEVER should have happened, and you NEVER should have taken it upon yourself to leave." Helplessly hypo and void of all phone manners, I said, "Miss, I cannot help but think you are accusing ME of doing something wrong. <u>I was told to leave.</u> **I'm the one** recovering from thyroid cancer. I am trying to make it through each day without any thyroid hormone. I'm doing the best I can! Naturally, I would have <u>loved</u> all of the info the day I was at your hospital- but I was **sent home.** I'd appreciate your help in repairing this matter. Can **you** find **someone** to walk me through what

I can expect tomorrow? Pointing blame is hardly helping the matter. I need you **to fix this** for me."

I think I was put on hold at that point because she didn't answer me back. Shortly after, a man's voice in full Boston dialect spoke on the line. "Hello, so ah yaH wah heaH yes-taH-day and no one helped yaH out, huh? Okay, well, heaH is what's goin' to happen'." He concluded with, "I'm really sorry no one called `ya! Someone should'aH met wit `ya yes-taH-day. That's not normally how we do things around heaH." I tried to accept his apology. I tried to accept the misinformed man in the white coat who blew me off and sent me home. I realized that I had to learn to go with the flow and let go.

At that point I called my husband to dump my radioactive fear all over him. Perhaps I was trying to contaminate both of us? After sharing how hesitant I was about taking the pill, he said, "I'll be home a little later on. Everything is going to be fine, Babe." I prepared the last of my radioactive iodine diet food, turned on the TV and tried to calm down. It seemed odd to me that Roger wasn't home for dinner. He mentioned having to run an errand after work, but I didn't expect him to be gone so long. After another half hour, I called his cell. When I heard his phone go to voice mail, I wanted to throw my phone against the wall. The ol' *let your phone go to voice mail* trick was all too familiar for a hopelessly hypo girl on a Wednesday night.

The story will make more sense if I provide a little history regarding my marriage. You see, on the first and third Thursday night of each month, my husband attends union meetings. Pre-cancer, our marriage struggled each time he drove home exhausted and slightly (or significantly) intoxicated somewhere between last call and 3:00 A.M. after one of the hallowed meetings. As an officer and delegate of the union, the monthly gatherings are never optional. Lord knows, attendance at the meetings is so imperative, it justifies skipping your spouses' birthday or even your wedding anniversary.

With great regret, I'm here to confirm that the boys club is still alive and thriving in several professions. My heart goes out to the spouses who sit home uninvited to gatherings and holiday parties because the "wives aren't going." I want to clarify a few things. My husband only behaves that prehistorically twice a month. He never drinks in our home. He never becomes legless when we are out to dinner. He is never an angry or violent drunk. He never so much as comes home from work late other than those two days a month.

In my heart, I knew that the root of his social drinking was a byproduct of pressure to network and stay abreast of what he needed to know in his field. In my head, I knew that I wasn't going to tolerate him risking his life, my life, and the lives of any passengers on the road the nights he drove home exhausted or "ham-maHed", as we say in Boston. So after talking about this until I was blue in the face, a few weeks after Dr. Smith found my lump, I saw a lawyer to discuss divorce proceedings. The day Dr. Smith felt my "*may* or *may not* be <u>cancerous</u>" lump- I felt something erupt inside of me. I needed to take charge of my life. I needed to fix everything that was broken.

Of course there were other extenuating circumstances (which I had neatly swept under a rug year after year) leading up to that appointment with the divorce attorney. In short, I had become unbelievably unhappy with the way things were going in our marriage. Most every moment spent in my home was a lonely one. Rog worked day and night often six days a week. I worked more and saw him even less. Although my husband had some amazing attributes, I felt certain I had made the wrong pick for a life partner. I wanted a companion. I wanted someone to take day trips with on Sunday afternoons. What I had was a housemate.

I sought a legal professional to get a sense of how clean, quick and easy, or dirty, long and difficult it would be for me to move out and move on. There was a business, property, a joint savings, furniture, items of value, and health insurance all wrapped around our eighteen year relationship. I didn't have the slightest idea of how divorce worked. One thing was certain; I was tired of the two ships in the night lifestyle we were leading. On top of that, I didn't want to stay awake another night wondering if my husbands head was smashed into a tree as his phone went to voice mail. I mourned his death in the wee hours of the morning on the first and third Friday of each month one too many times. As a child, I was surrounded by the wreckage excessive alcohol consumption leaves behind. There was no room in my adult house for such shards.

It took my endo running his fingers over my lump to help me realize that I wanted (and deserved) more. The **mere thought** of that lump bringing my life to an end me want to live the life I had always wanted. The life I kept putting on hold.

A week after I saw the lawyer, Roger called me inebriated from "somewhere in Boston near a gas station," asking for a ride home. "Where are you?" I said in my I cannot believe my ears tone. "I'm near a gas station. -In Boston." I knew it would be impossible to find him without more specific information. "Are you on your way home? What are you near? What are you looking at?" Just then, he stopped talking to me. I think he passed out. My next call was to our Boston cop friend. Turns out he wasn't on duty that night and it was too late for me to call him at home. Livid over the idea of getting up at 2:00 A.M. to find my husband's sorry ass somewhere "near a gas station in Boston", I paused while putting on my jacket. For years I have said, "If you cannot drive, CALL FOR A RIDE." For the first time in nearly two decades together- he did just that. Perhaps there was some hope for the relationship? The fact that he was willing to meet me half way convinced me to stick around long enough to give our relationship another try.

It would be unfair if I failed to mention that the night he called for a ride was also a tremendous day in Boston history. It was the night the Red Sox won the World Series! So if ever there was an appropriate evening to wake up your spouse and request a ride home -that was it. Our ride home was filled with incredible light from the full harvest moon. The breathtaking beauty of the sky was underscored by the aggravating sounds of snoring from "Sir Red Sox Fan Drinks a Lot" in the passenger seat. The intoxicated snorts were far less adorable than the almost childlike sound of his voice a few hours prior when he called to say "They WON! They WON!"

I'll skip the long version of how I found the gas station in Boston and just cut to the part that matters. His decision not to get behind the wheel that night was a sign of progress. So to further mark the relevance of that evening, I smacked him in the best place to leave a mark on a man- his wallet. I charged my husband $500.00 in cab fare for getting me out of bed.

You may wonder why I have gone so far-off track in the story. I promise this does all tie in. The 2004 World Series was the end to my husband driving home after consuming too much alcohol. Through a blatant series of "this is what I <u>want</u> and <u>need</u> from you if I'm going to stay," our marriage seemed to be back on track. - Just in time for my biopsy results.

At the risk of putting too much stock in cancer, it had appeared that cancer was actually saving our marriage. The mere idea of cancer reunited us. We were the team we had started out as nearly two decades prior to the lump in my neck. How's that for a good cancer? Six small letters of a little word c-a-n-c-e-r instituted more time together watching movies, having dinner, running errands, and late night chats under the covers of our bed. The idea of having the good cancer, brought the good back to our relationship.

Now that I've shared this story of hope and progress, one can imagine how stunned I was to hear my reformed soul mate's slurring voice as he entered our home the <u>night before my radioactive iodine radiation treatment</u> around <u>10:00 P.M.</u> "Hey, Babe. How are 'ya?" was all I could decipher through a mess of mumbles as the scent of beer wafted through our bedroom. "Where were you?" I asked. "I tried to call." I said, aching to hear his excuse for staying out and drinking the night before my **quarantine**. "I had to pay my dues at the ELKS." He went on to say, "I had a few drinks." I've never known him to hang at any local club. He's always been too busy with work. Parking his rump on a bar stool on the eve of my radiation was one of the most confusing and hurtful things he had ever done.

Void of the energy necessary to construct the perfect series of sentences to capture how truly disappointed I was, I rolled over and tried to fall asleep. My eyeballs rained down on the buttercup yellow flannel pillow case of my hypothyroid bed. We are both in hell. My husband didn't want to be around me, so he went out drinking on a Wednesday night. Cancer had replaced his attentive, loving, funny, thoughtful, and considerate wife with an angry bitch of a girl. Could I blame him for not wanting to come home to the house of cancer? Castle De La Cancer is the last place anyone in their right mind would want to be. He needed to be away from cancer…away from ME. I would have loved a night away. I just don't have that luxury. Cancer comes in a stylish travel bag and follows its' victims wherever they go. I could not escape the clutches of cancer. I envied Roger's ability to turn off his phone and hide from cancer.

Could the pill I was scheduled to swallow kill all of the dysfunctional toxins radiating through my house? Was the poison strong enough to destroy all of the hurt, anger, and pain in my heart? After weeks of misdirecting that rage on my husband, I decided to speak to the person who I was really mad at. –God. *You have given me the most fantastic test, Lord. I am failing you. I'm too tired to continue being your pupil. Your late night study sessions are frying my will to live. I find my anger over your decision to give me cancer impossible to overcome. I need you to make me well again. Please, enough already. Please God-**enough**.*

Still numb from the blow of spousal betrayal I took the night before, I opted not to engage in conversation with my man once the sun came up. I dressed for my blast of hazardously healing medicine and (ski-trip-belly and all) got in the Jeep. Ski-trip-belly is a term my friends and I came up with during the early Regan administration. After several 5:00 A.M. departures on the old exhaust smellin' ski trip charter bus, we named how our insides felt. Ski-trip-belly was the essence of pre-dawn nausea, mixed with a side of headache, a shot of dry heaves, chased with a touch of the chills and dizziness. Bear in mind, a sleep over preceded most every ski trip. The average amount of R.E.M sleep was around two hours.

This raw St. Patrick's Day morning, my ski-trip-belly was a combination of nerves, five weeks without thyroid hormone, and broken heart. I held back tears all the way into Boston. Rog was always good at listening and problem solving. If he had been home the night before my treatment, I could have worked through some of my fears out loud. I had too much pride to confide in him that morning. After all of the progress we made as a couple, I couldn't believe he elected to fall from grace on the eve of my radioactive iodine radiation. He knew how terrified I was. Pre-cancer, he was a good man who had been a typical husband. Since my diagnosis, he had become an <u>amazing husband</u>. His post-diagnosis dedication to our marriage motivated me to look at him through different colored glasses. Coming home drunk just seemed so below the man cancer brought out in him.

Just when cancer seemed to be doing something good for us, just when we seemed to be on a more authentic level of loving, just when we slowed down enough to really hear each other, just when we stopped working like dogs to spend more time together, just when I allowed myself to really lean on him, -he dropped the commitment ball. Had his cancer induced goodness expired?

As I signed into the hospital, I glanced at my husband. He looked tired. At first I thought *so what are you? Hung over? How would you like a little 131 in your coffee? That would perk you up. I have a special brew of radioactive breakfast blend coming right up.* Then I looked more closely at him. His skin was unlike any color I had ever seen. He looked white, pasty, gaunt, unshaven, and bloated. I know gaunt and bloated don't work in the same sentence, but that is what I saw. My cancer had kicked his ass. What a fine pair we had become. He didn't come home the night before because he didn't know where to put all of his pain. He needed a break. *We are going to have good and bad days.* I thought. *Yesterday was a bad day. Today may be better.* As we made our way into the Nuclear Medicine waiting room, I considered apologizing for the silent treatment. I couldn't find the words.

"Lorna Brunelle? Hello, you can follow me." As we walked behind the person in a white coat I contemplated going back to the car. *Shall I play Russian roulette? Take my chances that the cancer will not come back? Or just swallow the pill and put this all behind me?* The tech who helped me scan two days prior greeted us in a holding room. Not your typical exam cubical, the room had a few chairs, a computer, a pile of magazines, and colorless walls void of art. "How are you feeling today, Mrs. Brunelle?" the tech asked. "<u>Really</u> tired and <u>really</u> freaked out," I replied.

Just then, the series of questions began. "Could you be pregnant?" (Odd question to ask since they made me do a pregnancy blood test.) "Do you realize what radioactive iodine 131 therapy is? Do you consent to the treatment? Do you have any questions? Have you been on the radioactive iodine diet? Have you stuck to that plan? Now we will go over the precautions. Alright, now I'm going to go over the instructions for patients and families regarding Radiation Safety for 131 Iodine Therapy." Each section was read aloud. My head was spinning as the list of DONT'S seemed to be unending. (For a formal list of do's and don'ts, visit the thyca.org web site.)

"You must sleep in a separate bed. -Six feet of separation is a must. You must stay at least six feet away from children, pregnant woman, and elderly people." Then he asked, "Are there any children, pregnant or elderly people in your home?" I shook my head "No." He then went onto read the instructions. "You cannot sit near anyone on a train, bus, airplane or car over four hours at a time. You MUST avoid using disposable items that cannot be flushed down a toilet. All disposable items that come into contact with any bodily fluids cannot be disposed of in the normal trash. These items must be flushed down the toilet. You cannot touch any paper, plastic or Styrofoam. If you read a paper or drink from a plastic cup and dispose of it in your trash, the radar in your local trash truck will go off and you'll have to pay a fine. If incontinent, cloth diapers must be used. You cannot use a diaper service. If you need to take a short trip during the period of restricted travel, sit as far as possible from others. Avoid the use of public transportation. If possible, have sole use of one bathroom. Sit while urinating. Flush the toilet <u>three times</u> with the lid down. Clean the toilet after each use. Wash hands frequently, including after each toilet use. Shower at least once a day. Twice is preferred. Use and wash dishes and utensils separately for one week. Use separate towels, washcloths and toothbrushes from the rest of the household. Launder clothing and linen (sheets and towels) separately from the rest of the household for one week. If you blow your nose you must flush the tissue down the toilet. If you have any medical problems, call this number and bring your paperwork with you. Keep your paperwork with you at all times. We don't want you to share the house phone with anyone who lives with you. Try to use your own personal phone… like a cell."

When the list was finished he said, "Lorna, the radioactive matter is disposed the quickest through your urine. <u>Drink a lot</u> of water. Within the first forty-eight hours much of the radiation will leave your body. You have to stay quarantined for five days despite how often you are urinating. You may want to wait a little longer to be around children and the elderly. It is also our recommendation that you do not try to or become pregnant within twelve months. You may feel flu-like achy, crampy, and stiff. You may actually feel as if you have the flu. It is also common for you to be <u>very</u> tired. Do you have any questions?" *I could write a book on tired you moron* I thought *clearly you have never been hypo.*

As he continued to talk, I glanced at the bottom of the regulations sheet and read the last line: **Please note that you could possibly be identified by law enforcement personnel who are operating radiation detection equipment. In the interest of Homeland Security keep these instructions with you.** Just then I laughed at how ironic my life had become. In my early twenties, I was a pretty bombshell. In my early thirties I had become a toxic <u>**dirty bomb**</u>! So in a way, I had become a **dirty bombshell**! I could hardly wait to find out what my forties had in store.

He went on to say, "You may experience nausea. <u>Get right to a bathroom.</u> **No one else** can tend to the vomit if you get sick." Once we were done going over the rules and regulations, he placed a phone call. While we waited for the rest of the team to join us, I said, "I have a question. What about my cat?" "What about it?" he replied. "Well, if this stuff harms humans, what does it do to pets? Should I place her in quarantine while I'm contaminated?" "No, your cat will be fine." Completely suspect of that notion, I made a mental note to seclude my cat.

Just then a group of men entered the room. "Mrs. Brunelle, we are going to walk you through the final stages of your radiation therapy. Do you have any questions? I noticed one of the men was holding a cooler. The words POISON, TOXIC, and HAZARD were plastered on the sides. A skull and bones photo was in the middle near the lid along with the radioactive symbol. The pill was inside of the cooler. *You've got to be fucking kidding me! Are they for real? This is hardly the way to present something as medicine.*

Then a most *out of body* exchange began. The man who had been speaking to me for nearly <u>an hour</u> became almost Martian-like. In full robotic tones he said, "Are you Lorna Jayne Brunelle? Do you live at 96 North Street, in Middleboro, Massachusetts? Are you aware of the 131 Iodine therapy and all of the restrictions surrounding it? Do you willingly agree to take this pill? To the best of your knowledge, are you pregnant at this time? Do you have any questions?"

My mind kept drifting back to the phrase *in the interest of homeland security.* In the interest of my home and my security, I said, "Okay, let's do this." At that point the man in the white coat put on a pair of lead gloves. He then opened the cooler and pulled out a large lead egg. The eight-inch cylinder resembled a martini shaker. He untwisted the top and bottom. Nestled between inches of lead, sat a tiny purple pill. *It's purple! That must be a good sign. Purple is my birthstone. Purple is God's way of telling me it's going to be okay.*

"That's it?" I said in disbelief that I had feared something so small and unassuming. "Yes, that's it." The tech replied. "Now when I put this in your mouth, you have to <u>immediately</u> swallow all of the water in the cup. You cannot spit the pill out of your mouth. Are you ready?"

"I guess so," was all that I could get out of my mouth. "Are you *really* ready? I repeat, <u>you cannot spit it out</u> or hold the pill in your mouth. <u>You have to swallow it.</u>" I nodded my head then said, "I'm ready." As the pill went down my throat, my entire body became numb. Fighting tears, I tried to refocus my brain. All that kept repeating through my head was *what have I done? What have I done?* The man standing next to my husband took out a Geiger counter or Geiger meter and said, "She's registering." Then he walked back a few more feet and said, "Yep, she's registering." Then walked back a few more feet and said, "Oh yeah, she's registering." "What do you mean?" I asked. "You are showing up on the counter." he said. "You are already **radioactive.** -Pretty amazing, huh?" "How come you can be around me right now? Aren't you in danger?" I asked. "It's the nature of the beast," one of the men replied. "This is our job and besides, it's all about SPACE and TIME. You can only be around it for so long within so many feet. SPACE and TIME- remember that.

After a few more minutes of small talk, one of the men asked how I was feeling. Oddly enough, I wasn't feeling anything. I expected dizziness and nausea. "If you are feeling okay, you can gather your things. Hospital rules state that we have to escort you to your car. We cannot risk you stopping anywhere along the way. Are you ready to go?" "Escort me to my car? Oh my." I said. "Heaven forbid I contaminate anyone on the way out."

It was official. I had become a dirty bombshell. In the interest of homeland security, on Thursday, March 17th, 2005, I declared myself a dirty bombshell and vowed to embrace my dirty bombshell-ness.

$\mathcal{D}$arkness

$\mathcal{I}$N SILENCE TWO MEN ESCORTED US through the hospital parking lot. As a parting reminder one of the men said, "Don't forget-SPACE and TIME." As I loaded my weary self into the back seat of the Jeep, I had an overwhelming sense of self. I felt more present in the atmosphere. Not just on a psychological level, but on a literal three-dimensional sense of being. Perhaps it was an endorphin release from being so worked up? My mind drifted back to college when I read "The Unbearable Lightness of Being." The title always stimulated me. (Anyone who has read the text will have to pardon my play on words.) While leaving the hospital that day I couldn't help but relate to the title. I had an unbearable lightness of being.

Once I swallowed the pill I felt slight in body but massive in mind. That state of presence, that unbearable lightness of being, was unlike anything I had ever felt. If ever people ask what radioactive iodine radiation therapy feels like I simply say, "Very queer. You are yourself, yet not yourself. Don't suppose that helps?" During the ride home, I felt sea sick. I attributed my queasy belly to being hypo in the back seat of a moving vehicle. About thirty minutes into our commute I became unbelievably tired.

As Roger and I walked into our house, I knew something was wrong. There was a certain darkness in each room. A layer of smog seemed to hover a few feet below each ceiling. The chimney man was still on-site with his crew. The plastic tarp draping off the living room from the rest of the house was no longer hanging. "Something is off. This isn't right," I said as I stood in the doorway. As I entered my dining room it was very apparent an accident had occurred. My entire dining room was **covered** in soot. That morning, the chimney sweep had placed our invoice on the dinning room table before we left for Boston. I picked up the slip hours later and saw a perfect impression from the invoice on my table. The spot beneath where the invoice sat was perfectly clean. The entire rest of the table was doused in soot. My heart started pounding as I frantically ran through the rooms in the house. Every room was immersed in black soot. From floor to ceiling, every tea cup, every curtain, every rug, every piece of furniture, every plant, every piece of clothing, every piece of food in the fruit bowl, every crevice in the hard wood floors, every dish, every pot and pan, every pen, every antique, every photo, every linen, every decoration, every piece of paperwork, every piece of mail; even my cat was covered in black soot.

In a voice slightly raised above a whisper, I said, "What on earth happened here?" My husband didn't answer me. My whisper became a scream as I yelled, "You have to go outside and ask them what happened here!" At that point a member of the chimney crew came in and said, "Oh yeah, we saw this soot but we thought it was here before since you were having chimney issues." Holding back my rage, I said, "You've been here all week. My house was just cleaned three days ago. My cleaning lady worked around you while you serviced the chimney. Do you not remember seeing her here? Our house DID NOT look like this when we left this morning. Do you really think we would have been living this way?! I am sliding on the floor in soot. I will not allow you to say this black filth was here before we left for Boston today."

On the verge of smashing something, I stepped back and said, "I'm sorry. I am not upset with you. I need to speak with your boss. Is he still on site? Please go find him." At that point, my husband started moving papers and items around to show the owner of the chimney business how soot demolished our home. I heard him say, "You know our house didn't look like this when we left today. My wife has just received radiation. She is recovering from cancer. There is no way in hell I would have allowed her to live in this. This is uninhabitable. You cannot be serious in saying that our house was like this all week." The next sentence is what I refer to as the breaking point in my recovery.

"Well, I'll come back later on and help you guys clean, but how do I know it's not your old dirt? I mean come on, you guys had a chimney problem on the second floor. You saw some soot up there, right? What's not to say it was on this floor of the house, too?"

With respect to the six-foot limitations of quarantine, from the kitchen I screamed, "I cannot and will not clean any of this. This requires professional cleaning. MY HOME IS RUINED! Every room is damaged. **I AM NOT CLEANING THIS**. This isn't dirt, this is SOOT! I cannot clean sticky soot! I don't have the proper supplies. And as for the second floor, a few rooms had a light dusting of gray soot which was only visible on things like white plastic bags. The entire first floor is covered in a black smoky mess." In a full blown helplessly hypo rush, I leaned my head up against a wall in the kitchen and sobbed. I must have slid down the wall because I came to howling and shaking on the floor. A little puddle of tears, snot and soot welled up beside my leg. It was the lowest and darkest point of my life. In A.A. they say everyone hits rock bottom. For the first time, I truly understood what that meant.

I didn't have the option of going to a hotel. I couldn't stay with family. I couldn't flee to a second home. My radioactive iodine radiation caused a medically induced lock down. I was held hostage in a house destroyed by soot. The notion of being trapped in my dirty (and no doubt unhealthy) house sent me into a fear stricken panic.

I heard my husband on the phone with our cleaning lady. Within twenty minutes, she showed up to access our damage. Her diagnosis was, "This is beyond me. You need an industrial team to get in here with special products. You need to get the big guns in here." From there, my husband went through the yellow pages. I heard him say, "My wife has cancer. We just got home from her radiation and our entire house is covered in soot. We need someone to clean this. She is quarantined and cannot leave the house. It is not an option for us to go to a hotel. I recognize that this is short notice, but can someone get over here right away? I'm worried about her breathing this in all night."

I wondered how I could pull myself out from under the wreckage when the weight of the debris felt so profound. I remember crying harder and harder each time I looked around the house. Everything was dark and dirty. I felt as if the darkness of the external world around me was mirroring the darkness I had inside. When you cannot escape the physical horror and hell around you, and you have a mental mile-high pile of horror and hell inside of you, your mind has limited choices. Mine elected to break down. I was hyperventilating, trembling, yelling, and crying all while vigorously trying to wipe down the kitchen table. I needed to create one tiny clean soot free spot to house my somnolent soul. With each pass of the sponge, I cursed God. *Why have you vandalized my house? WHAT THE HELL ARE YOU TRYING TO TELL ME? HOW MUCH MORE DO YOU THINK I CAN STAND?*

Too tired to continue cleaning, I sat down with my head in my hands. I remember a moment when I was shivering and blankly starring out of a window onto my culinary herb garden. In a flashback-like haze, I remembered planting the garden with my step-son Brent. At the time he was about nine years old. Already a little man, he was unbelievably eager to help out around the yard. Roger and I had just moved into the house and we were preparing the yard for our wedding reception. The only care in the world I had that day was planting all of the flowers and herbs before it rained. When the last herb made it into the ground, Brent and I went for an ice cream. He ordered mint chocolate chip. I ordered chocolate. Life was **easy**.

My body was so functional back then. I had the energy to clean the entire house, work in the yard for hours, do a complete grocery shop, make a fantastic dinner and serve it out on the deck for friends and family. My mind was strong. I had a thyroid. I was happy, kindhearted, and loving. We were newlyweds in our first home. Life was good.

Flash ahead eight years later…I was a cold, damp, drizzling hypothyroid mess of tears, fatigue, cancer, devastation, and darkness. During that time in my life, I couldn't even buy groceries and cook them on the same day, let alone invite anyone over for dinner. For the first time in my life, I didn't have what it takes to clean up a mess. I'd been cleaning up messes and fixing the problems for as long as I could remember. It was time to take a break from fixing **things**…it was time to fix **me.** From the table I said, "I will not pick up a single tea cup. I will not wash one wall. I will not take this on. I didn't make this mess and I am not cleaning it up." Maybe that was the message God was trying to send? Maybe it was time I focused on myself and let go of the rest?

The next morning I had a team of professional disaster relief cleaners in my house. There were five men in total. I heard one man say, "This place is totally fucked. Even the ceilings need to be done. And the wife has cancer. -Tough break." I heard another member of the crew respond by saying, "What a friggen nightmare. -Poor bastard." *No shit,* I thought from the kitchen. Within minutes, all of my curtains were down, my bed was stripped, my rugs were rolled and a dry cleaning service was in my driveway to pick up all of our things. "We'll try to make the bedroom nice for her so she can at least sleep in there." I heard another man say. But this is going to take us about five to six days, maybe even a week."

My kitchen and dining room were converted into washing and drying stations. From morning until night, strangers washed the darkness away. Over eighty of my antique tea cups and saucers were set aside to dry. All of my 1940's molds and tins were shining again. As I watched the large men handle my grandmother's Havilland French Limoges Countess china, I wasn't concerned over the idea of them breaking it. The tears had finally stopped. I had become anesthetized. The blast of soot left me numb. For two days, I remained disconnected. The chimney soot was the straw that broke the cancer girls' back.

To make matters worse, I couldn't sleep or rest during my quarantine. My house was buzzing with people. I was contagiously radioactive so my job was to dress each morning and play musical rooms in the house. I had to stay six feet away from the bedlam so I bounced from living room, to dining room, to bedroom, and so on. Never before had lounging around made me so tired. The radiation tech was right, I felt like I had the flu. I also had a peculiar bleach-white discharge leaking out of my nose. Each time I'd pass by a mirror I'd notice a crusty stark white foam dried up around my nostrils. I never asked the doctors about it. I just assumed it was the radiation seeping out of my body through the mucous. That lasted about two weeks, so please don't be afraid if you experience that after your treatment.

Little by little our house was becoming a home again. Little by little I began to emotionally commit to my surroundings. Our sofa and loveseat smelled new. The fresh scent made me happy. The walls, floors, and ceilings were sparkling. Their glow made me smile. My plants were green again. Their emerald hues made me want to water them. All of my things were back in serene order. I sat down in my clean leather chair to take in the cleanliness. Just then my soot soiled kitty jumped in my lap. She was the only thing the crew did not clean. Much to my horror, I realized that we forgot to quarantine Mitzi when we returned from the hospital.

My cat wasn't the only thing the soot made me forget. With the carnival of chaos in my house, I totally forgot to massage the sides of my face and suck on lozenges. As a means to prevent the salivary glands from going dormant after the radiation, I was encouraged to do both. In a flash the little pocket of *clean house* happiness I had found faded.

The final days of my quarantine were filled with desolation and emotional muddle. The darkness impaired my vision. Some days were so dark it was hard to see that the soot was nothing more than a temporary set back. I found it impossible to distinguish the blessings from the rubble. I found it hard to commit to conversation. I found it hard to laugh. I found it hard to enjoy the taste of food with the metallic taste the radiation left in my mouth. Mix a little poisonous radiation on top of being hypothyroid for five weeks, add a cup full of severe soot damage, and you have the perfect recipe for the blues-and by blues, I don't mean Buddy Guy.

March 19th was supposed to be a turning point. At last, I was able to take my Synthroid pills! With my lovely amber prescription bottle in hand, I placed my glass under the ice maker of my refrigerator. As I heard water splashing around the ice I thought, *FINALLY...energy and happiness in a bottle...* Screw the fountain of youth! I was holding the fountain of sanity. I was on my way to saner days sans dry hair and skin, stiff muscles, freezing cold limbs, and sadness. I was saying goodbye to darkness. I knew it would take a few days to feel the benefits of the fake thyroid tablets. One would think on mere placebo, my emotional highs and lows would subside the moment I took the pills. -I wasn't that lucky.

As the meds made their way down my throat I sat on the porch. Trying to force moments of the peace, I read a magazine in the fresh air. I felt the spring breeze. I heard the young birds talking. I was out of doors but still in quarantine. Searching for happiness but still sad. As I watched the fat robins poke their beaks in the dirt, I thought *if only it were that easy to nourish and replenish my body.* I prayed for my thyroid hormone levels to resurface. As a means of holding onto my sanity, I tried to celebrate life on a smaller scale. With all of my might I clung to the simple things. My newest mantra was "Every time I swallow a pill, I am one step closer to happiness."

Pill time became the best part of each day! Bursts of euphoria rushed in like flash floods every time I heard ice cubes fall into my glass. I knew my pills were sure to follow. I serenaded each pill with "Have I Told You Lately That I Love You" -the Rod Stewart version because he, too, is a thyroid cancer survivor. I treasured the pocket of time I spent in front of the calendar. Crossing off days gave me a sense of elation. With each stroke of my pen, I was closer to my wellness goal. I drew a large sun on the daylight savings date knowing I was weeks away from warm days at the ocean's edge.

Desperately in search of some light at the end of my smoggy and polluted subway tunnel of cancer, I prayed for the clarity to put my darkness into perspective. Day after day, pill after pill, I prayed for a future filled with health, sunshine, laughter, and light. I wrote myself positive notes. One read: When is the last time you had your home professionally cleaned (furniture, rugs, curtains, ect.) from floor to ceiling? Blessings come in all forms. Learn to look beyond the darkness.

Another note read: My house was trashed and my body was broken, but I had a home to clean and a body to mend. The sun always comes up after a long black night. Out of darkness comes light. When cancer knocks on your door, I implore you to focus on the light.

Bidet the Bush

IN MY TEENS I WAS PERKY. I was nominated for SPIRIT QUEEN during spirit week each year in high school. Even my boobs were perky. They were so perfectly perky they didn't even need a bra! I was perky in college, too. As an adult, I remained perky. Even when my boobs fell victim to gravity and weight gain-I remained perky. In fact, I was pretty damn perky right up until I found out I had cancer. I missed feeling perky. I wanted to return to work with perkiness to prove to my team that I was back on track. I wanted to welcome the students with lots of smiles, love, lilt, energy, and **perkiness** in my voice. The perkiness is what leaves children with a sense of how truly special they are. Example: Try saying, "You did such a great job on that song!" in a perky voice. Now say, "You did such a great job on that song." in a monotone voice. Not the same message. All of these things, perkiness, lilt, smiles; all required one thing-energy. Even on Synthroid, my vigor cupboards were still bare. It was even harder to find my way back to being perky when a spot appeared on my follow up scan in Boston.

A week after my radiation, I returned for my series of after pictures.

We were hoping to see a clear picture to mark the effectiveness of the radiation treatment. This would also prove to be a tumor marker for future reference. By the grace of God, I had the same tech. He knew the drill, and we scanned in the same humane fashion from the previous week. As I waited for the scan results with my friend Reenie, I saw the tech talking to a woman seated at a computer. In <u>extremely</u> broken English, she called me over. "Hello, I am Dr. N. Okay good news. In thyroid region I see nothing. Nothing. Is good. But see spot here?" She pointed to the computer screen. A glowing spot as bright as the North Star gleamed at us. The doctor went on to say, "See spot? Do you see spot?" I remember thinking, *See spot what? See spot run? See spot jump? See spot skip? What am I looking for?*

I felt my lack of patience brewing. When a doctor is referring to something **wrong** on your scan you need to be able to understand what the hell they are saying! -Especially when you are only one week into thyroid meds after weeks of hypo hell. The doctor went on to say, "Well, umm spot may be two things. Umm, it may be radioactive urine in your underpants which show up on scan. Did you umm maybe dribble your urine today? That could be why spot is there near your bladder, sacral region." Trying to remain calm, I said, "How would I know if anything is down there in my underpants? I wipe well after I urinate, if that's what you mean!"

The ironic thing is that my husband is constantly making fun of me for clogging the toilet. I wrap the toilet tissue around my hand about seven times, creating a perfect baseball catchers mitt before wiping. I am forever spray-bleaching the toilet and keeping things clean. Her accusation of me being a messy pee'er, wasn't cutting it. As she spoke, my body became piping hot. "Can I speak to an American who actual speaks ENGLISH?" was on the tip of my ugly American tongue. "What do you need me to do?" I asked with great restraint. "Well, okay I need you to go to bathroom and remove underwear. Then I need you to wash bush. Wash bush extremely well, lots of soap and rinse. Do not urinate after you wash bush and we will rescan."

Almost crying and laughing with an overwhelming need to throw something, I said, "I'm sure you realize that we don't have **bidets** in the **United States.** So I have no idea how I can **wash the bush** without exposing myself to whomever might walk in to use the facilities! Plus, I don't have the proper wash cloth, soap or towel. I think I'll come back another day to retest. How's that sound?" With total urgency in her foreign voice, she replied, "Well you need to come back right way, how about Monday?" At that point I said, "What is the worst case scenario here?" "Well, it could be tumor or new cancer spot. But it could be radioactive urine showing up on screen. We have to see you with clean bush to tell." (My hand to God these are real quotes.)

The following Monday I urinated at home, took a shower and adorned my bush with brand spanking new "underpants", fresh from the laundry. I elected not to drink any water for fear of contaminating my bush region with radioactive pee. Ever the scanning pro, I alternated visits on the table with two talk radio shows while I scanned. The chatter coming across the air waves comforted me. I tried to imagine sitting in my Jeep listening to the talk jocks work the air waves. The scan table that caused so much grief ended up being a lovely little respite spot. I actually almost napped a little on the bed. Offended by the doctors' allegation, I walked down the hospital hall with my head held high. I tried preparing comeback lines incase there was a repeat attack on my bush. *I may have a contaminated bush, but at least I have a bush. OH wait, that doesn't work she has a bush, too. Try again; I may have a contaminated bush, but I bet I can sing better than anyone in here! So, there. Yeah, that works! So hats off to you, dry bush folk, at least this bush can sing. —Wait, well... back to the drawing bush...I mean board!*

As I waited for the scan results, I held in the urge to urinate. There was no way we were having a repeat performance in bush land. Once again, in busted English, the doctor called me in. "Did you keep bush dry or did you have to urinate?" *Lord give me strength, if ever I needed you to prevent me from clocking someone up side the head, it's now.* "Yes, I haven't gone to the bathroom since eight o'clock this morning. After I urinated, I showered, dressed and came here. Why, is there a problem?" I said clenching my teeth. "Did you dress in clean underpants?" She asked. *Are you kidding me, lady? Honestly...what the hell...this is America, in most households, we **wash** our panties before stepping into them.* My mind went into robot over-drive as I thought *MUST FIND AMERICAN TO TRANSLATE FOR ME…must find English speaking doctor…*Just then she interrupted my secret mission to find an American who was actually *born* in America by saying, "Well, I still see spot." Then she pointed to the screen and said, "See spot? It's in same place. See spot?"

The Hope Diamond shined back at me from the computer screen. "Okay, so this time I know it wasn't me. So what is it?" I said with a definite hint of *I told 'ya my immaculately-kept bush was dry* in my voice. Just then she said, "Well radioactive iodine can show up in your bladder on scan for up to six months. We will have to rescan early in fall time." Shocked I asked, "So, is there a test I can do or something to be sure I don't have <u>more cancer</u>? I mean, do I really have to wait <u>six months</u>? This is the last thing I need to have on my mind." Rather confused by what I was saying (or insensitive to my lack of patience) she called Dr. Smith and handed me the phone. "Mrs. Brunelle, so you are over at the hospital having some scans. So my guess is that radioactive urine stored in your bladder is coming up on the screen. This is quite common. I wouldn't worry about it. We'll rescan 'ya in a few months. The good news is we aren't seeing any thing in your thyroid region so that is really great. Take care."

The six month long probation sentence aggravated the hell out of me. How could I move on if I have to rescan in the fall? What if I had bladder cancer? My mind ran away from me, *it actually feels weird when I pee now. Is that from the cancer? My pee has been a different color, too. Is that from the radiation or **the cancer** in my bladder?* I'm going to cut way ahead in the book here…I didn't have bladder cancer. I just allowed the doctor to freak me out. So if ever you are given a trial period with a potentially bad verdict after your sentence, please don't get your panties or "underwear" into a bunch over it. In my case, I worried all summer over nothing.

I also need comment on the art of bedside manner. The non-English speaking doctor implied I had cancer in a new section of my body. My doctor, who just happens to speak English, assured me that radioactive urine creates spots on scans and not to worry. So here is another little tip for the medical training field: if you have physicians who do not fluently speak the language of the location of the hospital (in this case, the U.S.A.) they are practicing in, please consider **A**. telling them to always put a positive spin on the assessment through their broken language until they can find an English-speaking staff member, or **B**. bring in a translator to clearly set the record straight if the physician refuses to brush up their language skills. It is unacceptable to tell someone to "wash bush" in a public restroom of a hospital. It is unacceptable to say "could be tumor" is when in all actuality it was not.

Just to safe guard myself here from the immigrants who may be reading this book, please know that I am not against immigration. I applaud anyone who moves thousands of miles away from home hoping for a better life. My great-grandmother Jovanina Spadaro was born in Sicily. She moved to America and started a family in Boston. Her husband, my great-grandfather Joseph Gandolfo, also moved here from Sicily. In the North End of Boston, he opened an olive oil and produce store. Most everyone in that section of Boston spoke Italian. Both of their children (my grandmother Concetta "Connie" and my great-aunt Rose) were fluent in Italian and English.

Until I had cancer, I never cared what language people spoke. As a girl with childhood roots in the city areas of Watertown and Belmont, Massachusetts, I saw a rainbow of races and heard a symphony of assorted languages each day on the street. The varying dialects I heard at the local quick-marts were never strong enough to prevent us from purchasing a newspaper or filling up a gas tank. Most of those transactions could be achieved simply by smiling and reading the total due on the cash register. If you are going to move to America and seek a high-paying job with enormous responsibility (let's say in a hospital) where the primary language spoken is English you have to speak English. If people are relying on you to convey vital information, you must be able to clearly communicate. As a cancer patient in a hospital trying to receive crucial information regarding my health, I needed to hear the facts. I needed to hear them in the language of my country.

I think Teddy said it best in his address in 1907. Allow me to share the following quote by Theodore Roosevelt on immigrants and being an American.

"In the first place we should insist that if the immigrant who comes here in good faith becomes an American and assimilates himself to us, he shall be treated on an exact equality with everyone else, for it is an outrage to discriminate against any such man because of creed, or birthplace, or origin. But this is predicated upon the man's becoming in very fact an American, and nothing but an American...There can be no divided allegiance here. Any man who says he is an American, but something else also, isn't an American at all. We have room for but one flag, the American flag, and this excludes the red flag, which symbolizes all wars against liberty and civilization, just as much as it excludes any foreign flag of a nation to which we are hostile. . . We have room for but one language here, and that is the English language. . . We have room for but one sole loyalty and that is a loyalty to the American people."

Some say Teddy did indeed write those words, but not in 1907 while he was still president. Some believe the passages were culled from a letter he wrote to the president of the American Defense Society on January 3, 1919, three days before Roosevelt died. Either way, I think his words sum up what I am trying to say. -And to think they were written nearly one hundred years ago. I'm stepping off of the soap box now. I hope we can still be friends.

One week after my month of scanning, my friend passed away. She was fighting Non-Hodgkin's Lymphoma for quite a while. Years back when I was working in the public school system, she was in a few of my classes. Her sassy smile and mischievous eyes always caught my attention. It was as if she knew something the rest of us hadn't yet discovered. She was an old soul. After graduation, she went to school for massage therapy. Long story short, she needed to work on clients during the final phase of her education. Being the massage whore that I am, I was first in line. Anxious to get to know the girl behind those eyes, we talked during all of my treatments. In no time, we became friends. I followed her to the spa job she landed. We stayed in contact pretty regularly. After weeks of having a cold, she called and said, "Hi Lorna. I have some news...okay, don't be upset, but I have cancer. I need to take a little break from massages right now. But don't worry about me. I'm going to be fine. How are you?" Totally stunned by the news I flatly asked, "What <u>kind</u> of cancer do you have?" She had Non-Hodgkin's Lymphoma.

Two weeks after my radiation, I waited in a long line to say goodbye to my Princess Warrior friend. The way my friend fearlessly approached life, cancer, and death was astounding. I never saw her afraid. I never heard her complain. I never saw her give up hope. She was truly an inspiration. As I stood by her side looking into the casket I held back my tears. I held back tears when I hugged her family. They didn't need to see any more pain.

It's always hard to say goodbye to a friend. Saying goodbye to a friend who had cancer in her lymph system made it even harder. With my mortality ever present in my mind, I exited the doors of the funeral home thinking about the spot on my bladder. I wondered if my cancer had spread from the contaminated lymph node in my neck to my bladder. I envisioned my young mother standing in the receiving line at my wake. With my eyes drenched in tears, I searched through my bag for the keys to my Jeep.

I vowed to honor my Princess Warrior friend by living a good life. Long or short, the duration of my life needed to be fabulous!

Tigress

By April my energy resumed enough for me to put in half of a work shift without wanting to place my head on the piano and take a nap. (Again, everyone recovers at a different pace.) I am aware of how lucky I was to be self-employed during my recovery. I recognize that not everyone has the luxury of taking time off before returning to work full time. The downside to being self-employed was the financial hit on our home. From January through June, I was no longer teaching my full student load. Even after several weeks, I found it hard to work a full shift.

One night I shared my financial concerns with my husband. My retail therapy the weeks leading up to my surgery; my time off from work the weeks between surgery and radiation; the percentage of insurance we had to cover, in combination with all of the money I was spending on massages and healing energy treatments to restore my range of motion, started adding up in the back of my mind. After spewing out all of my worry, Roger very calmly said, "Lorna, they print more money every day and I can make it. Money should be *the last* thing on your mind right now. WE ARE FINE."

I found it grueling to sit around and watch money fly out of the windows because I caught cancer. Losing money thanks to cancer seemed unfathomably unfair. My entire life, I defined myself by work. I prided myself in contributing to the good life we had. For as long as I could remember, I had been infatuated with the concept of being a financially-independent woman. Dating back nearly twenty years, my work ethic has always been outstanding. My childhood memories of my step father pulling the phone out of the wall and wires out of the car in order to keep my mother isolated from help seared the importance of being self-sufficient. At a very early age, I vowed never to be stuck or financially dependent on anyone.

Money wasn't the only thing I missed. I missed my work. My career was fulfilling. I knew my work mattered on many levels. My job is to enhance artist awareness and foster creativity and self confidence in people. For months, cancer put the brakes on the creative aspect of my life. A life without creativity is, well, not very creative!

As a creative recovery incentive, two of my grammar school friends (Jen and Heather) planned a trip for us to visit Key West. The girls were quite clever in dangling that carrot in front of my nose. Around the time of my diagnosis they said, "When all of this is behind you, we are taking off. How about April vacation?"

I was having a hard time processing the idea of heading south without my man. I wasn't making any money. I was depleting our financial reserves. How could I pack my bags for sunny Florida and leave my husband behind in cold Massachusetts? He was working over-time to stay ahead of the game. In case his spouse, Miss Cancer Pants, had a relapse or two, no doubt. The old me, the girl with a thyroid, would have canceled the trip. She would have been level-headed and said, "This just isn't a good time. I've been out of work for months and it just isn't feasible right now. Thank you anyway." The new me, the girl without a thyroid, the girl who was recovering from cancer thought, *I have earned this trip. I have a battle scar across my neck to prove it.*

The horse chestnut trees on our property were filled with a chorus of singing birds as I hoisted my tired body into my Jeep headed toward Logan Airport. I couldn't help but think the Chickadees, Nuthatches, Woodpeckers, Titmice, Cardinals, and Juncos and were celebrating my departure to a warmer place. I saw my friends hopping out of the cab curbside at our terminal. I thought of my friend who had just passed away. I thought about what the word terminal really meant. By that point I had a few visible tears on my face. "I don't know if I should go," I said. "I don't know if I'm ready." Roger looked at me for a few seconds and said, "Honey you are going to be fine. You really need this. Go have fun with your friends. I'll be here Sunday to pick you up." I greeted Jen and Heather with a hug (by the way I was never a hugger) and said a silent prayer that they would accept me for the <u>new me</u> I had become.

Before I knew it we were flying over the turquoise blue waters of paradise. I was so close to weightlessly floating in that water. For months I had dreamed and waited for this day. *I'm going to float until my skin prunes. I am going to rest and bask in the warmth of the sun until every ounce, every cell of cancer evaporates from my soul...I am going to leave here well again. So help me God that is my mission.* As soon as I stepped off of the plane, I knew it was going to be a great trip. I felt lighter than I had in months (pretty miraculous since I had gained about twenty pounds since my surgery) and couldn't wait to submerge my body in the salt water.

As we sat waiting for our dinner we toasted to our health, friendship, and longevity. By the time our glasses emptied, we realized we had been waiting an eternity for our dinner. Just like old times, the girls elected me as the spokesperson for the group. "Lorna, it's been a l-o-n-g time. Did they forget our order? You should say something." Thrilled to have the responsibility of behaving like my old one of the girls self, I summonsed the hostess. My concerned heads up concluded with, "I mean really, waiting over an hour and a half between the appetizer and the entrée is unacceptable. What can you do to make this right?" Within minutes we were granted free drinks, dessert and 25% off of the tab. In the eyes of my friends, I was back. "Being back" wasn't about being forceful with a restaurant manager. It was about my friends relying on my voice to take on a situation they didn't want to address.

"Nice work, Lorna!" Jen said as we laughed over "make it right." "Good line, Lorna, where did you come up with that one?" Heather asked as we ordered another round of cocktails. Although I hardly ever drink, my glass of wine was not to blame for my boldness. I was completely serious about people making things right. From the nameless and faceless (like the wench at the grocery store who cut off my near empty cart to push her over-loaded cart to the cashier) to the far more germane people (like the doctor who couldn't speak English at the hospital) post-cancer, I needed everyone to do right by me.

The next day we awoke to the sound of The Big Dig outside our five-star, ever so pricey, ocean front island hotel. Anyone who survived The Big Dig construction project in Boston knows what I'm talking about. At the crack of dawn, we heard trucks, sirens and crashes of cement while our tired bodies tried to rest. I put on my glasses and tried to investigate the matter. There was a massive construction project adjacent to our hotel room. They were dismantling an old hotel and building condos. Heather asked, "Lorna, are you going to take care of the noise issue in our room?" Somewhat flattered by the request to put things back in order again less than twelve hours after obtaining free dessert and drinks at dinner, I asked, "Why me?" Quickly both girls said, "You have <u>always</u> been better at it." "Better at getting justice, or better at being a bitch?" I asked. "Better at getting your point across." Jen answered.

We dressed, ate breakfast, and walked over to the front desk. I requested a manager began explaining our predicament. "Hello, my name is Lorna Brunelle. I am in room _____. I have been coming here for a number of years, but this visit is of a different nature. This time, I am recovering from cancer. This time and I came here for rest and relaxation. I knew your hotel would be conducive to rehabilitation. Somehow we ended up positioned above a full blown dismantling site. The noise begins at dawn, and remains through the duration of the work day. Do we need to go to another hotel after you give us a full refund, or are you going to <u>make this right</u> for us?"

The new catch phrase flew out of my mouth with the ease of a rehearsed soliloquy. With the face of a person who had been sucker punched, the hotel higher-up handed me the keys to the ocean-front penthouse suite on the exact opposite side of the property. I triumphantly gathered my pocketbook and began to walk away. As I turned to leave the counter I said, "I won't forget your kindness. You took the time to make this right and that matters."

Before cancer, I was an aggressive woman fighting for the rights of the little people in the world. I was always there to speak up when an injustice had taken place. The quiet mouthed could rely on me to call attention to the smallest of offenses. "Excuse me, Miss, my friend wanted hash <u>not</u> bacon with her eggs. She'd like to send this back." Post-cancer, I was living in a world where everything felt wrong. I wanted everyone around me to make things right. Since the day God assigned my cancer, I was willing to suck up <u>every last bit of my energy</u> to get things close to <u>right</u> again. No longer fighting for my friend in the breakfast diner, I was fighting for my sanity and my right to heal. A get-a-way with the girls on top of a construction site was not going to bring me any closer to closure with my disease. I got on that plane in search of Mother Natures' nurturing and peace. I needed that hotel manager to do right by me.

The next night Jen and I went down to the restaurant bar while Heather dressed for dinner. I couldn't help but notice two really well-dressed women in their sixties seated at the opposite end of the bar. Feasting on an incredible looking dessert in a white crock, they smiled at us as if to say, "You have got to try this!" A few seconds later, the bartender slid the dessert toward us and said, "This is from the ladies. I'll get you some plates." As we spooned the most scrumptious warm chocolate soufflé (oozing with whipped cream and ice cream all over it) into our mouths, we enthusiastically thanked them for the slice of heaven. "Sometimes you have to eat dessert **before** dinner, girls. Enjoy!" they said, as they lifted their drinks to us. As the soufflé Gods shared their gifts with me, I sighed. I felt certain my days were going to be brighter.

My warm chocolate induced bliss escorted me to the ladies room. All of the stalls were in use. After about five minutes of paranoia over holding radioactive urine in my bladder, I opted to use the handicapped stall. After using the toilet, I washed my hands in the sink within the stall and walked out toward the exit door. As I made my way past a few ladies in line for other stalls, I heard a totally disgusted woman growl, "Eww…Gross! Wash your hands!" Then she turned to her friend and said, "She didn't even wash!" As I opened the door leading back into the restaurant, I realized that her hygienic command was intended for me. The girl with a thyroid and without cancer would have continued walking out of the door, dismissing her ignorance. The girl without a thyroid recovering from cancer, who wanted everyone to make things right, slowly turned around.

Nose-to-nose with an intoxicated stranger, I tried to set her straight. "Did you just tell me to wash my hands?" I asked, totally invading her personal space. "Ah, yeah!" she replied. With the breath of a drunken sailor she went on to say, "It's totally gross that you didn't wash up after you went to the bathroom. I saw you. You didn't wash your hands." With a body as still as tiger about to pounce, I crept even closer to her ear and said, "Oh I didn't wash my hands, huh? You are **sure** about that?" The drunken girl replied, "Ah, yeah, I'm sure! It's really nasty not to wash your hands." In a concentrated voice I replied, "Oh, I recognize the importance of washing my hands, Miss. I am recovering from cancer. Hand washing has reached a whole new level of importance since my radiation. My white blood cells are still pissed off. I cannot afford to skip hand washing."

With my jaw and fists clenched on each side of my body, I went on to say, "Which is why I washed my hands in the stall I was using a few minutes ago. That stall has its' own sink in it. Believe me, I don't need you to educate me on the points of bathroom cleanliness. Is there anything else I can clear up for you while I'm here?" I parted by pushing open the handicap stall door so she could examine the sink. As I passed by the drunken girl I noticed tears in her eyes. She was staring at my fresh hot pink shiny scar. I didn't want to make her cry. I wanted her to make things right. With a touch of guilt over bullying a drunk in a bathroom, I said, "Next time you go to pass judgment, do yourself a favor. Mind your own business. Things are not always as they appear. Are they? Stop living such a condemnatory life."

"Where the hell have you been? We were just coming to find you." my friends said as I made my way back to the bar. Drained from my bathroom boxing match, I tried to give them the short of the story. "Do I have a sign on my forehead that says "Recovering from cancer, step right up and take your best shot"? As the brazen sentence blurted out of my mouth I knew exactly what was going on. *I* was looking for a fight. *I* was looking for a reason to work through my anger. Never before had I been so willing to pounce. My zodiac sign is Aquarius. Normally we water bearers born between Jan 20th to Feb 18th are the peace-keepers or peace-makers. I had a key chain that claimed we are <u>the ones to settle the feuds</u>.

I must have been in my angry phase during my time in Key West. People say after traumatic incidents such as death, divorce, disease, or natural disasters such as fire, hurricanes or floods-that people experience stages of grief and loss. Doctor and author Elizabeth Kuebler Ross mapped out the stages of grief for us in her series of books. Although not always carved in stone, Dr. Ross suggests the stages of grief are: Denial, Anger, Bargaining, Depression and Acceptance. If you are dealing with cancer, tragedy, or have lost a loved one, I strongly urge you to read the work of Dr. Ross. You can find out more about her work at elisabethkublerross.com and ekrfoundation.org.

I was familiar with denial. One day I looked my husband right in the eyes and said, "I think the doctor said it *MAY* be cancer." From there I began bargaining. I remember promising God if he spared my voice, I'd never take my voice for granted again. I assured God I'd use my voice to inspire, educate, and bring positive change to the world all the days of my life. Third in line for me, was depression. As I told you earlier, my hypothyroid radioactive iodine days led to some really low moments. I was the stuff anti-depressant endorsements are made of. I spent most of my time pretending I was as happy as a clam when inside I wanted to stay in bed all day. Sure, much of my unhappiness was attributed to being hypothyroid. No one whistles Dixie all day when their hormones are off balance. Then slightly out of order, came the anger. The anger really caught me off guard. I had no idea how truly angry I was (a touch of denial, right?) until I was face-to-face berating a stranger in a public restroom. I wasn't bothered by the drunken girl's perception of me. I was bothered because she messed with me.

When and if the anger comes kicking in the door step to your soul, remember that you need a little of that anger in order to pull through. Being strong and having fight are two entirely different things. I know this may sound absurd, but it wasn't until I got my fight in me, that I started stepping away from the anger. My fight motivated me to live. In the Key West bathroom I felt a primal instinct to fight for my autonomy. To fight for my life. While penetrating that new echelon of my core self, I had found the fighter within. I was grateful for the opportunity to tap into my archaic primal surviving self. Thanks to cancer, I met my inner Tigress.

One would think the mere diagnosis of my cancer would unleash my Tigress. It did not. One would think the rain in my bedroom would unleash my Tigress. It did not. One would think my house covered in soot would unleash my Tigress. It did not. It took my hand washin' exchange with an intoxicated girl in a bar to bring my Tigress out of hibernation. Upon diagnosis, cancer ignited a rage within my body. A person can become as angry as a tyrant and still be a victim until they fight back. Once the fight comes in, victims become warriors. We have to find our Tigress (or Tiger) during crisis, death, disease, devastation and loss. That state of mind prevents us from curling up and emotionally expiring. When your anger comes, use your Tigress claws to burrow way down into your basin of pain and drag out your fight. By unclogging that channel of anger, fear, bitterness, and resentment you will find salvation.

I could tell you my bathroom brawl was the end to my yearning for people to make things right. That would make me a liar. Although it wasn't the end of the make it right phase, it was the beginning of a new phase -Acceptance. Acceptance was slow to come. By the grace of God, I finally got there. Once I lost my composure and let go, I began to accept how my world had changed. Acceptance allowed me to crave a better life.

Pre-cancer, I always wanted to be a little more bad ass. By more bad ass, I mean more risky. More adventures. More courageous. More daring. Less safe. I always admired the girls in the mud kickin' boots who rode Harley Davidson bikes. I was always more of a Manolo Blahnik high heeled girl. I liked things pretty and clean. Cancer taught me how dirty life can be. So as part of my acceptance of change, the day after my bathroom fight, I straddled my version of a Harley.

At high noon, I sat my bad ass on a moped. Normally, the idea of trying something that chancy, unfamiliar, dangerous, and precarious would frighten the hell out of me! I'd come up with a world class excuse as to why that amount of danger just wasn't going to work out. Example: "I wear contacts. I've heard they can fall out of your eyes while you are riding mopeds. Even with sunglasses on. I think I'll pass since I'm really blind without them." Exactly one year prior, on that very same island, I watched my husband parasail over the ocean. From my chair on the beach, I wondered why I didn't have the courage to join him.

As I pressed the gas on my bad ass moped I realized the days of coming up with reasons **why not** to LIVE were over! So the cage-less Tigress and I (adorned with our invisible Harley boots) hopped onto the back of a shiny moped and began spinning around the block on our test drive. I'll admit, the first time I had to bring my machine to a stop I thought *what in God's name am I doing? This is preposterous! Park this bike right back where you found it before you kill yourself!* But when the light turned green, I revved it back up. Before long I was leading the pack of my grammar school girlfriends along the coast of Key West! I was completely void of a care in my cancer recovery world. My Tigress and I were racing with the warm wind blowing on our backs alongside the turquoise blue sea. In all the thirty-four years of my life, I had never once felt that sense of boundless sovereignty.

Early in the book I referred to one of my most beloved memories with my husband. While snorkeling in Key West (a year prior) the current kept pulling me away from Roger. You may remember how he reached out and held my hand during the entire excursion. He sacrificed his adventure so I could enjoy the underworld sights. My fear of being swept away by the current was cured by Roger. **He** took away **my** fear. He solved my problem. During that pre-cancerous time it melted my heart to know that Roger loved me so selflessly that he'd relinquish his ocean adventure to make sure I felt protected. I say pre-cancerous but that snorkeling trip was in April of 2004. I already had cancer. I just didn't know it yet.

My point is that six months before my doctor found the lump, all I needed to feel safe was my husbands' love and allegiance. Sure, our marriage had ups and downs. At the end of the day, Roger literally had been watching my back since I was fourteen years old. He was the only constant man in my life.

Years earlier, my friend Rose and I lovingly nicknamed him Tug. One late summer, he pulled us through the crazy currents of the water off of Cape Pogue and Chappaquiddick so that we could enjoy the inlets without being dragged into the deep jelly fish zone waters. I learned first hand how a smart sting could ruin a lovely afternoon of floating in the same warm currents the jellies enjoy. Roger tugged us along the pure waves of that natural untouched slice of Martha's Vineyard. He was our tow and our anchor. He made me feel safe. Before cancer, that was enough.

Returning to Key West without my husband during my recovery was extraordinarily significant. It was more than just the buzz of the motor on my Ducati of a moped. It was about my decision to work past my trepidation and jump on the bike. It was about taking a risk all by myself, leaving my comfort zone, stepping out of my safe lifestyle and giving spontaneity a try. No one was there, physically reaching out a hand to pull me along. As precious as those snorkeling memories with my husband remain, I couldn't help but relish in becoming **my own tug** on that trip. Cancer, my Tigress, my fight, my Harley boots…they all taught me how to pull myself through the stalwart currents and swim directly into the uncharted waters without apprehension.

I think courage (the kind you never knew existed in your soul) is what helped to change my course. Once I found the courage to fight back, I began living a more fearless and fabulous life. My moped Tour De Keys was the first of many unpredictable steps toward a more courageous, healing, happy, spontaneous, risk-taking and accepting heart.

After several sumptuous days in the sun, we packed our bags to head home. While loading our luggage into the cab, I decided to call my husband. I hadn't called him much on the trip. Normally when I travel, I call my husband, mother, sisters, and nieces and nephews at least three times a day to check in. Normally, I am unbelievably home sick and cannot wait to get back home. Normally, I spend my days searching for presents and keepsakes for everyone at home. Once when I traveled to Mexico, I cried almost every night because I missed my family. Since December 15th, 2004, when Dr. Smith told me I had cancer, nothing about my behavior was normal. I didn't miss anyone enough on that trip to feel homesick. I didn't feel the need to call anyone. I didn't load my bags with gifts to distribute when I got off of the plane. I didn't even feel ready to load up the cab to head home. I easily could have stayed a few more weeks. For me, that wasn't normal.

Had cancer made me selfish? Or had cancer taught me to seize the day and forget about the things that aren't important. If I bought a coffee mug for my family each time I went away, they'd have a ridiculous amount of cups. Mugs don't matter. Roger called me several times to say he missed and loved me. Would it have been so hard to dial his number a few more times? Should I have bought Roger a mug?

Early into my diagnosis, I read stories about the changes brought on by illness and how cancer affects relationships. Some stories ended in a trial separation or divorce. I understood the need for change when life is out of control. The mere thought of having cancer brought me to a law office. I didn't really want a divorce…I just wanted my husband to get me.

Some cancer marriages endured acts of infidelity. The spouses who weren't ill strayed. The spouses with cancer strayed. I understood that, too. For a while I thought I was damaged goods. Would Roger want to love a sick girl? Would he want to find love in cancer-free arms? The idea of Roger seeing me (the girl formally known as super woman) sickly, made me sick. There were days when I thought he'd find my cancer too daunting.

A few months down the road to recovery, things began to change. I found myself more focused on what **I needed** to make it through each day. For years I focused on what the people around me needed from me to make it through their day. I feared my newfound emancipation from dependability would make me rely less on Roger's love in my life. I was slowly morphing into a girl who had to cross the finish line alone. For a stretch of time, it was me against the enemy. The enemy was cancer. I was the soldier fighting to win the war. Roger didn't have cancer. He wasn't part of my army. I questioned our survival rate. Would my independent moped riding soul still need him? After my surgery, I thought he'd emotionally walk out on me. As my recovery evolved, I wondered if I'd be the one walking.

Make no mistake about it; I always needed my husband to love me. While on that vacation, I realized that I needed to solve the every day battles on my own. During that phase of my recovery, I went from needing my husband to love me to just wanting my husband to love me. For years his love defined who I was. I no longer needed his love to find my way. Mindful of couples that stray, cheat, shut down, stop trying and walk away during change, I prayed we'd make it through cancer. I prayed we'd end up stronger on the other side of my illness.

Moments after I arrived home from Key West, I sat down in the dining room and began sifting through my pile of mail. I loved the smell of our house. I loved seeing our cat. I loved being home. As my husband followed me into our bedroom he began talking to me through the bathroom door. While I answered his questions, it occurred to me how odd it was for him to stand outside the door and converse while I was having private time. We aren't usually one of those couples who brush their teeth while the other one is using the toilet. When I came out of the bathroom, he stood in front of me chatting about my trip. His body blocked me in the bedroom. *Does he want to have sex? That's rather ambitious...I just walked in the door...why are we still standing here talking in our bedroom?* Just then he said, "Do you notice anything different?"

"You cleaned the house?" I asked. "No. That's not it," he replied. I went on to say, "You got me roses! They are beautiful. Thank you." "No, that's not it either." Then he said, "LOOK UP."

As my eyes met the ceiling of my bedroom, I gasped at the perfectly patched and painted image that gleamed back at me! "Oh my gosh, you fixed the ceiling. It's beautiful! You did an amazing job! I love it! You kept your promise! You fixed our ceiling." As I hugged him (and again, I was never a hugger) it was very clear to me that he, too, had changed. *He gets it. He finally gets who I am and how sacred a promise is.* He kept his word and followed through. For once he put our home first. It was the best present he ever gave me. Roger loved me, cancer and all.

In that moment, I was sure that we could survive anything. Cancer moped independence aside; I knew we would make it. I fell asleep certain no matter how much cancer tried to mess with us, we had the power to fight to make things right. We had the power to fight for what we wanted. We wanted love.

The Bad Cancer

*I*F YOU ARE DIAGNOSED WITH CANCER, I do not recommend committing to anything critical. By critical, I mean planning a political gala for three hundred people. Stick to short term projects to keep your mind keen. Start a garden indoors from seed, complete a 1000 piece jig saw puzzle or compile a scrapbook of your favorite poems and song lyrics. When the state rep asked me to plan his May 2005 event in December 2004, I thought for sure I'd be fully recovered by spring. I was wrong.

Somehow, I managed to make the event a success. The party went off without a hitch. I pulled it off. No matter how flattened my body felt, my confidence was administered a huge spoonful of reassurance. The gala made me realize that I hadn't totally lost my essence, organization, ability to lead, and most of all -sparkle. I knew my body would eventually recover from the event. It wasn't my body that worried me. It was my brain. My cognitive issues were at an all time high. I was still pronouncing words incorrectly, still replacing words with other words when I spoke, still blanking on words as I tried to pull them out from my head, and was still misspelling words and substituting letters with numbers when I wrote and spoke.

There was one scary moment toward the end of the gala. As part of the live auction, my state rep friend asked me to read the door prize ticket stubs out loud on the microphone. Having been a public speaker nearly all of my life, this spur of the moment request shouldn't have rattled me. On that night, it stopped me cold in my tracks. As I stepped up to the podium holding a fish bowl filled with ticket stubs, I prayed God would help me announce the numbers properly. *Please, please help me, Lord, if I invert these numbers or say them incorrectly, a big scene is going to take place when the crowd figures out there is no winner. What if someone else thinks they have won? Please give me the mind power to focus on these numbers and say them correctly!* With a huge deep breath, I very slowly began reading the numbers off of the first ticket. *Okay, the first number is a number three...Lorna SAY THREE OUT LOUD.*

"Three."

Good one, Lorna...your next number is eight...say EIGHT OUT LOUD just move your mouth and say the word eight.

"Eight."

Great job, Lorna...the next number is five. SAY FIVE OUT LOUD, but DO NOT SAY THE LETTER F-say FIVE, LORNA.

"Five."

You did it, you are home free...you made it past your hardest number... keep going, girl, you have this....focus...the next number is two...SAY TWO OUT LOUD.

"Two."

I didn't misread the numbers. The mental attention the task required yanked the final moments of liveliness out of my body. My ticking energy time clock had chimed the final hour. My human productivity for the day had ended. It was time to check out. In a fog, I heard my state rep friend sharing a few words about his exciting year. Just then I heard someone say, "Lorna, they are calling you up there. They just called you up." *I am shutting down quickly here...very little brain power left...I have to get home soon before the audience sees my melt down...The clock is ticking... any minute now the crowd will see my coach turn into a pumpkin...Why is he calling me up now?* In turtle fashion, I slowly made my way over to the podium. My state rep friend was holding a bouquet of roses. I saw the flowers. I saw his smile. I saw his arms reach to embrace me. My eyes were working but my ears were not. I heard mumbles. The tones were similar to the voices used in the PEANUTS-CHARLIE BROWN cartoons to portray the adults. I remember hearing, "Wahh wah wah wahh wahhh. Loorrrnnaa Bruunnelle...wohhhh wahh wahh" come out of his mouth. *Take the flowers, hug him and head for Roger* I thought as I felt the flowers touch my arm. *It's a straight line...flowers, hug, Roger. Flowers, hug, look at the crowd, Roger.* I did it! I made a strong exit. My work was done.

My body ached as Roger helped me to the Jeep. "I think I did too much today." I said near to crying in the parking lot. "<u>Everything</u> hurts." "We'll be home soon, Babe. You can rest tomorrow. You did it. I'm really proud of you." The following day I rested. And the day after. And the day after. And the day after. I spent the duration of May resting.

On the last day of May, I took my goddaughter out for her birthday. She was wearing the pearl necklace we were building together. On Christmas, her birthday and the day she was Christened, I give her a pearl. As we walked through the gardens of the restaurant, I glanced at the strand on her tiny neck. This was the first post-cancer pearl. I thought about all of the months represented by each pearl. Had I ever felt as tired? Had I ever felt as unsure about my future? Would her next pearl mark happier days?

She didn't see how much cancer had slowed me down. To the precious young people in my life, I remained the same~ precious to them. After beating myself up for being less of a wife, less of a daughter, less of a sister, less of an auntie, less of a granddaughter, less of a friend, less of boss, and less of a teacher during my recovery, it was nice to feel as if someone saw me as nothing less than who I used to be. That someone was my goddaughter.

During lunch she asked if my scar hurt. I assured her that I wasn't in any pain. I invited her to touch my healing wound. "No, thank you," she replied. Once lunch was finished, we headed for the children's toy store on the second floor. A few steps over the threshold of the toy room she said, "Auntie Lorna, I'll touch your scar now." I crouched down to her eye level and extended my neck. After a quick brush across my red and still slightly raised incision, she walked over to the dolls. She neglected to comment any further. I was her auntie and I just happened to have a pink line on my neck. Nothing more. Nothing less.

The next morning was the start to a new month. Just as every year before, I woke up with the song "June Is Bustin' Out All Over" from the musical Carousel in my head. I had made it to a new month. I was marching away from March 2005 and running toward a summer of wellness! I was in my fourth month of recovery from surgery and third month of recovery from the radioactive iodine radiation treatment. Life was close to being great again.

The beginning of the month was pretty mellow. I tried working in my gardens. Bending over to pull up weeds was bothersome to my neck incision area. For the first time ever, I hired someone to help me in the yard. The money it cost to pay someone to weed was cheaper than the money I would have spent on a massage therapist to restore my pissed-off neck. All of the flowers I craved during my surgery were in bloom. The roses were gorgeous, the lilies were proud, the heliopsus were as social as ever, and the lavender was begging for a blue ribbon. I spent several hours in the company of hummingbirds on the front and back porch. I delighted in the glory of each garden. I felt consistently happy.

Our wedding anniversary (June 14th) was the start of life moving back in the nasty direction from which I had been marching away from. Our friends took us to a local steak house to celebrate our special day. While I was eating my salad, I began to choke. No matter what I did, I couldn't get the food to go down my throat. The clogged sensation remained (preventing me from speaking or swallowing) for several seconds. In a total panic, I grabbed my glass of water and pushed the food down. *What the hell was that?* I wondered as my heart pounded out of my chest. *Okay, no one at the table noticed...keep eating but take smaller bites.* As I tried to recover from the incident, I pondered whether or not to eat my steak. *Oh, I'm sure that was just some freakish food going down the wrong pipe thing, you'll be fine.* I wasn't fine. As I chewed on a bite of very tender rib eye steak the choking sensation resumed. I felt like I was going to pass out. With the help of water, I got the food down. I decided not to eat the rest of my dinner. *What the heck is happening? Has it taken three months for my salivary glands to act up?*

After a few more episodes of chocking, I vowed not to eat unless I had a full glass of water on the table. If dining out, I'd ask the waitress to bring a pitcher. Foods that needed to be chewed a while in my mouth before swallowing caused the biggest problem. Steak and bread were the hardest solid foods to get down. Steak and bread also sparked pain on the sides of my face. I'd chew and chew but my mouth never seemed lubricated. My jaw felt like I had just won the National T.M.J. Tournament. A throbbing pain near my ears on the sides of my face lasted for hours after each meal. As if I had chipmunks for ancestors, my face actually looked puffy.

The other two foods that caused a chocking problem were lettuce (salad) and melted cheese. I was eating eggplant parmesan one day and the melted mozzarella clogged my throat on the way down. For seconds I was unable to swallow, talk, or breathe. I remember waiting to pass out. Eventually, the water I sucked through my straw pushed the food, giving my heart an open runway to fly out of my chest. After the fight between me and mozzarella, I went to the computer to research salivary gland dysfunction post-radioactive iodine radiation treatments. One would think I would have picked up the phone to ask my doctor. By that point I was sick of Boston and sick of being sick.

Turns out, <u>many</u> thyroid cancer patients experience food chocking issues weeks (if not months) after their radiation. For most people, it took up to nine months for the chocking to subside. There were reports of cases where people never regained normal salivary gland function. Their glands seemed to permanently dry up or stay dormant. I found that choking on food post-radiation also ties into dental hygiene. We have saliva that nourishes our teeth by serving as a mini car wash. Since my body wasn't producing that saliva, I ended up with a few pin-hole cavities. That stunned me because I was always the queen of dental hygiene. Hey that rhymes! I tried to stay positive and accept the new meal time challenges.

A few days later, we found out that Roger's maternal grandmother passed away. The sudden death caught all of us off guard. I was asked to sing at the graveside service. As I approached the music stand, I thought of Dr. Randolph. I silently thanked him again for saving my voice. *These are the moments when my voice matters the most. As always, I honor your work with each note.* After the song I joined my husband. The heat from the sun was relentless. I could feel my husbands arm pressed against my arm. I could tell by the rhythm of his jacket sleeve that he was crying. *Bring on the happiness, God! We cannot take much more pain.*

The next day I found out my grandfather Ray had lung cancer. The doctor said his tumor was grapefruit in size and ugly. Immediately, I called my grandfather. "Lornie" he said, "I'm in your club now. Can I have some fried clams? How did you say it? I'm gonna work the 'C'." He decided not to have surgery, not to go to the hospital for treatments, and not to take any medical precautions to slow down the process of his inevitable death. About a month prior, my mother questioned my grandfather's sudden weight loss. His doctor said, "It's good that he has lost some weight. Several medications curb the appetite, especially in older patients. I wouldn't worry about it." My mother demanded an X-ray and blood work. Turns out, cancer was the cause of his weight loss. It wasn't "good" at all. How is that for medical apathy?

In my mind, my grandfather was a giant. As a child I remember being hoisted up onto his shoulders. It was as if I could see the Boston skyline all the way from my yard. He was the tallest man I had ever known. His presence was even taller than his actual frame. Whenever he felt especially chipper, he greeted friends and family with the opening line of the 50's hit "Chantilly Lace" by the Big Bopper. Ray was famous for that boisterous salutation of "Hello Baby!" He dressed in dapper slacks, dress shirts, (always over a white t-shirt), fancy shoes and a black Greek-style fisherman's cap. My grandfather Ray turned thirty on July 19th, 1954. His gift was a baby girl. That girl is my mum.

Once the news about my grandfather's cancer spread through the family, we (my mother and sisters) kicked into over drive. Not everyone emotionally or intimately involved with the "C" steps up to the plate with the same piss and vinegar. The faint hearted step back, leaving the Vikings alone on the front lines. We took turns checking in on our new patient, bringing treats and the grandchildren to him. My mother assured him she'd do everything she could to prevent pain from ruling his body. Having worked with hospice, my mother was all too familiar with the terminally ill. She had seen her share of A.I.D.S. and cancer cases wherein disease had ravaged the bodies of her patients. I knew of the intimate care mum gave my uncle Ray (three years prior) when liver and pancreatic cancer took his life. All of these experiences would help her prepare my grandfather to pass.

In a very short amount of time cancer had changed his entire existence. It was revolting to watch disease diminish his grandeur. My grandfather's lifespan was ferociously present each time I'd say goodbye. I parted hoping he'd be alive the next time I knocked on the door. When someone you love is handed a death sentence life sits idle. You approach the daily grind relentlessly aware of the inevitable. Someone you love is dying.

Early into my diagnosis, I had convinced myself that one cancer led to another. In my mind it was only a matter of time until I, with my bald chemo head covered in a Coach scarf, would be picking out a casket. All of that madness ended once my grandfather got his news. His diagnosis forced me to stop questioning my time on earth and forced me to make peace with my good cancer. He was dying of the bad cancer -the kind of cancer that eats bodies leaving only skeletons behind to bury. Slowly his bad cancer made me grateful for my good cancer.

Early that July, we had a party in honor of my grandfather. He sat in the yard for hours conversing with his guests. He ate. He laughed. He listened to people protest their love for him. I filled the memory card in my digital camera. Forever preserved on a tiny chip were images of him relaxing with his family at his living wake. At one point he lit up a cigarette and said, "Something's going to kill all of us! It might as well be something I enjoy." I wondered if given the chance to do it all over again, if my grandfather would have stopped smoking as a young man. Did he regret his relationship with cigarettes?

I regretted my relationship with cigarettes. I felt like a selfish bitch for complaining about the smoke all of those years. I disliked visiting him thanks to the smell of his cigarette smoke which penetrated my clothes and ruined my clean hair scent. The cigarette smoke not only messed with my fashion, it actually caused my lungs to wheeze. Still, I felt guilty for not seeing him as often as I should have. For years he lived less than a half mile away. During our final weeks together, I tried to make peace with my regret. I needed my grandfather to forgive me for protesting his favorite pastime.

Less than two weeks had passed since the party and my grandfather's health had declined immensely. Eager to see him laughing and smiling again, I developed the photos from the party. There on every photo of Ray, sat his pack of cigarettes in the top left-side pocket of his dress shirt. I smiled at each image of the top of his "butts" sneaking out of the pocket. His pack of butts and his Greek style fishing hat were his trade mark and the essence of who he was.

One day I asked my grandfather if I could get him anything. In all seriousness he looked at me and said, "A coffin." My blood went cold as it was the first time I heard him vocalize the desire to die. "Well, I don't think I can pull that off today. I'm kind of busy. Besides, I've never really been that good at working with wood. Will a coffee frappe do?" I replied in my unshaken and nonchalant voice. Then I said, "Grandpa, I know <u>my</u> cancer is nothing like <u>your</u> cancer, but I do know what it's like to be afraid." He didn't respond so I left to buy the frappe.

By the end of July half of a glazed donut had become a complete meal for my grandfather. He spent hours in his bed sleeping. His face was sunken in, his breathing was hard, his color was gray and his skin seemed to be as thin and as dry as tissue paper. One day, I stared at his worn-out body wondering when he'd leave us. I tried to look beyond the diminished presence in the bed. I envision the man he spoke of from his youth. The man who sailed on the L.S.T. (Landing Ship Tank) ship during the war. I closed my eyes and recalled the photographs of him in Hawaii posing with the pretty girl he had tattooed on his brawny arm.

I pondered what physical look or form he'd elect to resume in heaven. *Will he look like a young soldier again? Or will he become the man in his 50's and 60's with the fuller frame and the big, laughing eyes? Maybe he'll look like the little boy on the beaches of Hull in the 1930's playing with his sisters with his mother on the shore.* My mind floated over an imaginary journal of questions for him. *Grandpa, when were you the most happy in your life? Do you remember those days on the beach? You were the cutest baby back then. What are you most proud of? What do you want to be remembered for? Do you have any regrets? Who was your one great love? Did you have many true loves? Do you hope to see your mother first when you cross over? Will you check in on us from time to time? Were you happy toward the end of your life? Do you prefer chocolate or vanilla cake? Are you afraid? Do you know when you are leaving? Do you believe in God? Do you know how much I love you?* I spent hours silently conversing with my near-dead grandfather, ashamed that I never made the time to question him while he was truly alive.

On August 20th, my grandfather left his home and moved in with my mum. He needed round the clock care. Again I asked, "Is there anything I can get you grandpa?" After a short pause he replied, "A white Persian kitty cat." While mum put the finishing touches on his new room, my sister Liz and I raced through several stores to find him a stuffed fluffy white cat. Sadly, all we came up with was a small white (rather fancy) cat. He adored it just the same. "You hot shit!' he said, as I handed him the toy cat and an order of fried clams. "Why are you so nice to me?" he asked as if he truly didn't warrant such attention. *Because you won't be here much longer and because I love you,* I thought, but "Because you are the cat's meow!" is what came out of my mouth.

I watched my grandfather from 8:00 A.M. to 11:00 A.M. while my mother was at work. At that point, my visits involved finding the best game show on his TV, bringing him a treat, and talking about the weather. "They said it may rain tonight. That'll be good," he'd say, letting me know he was still in the loop of life. His hospice rep and my mother share the same name- Wanda. Shocked by the coincidence of sharing the uncommon name, we knew it was a sign that she would be the one to provide daily care. My grandfather instantly took to Wanda. "I'm going to teach you how to roll him with me," Wanda said. "He is very tall and that is the only way I can bathe and change him." The

<u>definition of bad cancer</u>: when a total stranger has just changed your diaper with the help of your oldest granddaughter.

Less than an hour later, the woman walked out of his bedroom and said, "You can expect that he will be afraid to sleep during the evening. He may rest a lot during the day." Silly me, always with the questions, I asked, "What do you mean he may not sleep during the evening?" As plain as the nose on her face, the woman replied, "Most often they are afraid." "Afraid of what?" I asked. "Afraid they won't wake up."

The next day I arrived at 8:00 A.M. with a car full of groceries. I said good morning to my grandfather, was briefed on how his night was, and began cooking a feast of soft scrumptious treats to entice his appetite. I wanted him to smell food being prepped in the kitchen. I thought the home cooked aromas would make him feel better. As the hospice rep worked with him, I began preparing a granny smith brown sugar apple pie, chocolate banana cream pie, beef stroganoff, roasted chicken dinner fit with mashed potatoes, gravy, cranberry sauce and corn, apple dumplings with custard sauce and big pot of American Chop Suey. I felt an immense responsibility to fatten him up and prolong his life.

I heard laugher coming from the bedroom. Excited to see him happy, I entered the room. After having his genitals anointed with diaper rash cream my grandfather said, "Since you have been all around my testicockales, don't 'ya think we should get married?" I am not sure which was more atypical - watching a stranger rub cream on my grandfathers' privates, or actually seeing my grandfathers' privates. There was something organic about the way he found humor under such embarrassing circumstances. One thing was certain, I loved hearing him laugh. The laughter stopped when Wanda's shift ended.

<u>Crumbled</u>: That is how I felt when my grandfather politely refused to eat any of the food I prepared. I tried not to crumble in front of him. Completely exhausted from the stress of the daily death watch (and my lack of natural thyroid hormone) I turned my back in tears. I escorted the luscious piece of hot baked pie back to the kitchen. Thoroughly missing my thyroid and my healthy grandpa, I cleaned the pots and pans praying to God for the strength and energy to properly serve my grandfather during the final phase of his life. As he napped, I ate his piece of pie. I tried to flip through the pages of my latest purchase: "Natural Cures *They* Don't Want You To Know About" by Kevin Trudeau. I selected an especially large book to keep me busy during my shifts with my grandfather. I wanted the book to end before his life.

Day three with my grandfather was a lot grimmer. He spent most of my visit sleeping. Wanda taught me how to prepare a syringe of liquid <u>Dr. Feel Good</u> and explained that she did not have the authority to administer medication. Once I squirted the meds into his mouth, I sat at his side. In fear of killing him, I watched his chest move up and down to make sure he was breathing. After an hour, I headed out onto my mother's deck with the baby monitor turned on high. With my face in the sun, I began to pray. *Please God…if the end is here, make it quick and clean.* Clean. As if I hadn't seen how dirty cancer was. As if the filth and grunge of disease and death wasn't tattooed on to my skin. As if the grime of mortality hadn't permeated into my cranium. As if the scar on my neck was an antiseptic indication of how **clean** cancer is?

I noticed something in the trees. It was a strange flicker of light reflecting off of the bark. As my eyes focused on the light, I noticed the bust of an apparition. It was an Indian man staring back at me. The sunlight created the outline of a long, gorgeously strong and brave face that seared his eyes onto mine, demanding my attention. The vision remained perfectly still as I spoke. *Are you here to take my grandfather? Are you his spirit guide? Are you of the Penobscot tribe? Is he going today? Please let my mother get here before goes. I'm happy to see you. Thank you for showing yourself to me. Is he ready? Does he know you are here? Have you met him before today?* I could see his entire face and part of his neck. He felt very wise. With my eyes locked on the image, my body became very calm. I felt as if I had a thousand hours of sleep. I was restored and energized. Then, after a few more moments, he vanished.

Instantly I called my mother. Then I called my friend Rose. Neither of them doubted my testimony. My friend Rose said, "He might be there for <u>you</u>, Lorna, to reboot your energy." As phenomenal as it was to see a guide, I kept the summit with the Sachem under my hat. I knew very few people would believe me. The vision in the tree marked the end of my grandfathers' coherency. Most hours he mumbled a few words, took a few sips of water, nibbled on the corner of a glazed donut and slept.

On morning number five I reached over to fill his mouth with the meds. He said, "Can we just **do** this?" "Do what?" I asked. "<u>Fill that thing up!</u>" he said. "Grandpa, I'm sorry. I cannot do that." At that point he looked at Wanda and said, "Can **you do** this?" "No, I prefer my life on the other side of the bars!" She said. "As much as I luv `ya, I have no desire to go to jail for you." As long as I live, I don't think I'll ever shake what that moment did to me.

On day six of my bedside vigil, his breathing was very shallow. His nights were terrible and my mother was running on empty. I remember stroking his hand and running my fingers down his long well-designed legs and model-worthy feet. I covered his skin in cream over and over again to hydrate his parched, frail feet. *You are a beautiful man.* I said without words knowing that his soul could hear me. *And you have lived one fascinating life.* His charming frame reminded me of my high school and college frame when I was several pounds thinner. *We have the same hands and feet…there is so much of you in all of us. We will be in all of us forever. You'll live on in your children, grandchildren, great-grandchildren and great-great-great grandchildren-you will live on.*

Later on that day, we gathered as a family and assured my grandfather that it was okay to go. One by one we kissed him goodbye letting him know we were ready for him pass. For many minutes his room was filled with choruses of, "We love you, Grandpa G.G.-its okay for you to go. Your mom is waiting for you in heaven. And your son, Uncle Ray is there. It's okay to go. You don't have to stick around here for us. <u>We will be okay</u>. <u>We love you.</u> For the last time, I kissed his precious head. For the first time, I turned to leave his side without asking if there was anything I could get for him.

On Sunday, August 28th, 2005, at five o'clock in the morning, eight days after we moved him into my mothers' house, my phone rang. I heard my mother's voice plainly say, "He's gone."

God had finally set him free from the bad cancer.

Forgiving God

My Jeep was the only vehicle on the road the morning my grandfather died. Mum quietly walked me through his last night, and the moment when she realized he was gone. As she spoke, I noticed how truly worn out she looked. Cancer had kicked her ass. It didn't seem fair that a woman should have to nurse her daughter's good cancer in February, only to nurse her father's bad cancer four months later. If anyone was in need of a break, it was her. Within an hour or so my sisters arrived. Suddenly, there was nothing left to do. Mum had already stripped the death bed and discarded the linens. His funeral was already planned. Most of the phone calls had been made. His obituary was already written. Photos and music had already been selected. Passages were assigned to be read. Other than emptying out what little was left in his house, it was simply time to mend.

I decided to take the children to my mum's little private beach on Buttermilk Bay. As I floated in the ocean listening to the laughter of all four grandchildren, I knew their great Grandpa G.G. was at peace. The crisp, detoxifying ocean water brought my body to a still place.

No more tears I thought as I swam. *From here on out, I celebrate his life through memories and work that makes a difference in the world. No more tears. I will not permit cancer to pull one more tear from my head. Do you hear me, Cancer? You have taken far too much from me…I will not give you any thing else.*

My three-year-old niece Taylor tapped my shoulder and asked me if I wanted to swim with her. In her world swimming meant floating in four-inch deep water on the boogie board. Her petite, frigid body pressed against my tired limbs. Together, side by side on my boogie board, we drifted down the beach. *This is what it's all about* I thought. *The moments when nature rescues us from pain…When the sea pulls rank over cancer, restoring all of the victims in the world. Screw you, cancer. I am gliding on the waters of God's natural spa… there is no room for you here. We are moving on without you.*

On the first day of September, we buried my grandfather at the Massachusetts National Cemetery. His prayer and service cards had a lovely tranquil scene with a boat on the water. Mum said the people in silhouette on the boat were her father, his mother and my uncle Ray. As I approached the multi-colored rose arrangements (his favorite) to sing "Amazing Grace", my mind momentarily drifted to Dr. Smith and Dr. Randolph. How blessed I was to have them in my good cancer life. Next we played my grandfather's favorite song, "Chantilly Lace." The familiar sound seemed to bring a smile to everyone's face. We even had "Hello Baby" (the opening line of the song) engraved on his marker to ensure smiles each time people visit his site.

As we pulled away from the funeral, my mother and I noticed VOLUNTEERS NEEDED signs along the strip to Otis Air Force Base. In lieu of my grandfathers' death, I spent most of my time at the ocean and very little time in front of the TV. We knew Hurricane Katrina had devastated a region but were not up to speed on the American crisis. Turns out, hundreds of displaced residents of New Orleans were coming to stay in Massachusetts at Camp Edwards a few miles away from my grandfathers' grave. Ironic -the day before we saw that sign, mum said, "What am I going to do with all of my free time? I saw my father every day. What will I do with myself now?"

The next day we drove to the Barnstable County Sheriff's office and filled out the paperwork to volunteer on the military base. I was thrilled to see my mum excited for something new and meaningful. Within minutes we were seated having photos taken for our identification badges. In order to be allowed access to the base, everyone involved with the project needed to be screened and approved. Mum got quite a thrill out of having the formal badge. She was even more ecstatic over the idea of helping so many people who were down and out. In some ways (with all due respect to the families who lost everything) my mother was on the same emotional level as the victims of Katrina. She, like them, was feeling incredible loss, sorrow and displacement. The compassionate connection with the residents on base was sure to be Kismet.

Two weeks later, I received a call from the director of "Operation Helping Hand". Mum and I were assigned to the early evening shift. Our job was to make the guests more comfortable. We were asked to keep track of what the people needed. (Fans, shorts, books, toiletries) Other days we were asked to try to locate specific items. Some days we were encouraged to make conversation. If anyone seemed distraught, we were told to direct them to the volunteer social workers, therapists, and clergyman.

The first woman we met was named Gracie. She was a beautiful black woman in her mid-seventies. She and her two adult children were living on the base. Gracie's big request was a fan for her barrack room, a few summer shorts and t-shirts, and a bra for her daughter. She had developed incredibly painful boils under her breasts from living braless in the Super Dome in Louisiana for nearly a week in sweltering temperatures, unable to bathe. We sat with her for quite a while, talking about her happy life back home. Eventually, the conversation ended up at the worst phase of her life: the breaking of the levee.

She went on to say how grateful she was to God, Massachusetts Governor Mitt Romney and all of the kind people in Massachusetts who took in the people of Louisiana. Her genuine smile and gratitude gave me pause. At the end of her story, she proclaimed, "Praise Jesus!" *If you say so*, I sarcastically thought to myself, in total awe of her faith and forgiveness. I mentally exited the conversation while reflecting on my own life. *This woman <u>has lost everything</u>. She hasn't spoken to her other daughter (or grandchildren) in weeks. She has no idea if they are okay. She is living in a hot house barrack with hundreds of strangers. She has the audacity to thank GOD in front of me. This woman, who walked bare-foot through the contaminated waters of her home town as dead bodies floating by her, who remained bare foot until her plane landed in Massachusetts… just thanked GOD. Forgive me, Lord, but how the hell did you pull that off? Are the Swamp Yanks of Massachusetts the only people who get pissy with you?*

The next friend we made was named Dee. She had been separated from her children and was desperately trying to locate them. She wanted to arrange for them to be flown to Massachusetts. Again, I found myself staring into the eyes of someone unafraid. With the strength of a freight train, she shared her faith in God. She knew God would find and return her children. Just then, my mother said, "You haven't found your children yet?" With shocking serenity she said, "Yes, but God will bring them to me soon. I was taken off of my roof, but my kids were staying over night with family at the time. We weren't together when they saved me, but they'll get here."

I couldn't believe her positive attitude. Locally the media was referring to the residents of New Orleans as the forgotten ones. People in my part of the country were blatantly declaring President Bush a racist. The media made it clear that he neglected to act rapidly immediately following the disaster, consequently leaving the people of New Orleans in distress. But there, standing at a welcoming cookout (on lovely Cape Cod), a few feet away from our Governor, all Dee had to offer was praise to everyone who helped her land in Massachusetts. She literally didn't have one bad word to utter about the government, the President or her luck. Her soul seemed free of bitterness. It was clear her immeasurable faith in God prevailed over all loss. For some reason her level of faith floored me.

My first night at Camp Edwards was spent on a field with hundreds of Katrina guests laughing and dancing to a Creole band. Everyone seemed so happy. I had been walking around pungently bitter and angry at God since December 15, 2004, because I had <u>the good</u> cancer. I suppose I had the right to be pissed off over getting cancer-but thousands of people get cancer <u>and live</u> every year. Sure, I had the right to be pissed off about my grandfather dying of cancer, but sooner or later, everyone loses their grandfather. It's the circle of life. Difference is most people who have cancer and lose their grandparents have a house to comfort them during their hardship. Every person seeking refuge in Massachusetts had lost everything and yet they were filled with thankfulness and gratitude. It wasn't until I stepped on the base that I truly understood how blessed and how spoiled I was.

Talk about a wake-up call! My higher power seemed to have summonsed me to the base to put things in perspective. I had a minor set back in my health but I still had a home, a car, a business, photo albums, clothing, friends, and most of all: family. I knew where my nieces and nephews were. They weren't taken off of a roof weeks ago, only to remain among the missing. The people I met had nothing left but the clothes on their backs. There wasn't an ounce of self-pity or anger. An abundance of faith and gratitude seemed to emanate from every person. *LEARN FROM THEM.* I thought *THIS is why you are here.*

Over the next five weeks, we volunteered at the base in the evening. I left work early each night and carpooled with mum. The most inspirational conservations took place outside at the picnic tables. Everyone willingly shared their stories of triumph over the hurricane. What began as a group of displaced American citizens in crisis quickly became a community of strength and hope. Their acceptance of the abrupt transition after the destruction encouraged me to ascend to a higher plain of trust in God. By their example, I navigated my soul toward unearthing a plethora of hope for my own future.

The camaraderie, faith, and goodwill on the base became contagious. I carried photos of my Katrina friends in my handbag and shared my stories with everyone who would listen. By voicing the lessons I learned on Camp Edwards, I hoped others would experience the same awakening. I needed to use the voice God spared, my voice, to spread the motivating message of the survivors of Katrina. I prayed the power of each story of hope would help others move forward with an intention to live more consciously, gratefully, willfully, and deliberately.

By the end of October, all of the guests of Hurricane Katrina had moved onto their next destination. I was left with photos, my expired badge, a thank you booklet, a lifetime of lessons, confirmation of how fleeting each moment is, and the challenge to live a more meaningful life. A framed picture of me and mum on the base hangs in my office. Each time I walk by the photo, I pray the guests of Louisiana realize what we gained thanks to all they lost.

A few weeks later the volunteers were invited to an appreciation dinner on the base. During a slide show I saw a photo of a woman without any shoes on her feet. She was triumphantly holding her fists up to the Lord. As I looked more closely at the lady I exclaimed, "That's Gracie!" I will never forget the look of salvation on her face. The memory of the massive image of Gracie smiling across the back wall of the dining hall still brings me to tears. Gracie helped me become a more grateful woman. Gracie helped me to forgive God.

Cancer Made Me Selfish

By mid September, I was back to work full-time at the casting company and my school. As we said goodbye to summer, we said hello to my husbands' ninety-year-old grandmother. She moved in with us the exact same week my mother-in-law took a temporary job in Atlanta, Georgia. My plate was literally overflowing with projects. On the subject of plates, I prepared fourteen low-sodium meals each week for my new housemate. I became her personal chef, nurse's aid, and companion. I couldn't get over how tired I felt. I wracked my brain wondering why I couldn't make it through each day without intense leg cramps, fatigue, and an overall lack of concentration.

I shared my level of fatigue with Dr. Smith. I neglected to fill him in on how much I was trying to fit into one day and limited my plea to, "By the end of the work day, I am in a hazy fog- again. I am unable to concentrate- again. I am crying a lot- again. My legs are cramping-again. My body feels stiff-again. It's been eight months since my surgery, what's with all of the post-hypo feelings of being hypo?" "Lorna, you have had a life changing ordeal. It's perfectly normal to find that you are more emotional now. If you are experiencing fatigue we can try adding a little Cytomel which is T3 to boost your T4 in the Synthroid. Patients have experienced an increase in energy on this drug." I gladly agreed to try the new fake me pill.

Six months had passed from my radioactive iodine radiation treatment. It was time to retest to make sure new cancer wasn't in my lower body or **bush** region. Dr. Smith assured me that the spot was most likely left over radioactive matter stored in my bladder. He told me not to worry. I worried anyway. The last time he told me not to worry, I ended up having cancer. That's a hard hit to shake off. From the moment I went down to X-Ray to pick up two jugs of banana flavored Barium Sulfate, I was sick to my stomach. (And to think, that was BEFORE I drank the sludge!)

"Had a bit of pelvic uptake consistent with bladder." is what Dr. Smith wrote after our last visit. I was rescanning to confirm the uptake was negative. On November 8th, (Election Day) 2005, I found myself back in the hospital exactly a year to the day after my ultrasound on Election Day in 2004 after Dr. Smith felt my lump. *This is so freaking eerie* I thought as I pulled into the hospital through a channel of constituents loyally holding signs for their candidates. *Talk about history repeating itself! I don't want anymore bad news…please let this scan be negative.* As I placed the sexy hospital gown on my body, my mood began to diminish. *Here I am again…more tests, more scans…more terror…more cancer-related concern in my life…just when I found a Zen like place after working on the base with girls like Gracie, I'm right back in hell with words like SCAN and TUMOR and SPOT and BARIUM SULFATE and UPTAKE and CONTRAST and DON'T MOVE and "SORRY IT'S SO COLD IN HERE, you can leave your socks on".*

When I had my CT scan at pre-op, I couldn't have contrast because I had trace amounts of Metformin in my body. Metformin is prescribed to women with P.C.O.S. to help prevent miscarriages in the first trimester of pregnancy and to help with weight loss. Patients taking Metformin aren't supposed to have contrast. I stopped taking the drug once I realized I had cancer. (Pregnancy and weight loss were the last things on my mind.) My body was no longer at risk of a dangerous Metformin induced contrast reaction. It was time to add contrast to my life. I had heard a scary story about a woman who wasn't on Metformin yet had a reaction to contrast. Here is a snippet of what I overheard: "I was allergic to contrast. My entire body went numb. I was shaking and going crazy! They had to CODE BLUE me. Then I was injected with adrenalin. I was okay, but it was the most terrifying moment of my life, I thought I was going to die." If you know me, you know that is the LAST thing I needed to hear the same week as my blind date with contrast.

Once in the scan room, I asked the nurse to walk me through the pros and cons of having contrast. I'm going to cut right to the chase. The lady was a witch. After a few minutes she said, "LOOK, are you allergic to shellfish?" I said, "No, but I'm allergic to <u>everything</u> I put on my skin. I received allergy shots for like four years for environmental allergies. I get a U.T.I. infection every time I change soap or use bubble bath. My face blew up once when I changed skin cleansers. I ended up on prednisone for a week to break down the inflammation. My eyes were swollen shut. I have a problem with sulfur- I break out in big red dots when I take it. I guess I'm trying to tell you that I am <u>usually allergic</u> to <u>anything</u> that has an allergy warning on it. -That's all. I was just sort of hoping that you could shed some light on this. You know more about contrast than I do. I'm looking for you to comfort me. Can you tell me that I won't end up a code blue?"

At that point she interrupted me and said, "You know what, I'm not even going to use contrast on you because you have freaked yourself out. <u>So forget about it.</u> No contrast, OKAY?" After a long pause I said, "Well, if it isn't necessary- WHY DO IT in the first place?" After another pause she said, "It gives us a clearer picture. If the doctor sees anything without the contrast, we'll come back and do it with contrast. You'll have to take a sedative first." She had total disgust and contempt in her voice when she spoke to me. I wondered how I could have reworded my concerns about allergies to the empathetic-free nurse. Should I have said, "Is it true you code blue people who have a reaction to contrast? What does the reaction feel like? Can you patch test me?" Did she have to be so rude? Medical personnel have to realize patients aren't just bitchin' about contrast. Some of us are sitting in the scan room wondering if our **cancer** has returned. The nurse was aggravated by the information I needed in order to feel safe. That is not okay.

I held back tears of frustration on the table. Try as I may, water began to fall on my cheeks. I sat there quietly crying over how pathetically low the standard of public service in America has become. *When this is over, ask her if she has ever had a scan…better yet, ask her if she has ever had contrast…ask her if she has ever had cancer…better yet, thank her profusely for all of her assistance and wish her a wonderful day. YEAH, that is the best thing to do. Hell, compliment her on her scrubs even…give her the care she hasn't given you. Lead by example.* When I got off of the bed, I told her how much I appreciated her time. In my most sincere voice, I reminded her of what an important role she plays in the world of medicine. I told her that deep down the root of my panic was my fear. Fear of a recurrence of **cancer.** Somewhat taken aback by my words, she shockingly said, "Oh, thanks. Sorry if I…You take care."

For the record, in my medical report there is a note from the nurse stating that "The Patient refused contrast." I did not refuse anything. She decided to skip the drama because she wasn't up for calming me down. She is on record in my file stating that I am hard to work with. As if I go about the scanning rooms of Greater Boston refusing contrast. Well I never! (I pray you hear the Scarlet O'Hara tone in the last sentence!)

A few days later Dr. Smith called to say, "I have good news and bad news. The good news is, it is not cancer. The bad news is I see some arthritis in there." Turns out arthritis can resemble cancer on scans? Who knew? A drunk driver hit me when I was in the forth grade. His car sent my body through the air, crashing down on the pavement. Since college I had gained about eighty pounds. Even worse, the weight came on in under four months. Who knows why I had arthritis in my lower back? It could have been the weight or the car accident. All I cared about was that I wasn't sick again. I could take a pill for arthritis but I could not take a pill for bladder cancer.

I met up with several grammar school and post-college friends in Bristol, Rhode Island to celebrate my friend's birthday. After a fabulous Indian dinner, I mentioned being excited about an upcoming trip to Venice, Florida. My friend chimed in with, "Wow, Lorna, do you remember when you hated traveling and how you used to get really home sick? What happened? Now you are going all over the place. You travel more than anyone I know! What changed?" After careful consideration, I said, "Well before I got cancer, I was afraid. I was afraid of dying in a plane crash. I was afraid of going over seas and being killed in a terrorist attack. I was afraid of a family emergency back home and how long it would take me to return. Then I got sick with cancer, and I was afraid that I wouldn't live a long life. Once I made it through the surgery, all I wanted to do was LIVE. Before cancer, I was afraid of dying...which prevented me from living. Now after cancer, the reality of dying makes me want to live."

If only we had ordered one more pitcher of Sangria, the entire topic would have blown over. "Wow." One friend said. "Well... good for you." Another friend added. The silence in between each comment made me pause. Perhaps I had fallen victim to providing too much information? With a self-induced pressure to put a more positive spin on my grave declaration, I concluded with, "I prefer how liberating my life is now, thanks to cancer. I'm a lot happier this way. I guess I've become more selfish. Instead of worrying about everyone back home when I travel, I focus on myself and my needs. The need to relax. The need to stay well."

Finally, I had said the word out loud-**selfish**. I was a lot more selfish post-cancer. After years of loathing the it's all about ME crowd (a very popular clique in the performing arts realm) I had finally crossed over to the <u>this is what I need</u> group of people. -The people who put themselves first. Pre-cancer, I'd begin Christmas shopping in August. By December 1st, I'd deliver beautifully wrapped gifts (worth hundreds of dollars) to everyone's house. I thought I enjoyed living that way. Post-cancer, I no longer had the energy for that fine attention to detail. All of the children in my family received cash money wrapped up in decorative boxes. No one seemed to miss the presents, pretty paper and bows. The lack of holiday stress was delightful.

I selfishly stopped doing other things like calling my friends every day to say hello. For years I was the one initiating much of the phone work. Post-cancer, I just didn't have the energy to place casual calls.

Other than a Sunday afternoon when I had the chutzpah to reach out, I relied on my pals to dial me up to chat. Even my snail mail and email correspondence slowed down. I realized I had to cut back on my amount of energy zapping responsibility. I made a promise to set boundaries to protect my health for the long run.

One of the best things to come out of my selfishness was this book. With the help of my new best friend Cytomel, I had enough concentration and liveliness to write. Daily, between the hours of 6:00A.M.-9:00A.M., I ignored emails, errands, housework, and phone calls to work on this book. Some days I wrote until my eyes were bloodshot red and my forearms were stiff as steel from typing. Other days I wrote through tears and contemplation about how much my life had shifted. I collected all of my emails, notes and scribbles about cancer and began formatting a timeline for people recovering from thyroid cancer. I wanted to offer patients a tool to mark their progress. I wanted to shed light on an unfamiliar cancer. Day after day, I selfishly sat at my computer typing my way toward wellness.

I typed through the seasons. In no time, my one-year diagnosis Cancerversary was at my door. On December 13th, two days shy of my cancer call, Dr. Randolph invited me to speak at a Thyroid Cancer Convocation. In remembrance of the 20th Anniversary of the Chernobyl disaster, the event was slated for early May, 2006. Dr. Randolph said that he'd love to have me involved with other thyroid cancer awareness projects throughout the year. He was looking for a patient to serve as a spokesperson. He thought I was perfect for the job. I was ecstatic! From there he offered a lovely sentence about making peace with adversity through education and helping others with messages of hope.

Since we were chatting like old friends, I mentioned that my anchor friend (Jen) did a story about the Chernobyl Children Project U.S.A. Ever the small world, my surgeon was at the event she covered. The entire appointment was filled with coincidences and perfectly placed seeds of hope and enthusiasm for the future. I felt like someone else was cultivating our conversation by sprinkling holy water on our garden of goodwill for the future. As we parted, I thanked him for extending the opportunity to work together. My surgeon closed our meeting by saying,

"So my office will contact you regarding the convocation this spring... Again, you really have done beautifully, Lorna. I couldn't be happier for you." I left his office floating on air, sort of skipping down the hall just as I did nearly a year ago when I met him.

Selfishness provoked me to get a second opinion. Selfishness appointed me to my surgeon's thyroid cancer awareness team in Boston. Selfishness is why you are reading this book. Selfishness is the origin of great things. Selfishness made me want more.

More

I AWOKE ON DECEMBER 15ᵀᴴ, WITHOUT RESERVATION in my heart. My house was still. My phones didn't ring. No one came to my door. There weren't any pressing emails on the computer. Life was calm. Life was cancer free. Life was good.

Twelve months prior, Dr. Smith's phone call broke me down. A year later, I was stronger, more powerful, more determined, more dynamic, more empathetic, more aware, more grateful, and more excited to live. My one year cancerversary was a marker. Not a tumor marker, thyroid globulin marker, THS, T3, or T4 count marker, but a marker of how much progress I had made. Within a few months, I'd be sharing my progress with an audience of doctors and patients in Boston. My one year marker was a day of celebration. A spa day was planned in New Hampshire with one of my truest and dearest friends-Jen. I couldn't wait to sing along to my favorite CD's during my commute. I couldn't wait to close the hardest year of my life.

As I crossed the state line to New Hampshire, I mentally piled up a list of all the lessons cancer had taught me. "Things I Learned in Cancer-garten" *I have learned to ask for help. I have learned to fully commit* *to loving someone. I have learned to approach each day as if it were the last. I have learned to set boundaries and say no. I have learned to listen to my body. I have learned to be more selfish. I have learned just how much I mean to my friends and just how much my family loves me. I have learned that warts and all, Roger is a champion and loves me more than I, at times over the past year, have loved myself. I have learned that I can only do so much in one day and that is fine. I have learned that an afternoon on the loveseat in my bathrobe is **not** a wasted day. I have learned that the sky will not cave in if I leave the watchtower and that no one will be in danger if I branch out, travel, and enjoy the world. I have learned that I cannot be responsible for the happiness of everyone in my life. I have learned that I need a lot more rest now and that does not make me lazy. I have learned that I am my best advocate when dealing with the medical world. I have learned that I have the power to help other people heal by talking about how truly remarkable this past year has been. I have learned that God makes no mistakes and nothing is random. I have learned that cancer has been one of the greatest teachers in my life. I have learned that this illness is the most significant thing that has ever happened to me. I have learned to live more consciously, willfully, and deliberately. I have learned never to take anything for granted.*

Jen greeted me on her front steps, ready to hit the spa. As we drove through the windy back roads of New England, she said, "Lorna, I am so proud of you. I mean, who thought you'd be driving up here on a Thursday afternoon for spa treatments and dinner? Do you remember how freaked you used to be about driving out-of-state? Never mind at night-alone! You have really come so far. It's great!" As I candidly filled her in on how liberating cancer was, we laughed about what a silly mess I was pre-disease.

We rehashed all of the ridiculous excuses I'd use simply to avoid driving in unknown, out-of-state territory. At the time the excuses didn't seem ridiculous. "What if I break down on the highway in the dark somewhere between Massachusetts and New Hampshire?" (As if my brand new Jeep would break down?) "What if something goes wrong at work and they need me?" "What if someone in my family needs me?" "What if Roger gets home and needs something?" Although we were both laughing, the verbal recount of how my mind used to think sickened me. I'd wasted so many years and missed so many adventures because I was afraid to take a chance on something foreign. Afraid to want more out of life. Gone were those days.

On the ride home, I watched a spectacular sunset of purple, orange, pink, and blue hues fall over the mountains. I couldn't help but think about the evening of my ultrasound, the morning of my fine-needle biopsy, and the morning of my surgery. During all of those turning points in my life, nature and God seemed to couple up to provide heavenly sites to ease my troubled heart. So much had changed over the past year. Even my taste in music changed. During my year of cancer, I found the music of my not-so-happy childhood comforting. My time growing up at mum's house was filled with Motown, Diana Ross, and the Leslie Gore and Connie Francis-types. Weekend stays at my father's house were filled with Jim Morrison, Led Zeplin, Lynyrd Skynyrd, The Stones, and countless other now classic rock bands. During my illness, the familiar sounds of my younger days made me feel rooted. Daily, I stopped the radio dial on those genres of music.

After my diagnosis, I replaced my modern CD's with the more dated sounds of Van Morrison, Carol King, and Eva Cassidy. Their mellow resonance soothed my healing soul. I craved rhythms and lyrics that induced hope and truth. Pre-cancer, I was a fan of Billy Holiday. Her less known renditions of "Willow Weep for Me" and "Lover Man", and Ella Fitzgerald's "The Blues in the Night", sent me into a trance. I was also a sucker for every arrangement of "Stormy Weather" and "The Man That Got Away." When crooned out of the pipes of those incredible yet painfully powerful singers, a blues ballad could take my breath away. I was hopelessly moved by the wounded sentiment that seeped out of each song. I coveted their ability to tell a story through music.

As a singer, my own repertoire consisted mainly of Torch Songs. I loved wailing out the cries of the women done wrong across audiences filled with faces of women who had *been there*. "Since I Fell for You" and "Stormy" were some of my favorite crowd warmers when I sang on the Spirit of Boston Cruise Line back in college. The irony about my passion for the blues is that I've never had a man love and leave me. I married the man I attended my senior prom with. In truth, I've never had a guy break up with me. Regardless of my personal plight with romance, for years I related to every blues singer. I channeled all of my childhood pain through their music. For me, "The Man That Got Away" was not about a lover walking out on me, but rather my biological father walking out on my mother when she was pregnant. Cancer disconnected my relationship with the blues. Victim songs no longer appealed to me.

At 1:00A.M., on December 16th, I woke up and looked at the clock. I smiled in my bed thoroughly impressed by my milestone. I was officially in my *second* year of recovery. I felt a major sense of accomplishment! With New Year's Day a few weeks away, I eagerly awaited the close of 2005. I could hardly contain my enthusiasm for things to come in 2006. I've always been more of a birthday girl, but I was excited to hit the Christmas circuit without cancer. -Until I attended a holiday party. A very distant acquaintance approached me to discuss my **throat** cancer and to see how I was doing. Word on the street was that my chemo had really knocked me on my ass. (Don't `ya just love small town gossip?) In the middle of explaining what form of cancer and radiation I had, she blurted out "I HOPE YOU FROZE YOUR EGGS! It's near impossible to get pregnant after chemo." Completely amused by America's obsession with married woman over the age of thirty procreating, I tried to ease her panic over my eggs.

I want to go on record saying that I appreciate the magnificence of starting a family. Hell, if my mother hadn't been pregnant, you wouldn't be reading this book. After sleeping with my husband for the past nineteen years, during phases of both protected and unprotected sex, I think it's time for society to back off the baby stuff. If you see a woman in her mid-thirties at a party a week before Christmas, and you know she's been married for nearly ten years, and you know she doesn't have any children, and you know she's recovering from **cancer,** and you have no idea what town she resides in; then you have <u>no business</u> asking if she froze her eggs! Unless you are speaking to your sister or best friend, you have no right to go there.

There have been phases of my life when the idea of having a baby was simply enchanting. Like most girls, I've spent moments daydreaming about the names I would select for my little girl or boy. I even daydreamed about the proper middle names to ensure my child's initials didn't spell out A.S.S., D.I.C., or F.U.K. There have also been phases of my life when the idea of becoming a mother was down-right creepy, invoking fits of claustrophobia the more I entertained the notion. There was a period of time when Dr. Smith encouraged me to seriously consider my age and the idea of getting pregnant. He even prescribed Metformin a drug known to help prevent miscarriages in cases of Poly Cystic Ovarian Syndrome, a well known hindrance to conception. I was also told the key to getting pregnant was keeping stress levels down. Since my life of self employment never really seemed to be stress-free, and since I never ended up getting pregnant during my unprotected married sex, I assumed a baby wasn't in the cards.

If I had been told I needed chemo, I'm not totally convinced freezing my eggs would have been on the priority list. If this makes me a bad Catholic or less of a woman-so be it. Oprah doesn't have any babies and she kicks ass. (Can I get an Amen for Oprah? Amen!) What if (God forbid) I did have throat cancer? What if I did have chemo? What if I didn't freeze my eggs first? What if at the time <u>staying alive</u> was about all I had time to worry about? What if all of that gossip about me was true? How gut wrenching would it be each time someone at a holiday party asked if I froze my eggs? The very eggs I potentially destroyed during the chemo I absorbed in order to stay alive? Can you even imagine how hurtful a question like that would be?

On New Years Eve I bid farewell to cancer. I sent a 2006 wish into the universe hoping that God would spare the people in my life of disease. I vowed to do great things to balance out the shit assigned to the human race. To most, the first of any month is just a number. To me, January 1, 2006, marked the mass exodus of all things cancer from my life. I yearned to begin the New Year with a clean bill of health. I officially evacuated every ounce of sickness from my psyche. *Here's to putting cancer behind you…here's to fewer doctors appointments…here's to less worry…here's to fewer leg cramps and more energy…here's to less sadness….here's to life, health and the pursuit happiness… Here's to 2006! Here's to more time to finish my work on earth. Here's to more time with the people I love. Here's to more of MORE! I feel great things to come…*

Hardly Recognizable

I STARTED THE NEW YEAR BY LOADING two bags of luggage and my chilled New England in January body into my Jeep headed for Logan Airport. Rose and I were about to board a plane for Naples, Florida. We were in search of sunshine and relaxation. The two of us were determined to return to Boston restored and ready to face the duration of a wicked winter. Our friend Marsha opened her house to us for our week long spontaneous stay. Marsha and I have a lot in common. We are from the same home town and have both survived cancer. I craved stimulating conversations with her over exquisite dinners on decks stretching across the various marinas of the gulf coast. Episodes of perfect escapes raced through my head as I waited in line to exit the plane. *Where will we have dinner first? In Naples or on Marco Island? Perhaps Bonita Springs better suits us tonight? Who knows, maybe we'll drive to Sanibel for dessert? This week is all about US! Let the fun begin!*

My Godmother (a former Bostonian) lived around the corner from my friend and was on the must visit list. Another friend and former Bostonian Vivian (a breast, lung, and brain cancer survivor) picked us up at the airport. Vivian was known as a miracle. Even her medical team referred to her as a miracle. A rare concept for physicians. Early on my quest through thyroid cancer, she was right there giving me advice. She encouraged me to keep my mind active as I walked down the hellacious hallways of disease. Prior to my Naples visit in 2006, I had only seen Vivian a handful of times. We met in October of 2004, and had dinner a few times. We were by no means life long friends, but rather soul-sister acquaintances thrown together by fate. I think it's important to note the irony of our connection. I, too, had cancer when I met Vivian. I just didn't know it yet.

"Well Hello, My Darling!" Vivian said in her smooth Jackie-O sounding voice as she made her way through the airport. I was thrilled to see sparkle in her eyes as we embraced. "Lorna, you've lost weight since I last saw you," she said smiling at my frame. *Note to self, this is the best vacation evAH!* When I asked how she was feeling she said, "I'm fine. Just a little slower than I used to be, that's all." She was wearing a white fitted jogging suit that displayed her long, elegant body. Her chemo head was topped off by an adorable floppy blue hat. She had the spirit and style of a sassy teenager. Other than her short incoming hair, no one would ever suspect what she had been through.

The stay allowed us to pause long enough to refuel our souls. We walked the shores of Sanibel collecting bags of shells. We marveled at an art show in Bonita. We ate earth shattering chocolate soufflé after watching the sun go down in Naples. We prepared and feasted upon breakfasts fit with fresh peaches, pork chops, eggs, French toast, and honey bell oranges. We lounged in the lanai overlooking the pond. We had darling late night chats. We giggled under the sheets of our twin beds with tears of laughter strolling down our faces. We submerged ourselves into philosophical conversations about love, relationships, cancer, and life.

One of the most emotionally impactful days of the trip took place on Sanibel Island with Vivian. Over ice cream on a bench, Vivian spoke about surviving three major cancers. I sponged off of her words of power, resilience, and wisdom. Establishing a pattern of strength, Vivian shared the passing of her mother. A man jacked up on drugs, broke into the home of her elderly mother and killed her. Vivian made it clear that she had no desire to convince a judge to send the murderer to death row. This display of clemency forced me to look within. If someone killed my mother would I exonerate them? Would I be strong enough to pardon God for taking her so violently?

As if that heartache wasn't enough, Vivian lost her father at an early age to a shellfish/food poisoning incident. On top of all of that, she was diagnosed with breast, then lung, and then brain cancer. What kind of woman…what kind of person forgives God for all of that pain? I've never heard Vivian utter one negative word. Her tremendous trust in God was marked by her ability to remain dedicated to her faith. On the subject of faith, I know God sent Vivian to me. As she elegantly held her ice cream in her long pretty hands, recounting all of her tribulations, I was in awe of her. She was an earth angel sent to narrate her story of strength. She has managed to stay on this planet in spite of three often fatal cancers. She is the face of every survivor. Her eyes are rings of hope linking mankind together.

I recognized her hope. Worn, but still shining, Vivian's light mirrored every survivor I knew… The Hurricane Katrina victims on the base, the parents of a young girl who died in one of the towers on September 11th, the father just back from Iraq picking up his daughter after a voice lesson, my childhood friend whose sister was brutally murdered less than a mile away from our homes, the son of my friend after his tour as a Marine sharp shooter in Afghanistan, the Vietnam veterans I interviewed (including the father who raised me) for a school project, my friend Rose after her son died, my mother after her father died. I firmly believe that our ability to manifest hope for the future is what rescues us from the sorrow. Hope shines through pain.

Vivian had the soul of a prophet. I believe God spares the prophets to teach us. We, the students, need to walk away smarter, more attentive, and grateful for our abundance. Vivian's lessons stayed with me long after we shared soft serve on the island of Sanibel.

Our trip infused my body with positive energy. For the duration of that month, I was on top of the world. I was so caught up in being happy I hadn't emotionally prepared myself for the surgical one year date. The no more thyroid blues crept in when I least expected them. One would think my one year marker would have been cause for celebration. To the contrary, as February 2, approached I was overcome with an all too familiar sense of loss.

The week of my surgi-versary, my friend knocked the wind out of me with honesty. She was talking about the diet she and her husband were on. She said, "Guys lose weight so much faster." My authentic response walked us into the den of truth. "I know, just the other day Roger found fishing pictures from 1994 in Key West. He kept saying, "Babe, look at how ripped I was." Much to my surprise my friend countered with, "Yeah, it's unreal. Roger has had such a transformation in the past year. If ever a spouse was physically a product of cancer in the household, it's Roger. He looks so different."

Roger has always had short hair and has always been very fit. Since my cancer, he had put on a few pounds and was growing his hair to donate to "Locks of Love." Rather than become defensive, I said, "Once he cuts his hair, he'll look more like himself."

"I think of him often," she said, "Because he, like me, is basically getting to know you all over again, Lorna. You are totally different. It's very strange for me. I cannot imagine what it's like for him." At that point, my body was tingly and my head felt light. "How do you mean I'm different? What do you mean?" By now my friend's Irish skin was becoming a blotchy and pinkish red in color. "Whatever, Lorna, I cannot explain it. It's just that you are so different. It's like I don't know where to find you in there. For a moment or two you seem like you are you, but then I cannot recognize you. It's not a bad thing- it's just hard to explain."

"Have I let you down? Do you feel as if I'm not here for you?" I asked, desperate to get to the root of the matter. "No-no-no, it's not that. It's the little things…you not putting up a Christmas tree this year, things like that. It's just so different. Forget it, I cannot explain it."

If I can digress for a moment…Christmas post-cancer felt different. I wanted to have friends over for caroling, great food, and a bon fire, but I no longer wanted to the pressure of decorating the house. December 2006 marked the first year we put up a three foot artificial tree. It was adorned with one single string of colored lights. For years colored lights were the nemesis of my white light tree fashion. Roger loves colored lights. He also loves STAR WARS. Each limb of our new little tree boasted the limited edition STAR WARS and STAR TREK ornaments. For years the collectables remained in their respective boxes. I blatantly refused to provide space for Sci-Fi on my picturesque and magazine-worthy Christmas tree. After cancer a pretty tree didn't mean much to me. Roger **loved** our 2006 Sci-Fi tree. Where the harm is in that?

My friend went on to say, "Okay, Lorna, here is an example of what I mean, normally we have conversations about the craziness of your day to day life. We don't do that anymore. Again, I'm not saying this is a bad thing, I'm just saying you aren't the same." As I listened to her explain how much I had changed, I felt my blood boil a bit, remembering the time I spent mourning the loss of all my friendships. Each time one of my friends had a new baby, I sincerely grieved the loss of our relationship. Once the kids came, we didn't see each other as often. We lost all spontaneity. We were unable to grab a bite to eat before scheduling in a time. We were never alone shopping or poking through a bookstore. We never had uninterrupted phone conversations between the hours of 7 A.M. and 11 P.M. Talk about change? Each and every one of my close gal pal's changed when they became moms. Never have I heard so much talk about breast pumps and organic food! I never commented on the changes. I accepted the transformation in each friendship and found ways to make our new relationship work.

As my friend continued to explain how unrecognizable I had become, I tried to analyze what was happening. Was she simply trying to say she missed me? Does she think I don't need her as much? Maybe she preferred the crazy, erratic girl I used to be? I have always shared every dark corner of my life with her. I never truly invited my friends into my annex of cancer hell. Perhaps she feels left out? Rather than put a wall up I tried to explain how I felt. "A few things are happening here," I said. "To start, I have lost a part of my body that two surgeons referred to as the "thing that makes us go" in our body. It's our gas pedal. Our thyroid is responsible for our energy, hormones, body temperature, emotions, highs and lows, skin texture, hair texture, weight, metabolism, our calcium, ability to reason, to problem solve; I could go on. In short, it's a really important part of **who** we are. I have had that part of my body removed. I am taking synthetic hormones to replace all of the wonderful things the thyroid gland does naturally. Doesn't it make sense that I'd be a <u>slight bit</u> different? I no longer have a part of my body that creates, decides, or makes up **who** I am. That alone may explain the changes you are witnessing. My body is no longer the same. They didn't fix a broken bone or repair my existing heart; I literally have lost a piece of me."

To further explain my new unrecognizable life, I went on to say, "Some days I don't even recognize who I am. I completely understand where you are coming from. I'm sorry. That's all I can say. We are at an age where <u>everything</u> is changing around us. Our grandparents are dying. Gosh, someone in our circle has buried a child. Our parents are starting to get sick and are having major surgeries. Our friends are getting divorced. Their children are growing up. **WE** are growing up. Part of that involves cancer and set backs and illnesses. It also involves fabulous things like babies becoming teenagers and going off to college, second vacation homes on the beach, trips around the world, and 40th and 50th birthday bashes. Everything is changing. We cannot change that. I'm sorry I'm not the same. I don't know what I can do to make it better for you. This is who I am now."

After bouncing her unrecognizable allegations off of my husband, he said, "Of course we have changed! Of course you aren't the same. Nothing will ever be the same-but that's how life goes. CANCER HAPPENS and people change. It's good that she talked about this to you, Lorna. At least you know how she feels. That's a step in the right direction." As usual, he was right.

The following week our pet cat Mitzi (of sixteen years) displayed alarming behavior. We scheduled an immediate vet visit. With a vast investment in the power of life-sustaining medicine, I assumed she'd be fine after a treatment for whatever was ailing her. Remember how I asked the nuclear medicine team if my cat would have to be quarantined during my quarantine? Remember how they assured me animals would not be affected by my, for lack of a better word, dirty bomb shell-ness? Shortly after being radioactive, Mitzi was diagnosed with a **thyroid disorder**. I know cats often have thyroid disease, but the coincidence was enigmatic. One would think an animal who had never missed an annual vet appointment would have presented a thyroid issue prior to my radiation.

Bottom line: an otherwise healthy cat of sixteen years, passed away on Valentine's Day 2006. We lost our precious pet in the vet's office on a cold metal table under a blinding light. As my husband and I sobbed together stroking her tiny deceased body, I hated myself for not separating her from me the day I came home from the hospital. If the chimney soot hadn't saturated my house I would have been in clear mind. I would have remove Mitzi from our first floor. Because of my selfishness, our cat was dead.

As my husband dug a grave for the small white cardboard box coffin, my sister Elizabeth pulled into our driveway for the makeshift funeral. As soon as I saw her somber face, I hugged her (I was never a hugger) and began crying on her shoulder. We'd known Mitzi longer than all of the grandchildren in our family. Our embrace of tears in my driveway was more extreme than all of the crying we displayed at both my uncle and grandfather's wakes and funerals. What is it about the death of an animal that releases our primal sense of loss and grief? Long after the funeral, Roger remained outside smoothing the dirt above Mitzi's body. We weren't even cat people when Mitzi made her way into our lives. My husband spent his entire life with big 'ol mixed breed dogs with names like Brandy. On a November night, some sixteen years prior, a cat invited herself in our home through an open window. We were instantly smitten with the kitten. The house was very quiet the weeks that followed Mitzi's death. Her passing was yet another change we had to accept.

A week later, I returned to Boston to have an ultrasound on my neck. I sat still in my Jeep waiting for my legs to walk into the hospital.

It's just a scan…the cancer hasn't come back. Walk inside. Put one foot in front of the other and move. I remained standing in the waiting area for several moments hoping the tech would call my name. *It's just a scan…you are fine.* My thoughts reverted back to the ultrasound I had in November of 2004 when things were not fine. That scan is what got the ball rolling down my candlepin lane of cancer. Suddenly, I heard an unusual sound. In a Russian accent a tender voice said, "Lorna Brunelle?"*Oh my gosh, she's from Russia. She's about my age…I wonder if she lived near the Chernobyl region. I wonder if she was exposed to the radiation. She must know all about thyroid cancer if she is from Russia.* "Hello, I am Jane." "Where are you from?" I asked. "The Ukraine," she replied. "Oh, that's funny, Jane from the Ukraine! It rhymes," I said, nervously trying to bond with her.

As we made our way over to the table, I shared my interest in the Chernobyl Children Project. Within minutes I was blabbering about the C.C.P. I got the courage to ask if she had been affected by the disaster. "I was younger when it happened. I get tested every few months. I was exposed to radiation as so many of us were. My family members were worse off than I was. I came to this country to leave the contamination. What are you here for?" she asked. "Thyroid cancer. I'm a year out and pretty worked up about this test."

Her warm smile and wonderful command of the English language eased my nerves as she walked me through the ultrasound. *Oh, please, let this be clear. Please…no more lumps or clusters or tumors…please, just a clear scan…* Just then, as if an angel had floated down to earth and landed at my bedside, Jane from the Ukraine leaned over to my right ear and whispered, "I tell what I see, okay?" Totally still and silent, I looked at her as if to say *Thank you, kind girl, thank you for understanding my soul.* Her steady voice continued on with, "I see…I see no cancer…I see only muscles…muscles only…no cancer…I see…no cancer…I see nothing but good. Okay, you can get up now."

Our precious meeting of intimacy was the most beautiful clandestine moment I have ever had with a stranger. Jane from the Ukraine understood the panic of cancer. As I toweled off the ultrasound gel from my neck, Jane said, "It was so nice to meeting you. I wish you luck.

I want you to please thank all of the people that you know helping my people. Now, I would like to God Bless you." I threw my arms around her (once again, I was never a hugger) and thanked her for being so special. I knew she risked her job by telling me what she thought she saw on the screen. I knew she wasn't authorized to comment on what the ultrasound recorded. I knew she wasn't a doctor and therefore may have been wrong in her assessment. I knew none of that mattered because regardless of whether or not Dr. Smith agreed with her findings, in that brief instant Jane restored my faith in a medical world.

After long runs with impatience and impoliteness Jane was a breath of fresh air. Jane from the Ukraine made me want to believe in the power of medical optimism again. Jane from the Ukraine erased the nasty nurse who lied on my form about contrast. Jane from the Ukraine gave me hope regarding future scans.

A few days later, Dr. Smith confirmed Jane's good eye! On an upbeat phone call, he said he thought I was an excellent candidate for Thyrogen injections. Once a year, most thyroid cancer patients have to go off their thyroid hormones (otherwise known as their lifeline) to prepare for a series of tests. For several weeks leading up to the testing period, patients experience symptoms of hypothyroidism. I don't need to remind you how horrid it is to be hypo. Dr. Smith explained how Thyrogen was being used as an alternative to weeks of hypo hell. Using Thyrogen in combination with imaging and lab tests provides patients with an option of complete thyroid hormone withdrawal in shorter amount of time. Thyrogen also provides doctors with an effective follow-up tool in the management of well-differentiated thyroid cancer.

Rather than feeling hypo for over a month, I'd only have to go off of my meds for a week. I thought the job of the radiation was to destroy the contamination in my body. I asked Dr. Smith why, after becoming a dirty bomb shell, I needed such extensive tests. "Well, Mrs. Brunelle, you did have that positive antigen. It's best that we stay on top of this." *Damn that positive lymph node.*

I went to the computer and typed in Thyrogen. Turns out Thyrogen is made from the ovary cell line of Chinese hamsters. For the record, whenever I walk by hamsters in a pet shop, I now feel a certain kinship to them.

Dr. Smith's verbal reminder about the severity of my disease threw me into "Carpe Diem" mode. My life went into a tailspin of making time for the things I'd always wanted but never got around to doing. **Seize the day** became my mantra. It's amazing how much one little negative phrase like positive antigen can positively motivate us. I picked up the phone and purchased four tickets to Florida. Eager to thank my mother for taking care of me and my grandfather, I went into her office with a photo of Naples, Florida. I told her that we were going to visit my godmother (one of her best friends) at the end of the March and that we were bringing my niece Paige and my nephew Tyler. We had talked about going to Florida together for years but never booked a trip.

My mother hadn't been on a plane since 1979. Paige and Tyler had never flown. Out of the four of us, I was the most excited! I couldn't wait to see their faces as we soared off of the runway. The past year consisted of a series of emotional cancer highs and lows. Just once, I wanted a high to last longer than a low. Life can change in an instant my friends. As a thyroid cancer survivor, I hereby declare spontaneous trips to lovely places. Dear people who say "I'll get there next year" or "I just cannot afford it right now," please do not put off the things you have always longed to do. Make the most out of each day. Each passing of someone we love reaffirms the importance of being happy. Get a jar for your spare change. Two years from now, you will have plane tickets.

I was proud as punch over planning the trip. For the first time in my life, **I** was the captain of the vacation. It was my responsibility to lead the group to the luggage check in, the terminal, our seats, the rental car station, the parking lot, onto the highway in Ft. Myers, through the roads to Naples, through the parking lot to the hotel, and all over the map for site seeing, meals and merriment. Never before had I been responsible for making it from point A to point B on a trip. I had always been in the company of my husband or side-kick savvy traveling friends who were Ace's at jaunting to warmer places. I relished in my personal growth. I considered the entire adventure a testament to how much I had changed for the better.

As the plane took off, my entire body tingled with exhilaration as I watched the eyes of my co-travelers light up. "Here we go!" I exclaimed, as we tilted toward heaven. Completely caught up in my marvelous moment, I provided underscoring in my head by recalling a verse from "Come Sail Away" written by Dennis De Young for the rock band Styx. I encourage all readers born before 1980 to join me by allowing the piano accompaniment to stream in as we hear that flawless tenor voice sing the following lyrics he wrote.

I'm sailing away, set an open course for the virgin sea
I've got to be free, free to face the life that's ahead of me
On board, I'm the captain, so climb aboard
We'll search for tomorrow on every shore
And I'll try, oh lord, I'll try to carry on

I look to the sea, reflections in the waves spark my memory
Some happy, some sad
I think of childhood friends and the dreams we had
We live happily forever, so the story goes
But somehow we missed out on that pot of gold
But we'll try best that we can to carry on

A gathering of angels appeared above my head
They sang to me this song of hope, and this is what they said
They said come sail away, come sail away
Come sail away with me
Come sail away, come sail away
Come sail away with me

It was a blissful moment! Just when my life couldn't have gotten any better, just when I thanked God for giving me cancer, just when I was floating on top of the world, the kids began freaking out over their ears popping! At one point my thirteen-year-old niece was holding the sides of her head and moaning in pain. Soon after she calmed down, my nephew asked about snacks, drinks, and money to order a movie. Reality reminded me that the trip was about *my* growth and evolution into a stronger, more adventurous woman. It wasn't about how spectacular the children would feel about being a part of my maiden voyage to Florida.

I remained very calm the following morning as my nephew vomited all over the bed, floor and bathroom of our hotel room. Around 3:00 A.M., I found myself at the front desk in search of bedding and cleaning products to disinfect the room. While my mother stripped and remade the bed, I (in full blown dry heaves) tried to tend to the carpet and bathroom. *Please let this be a temporary upset stomach from flying. Please, Lord, if this is a one-week-long virus type thing that makes its way through all four of us, I'll lose my mind. I came here to heal with my family. Lord, I need you to work with me.*

With the hurlin' fest behind us, each day on our trip became increasingly more enjoyable. Together we walked the beaches of Marco Island, Naples, and Venice, laughing and relaxing in the sun. The entire excursion was a success. The most unforgettable moment took place on the car ride home from the beach. All of my passengers fell asleep. While the noiseless car moved along the highway, radiant sunbeams cast a golden glow on my family. Each of them exhausted from swimming, walking and mending; the stillness of the commute gave me time to reflect. *Everything is okay now...I am going to be fine...everyone is going to be fine...this trip has proven how strong cancer has made me...I get it now God...I got the message. Cancer has brought out the best in me.*

Just then, I felt a beautiful presence in the car. I knew someone familiar had joined us. I felt as if my grandfather's spirit had taken a blanket of love and protection and covered all of us. The heavenly coverlet of care had a profound healing effect on my body. As I type this memory, my cell phone is tapping out a steady stream of sound. The tap-tap, rhythm bears a resemblance to a human heart beat. It's no secret that phones act up near computers, but this undeniable cadence began the moment I reenacted that afternoon in the car. I am certain my grandfather is acknowledging his attendance in Florida. Just as I finished typing that last sentence, the noise stopped. Little signs from above are all around us. We just have to slow down enough to *tap* in.

I returned home from Naples feeling as though I could achieve anything. One would think after graduating from one of the toughest colleges in the country, opening my own business at the age of twenty-four, making a positive impact on countless community service projects, and working at a major casting company in Boston, that I would have felt pretty damn good about my accomplishments. Revealing the beauty of the Gulf Coast to my family made me feel like the most successful person in the world. I got more joy out of bringing my mother to Naples with her two oldest grandchildren, than accepting my college degree on stage in Boston.

The funny thing about cancer is just when you think you know yourself, just when you think you have discovered what you want out of life, just when you think you understand what really matters; **everything changes**. The things that previously took precedence seem irrelevant. Cancer sears the core principals of survival on the hearts of those afflicted by the disease. Family, friends, love, health, joy, adventure, laughter, security, and wellness, become paramount. Those core principals of life are food for the soul. A person can work seventy hour weeks and obtain gold watches, trips, awards, new kitchens, degrees, beach houses, country club memberships, status cars, corner offices, and seven figure salaries; but without those principals, I bet their soul remains hungry.

For me, cancer offered super hero vision. Through the eyes of cancer, I was permitted to see the spectacular horizon of an entirely new life landscape. Beneath a brilliant sunrise of hope, shining over a disease-free kingdom, I was able to see the life I wanted to live. There are still moments of doubt and sadness, but they are overshadowed by beautiful moments of clarity. I implore you to flourish in your new existence and embrace the possibilities your new cancer-free life will afford you.

My friend was right. I had changed. And perhaps to her, I had become unrecognizable. As survivors, we have to trust the positive power of change. In time, your loved ones will be able to find you on the other side of cancer.

Part of the Human Heart

WITH MY PORTABLE COOLER IN HAND, I drove to the pharmacy to pick up my Thyrogen. Normally, insurance companies approve the direct delivery of the medication to the hospital or office that is administering the injections. For some reason, my insurance denied that luxury. I had to pick up the vials, store them in a cooler, and drive them into Boston for the injections in my ass. Rather ass-backwards, don't 'ya think?

Once the meds came in, I called Dr. Smith to review the plan. "When you get to the hospital, go to oncology." As soon as he said oncology, I lost it. My heart started to race. As Dr. Smith gave me instructions, I did everything I could to hold back tears. My snap of emotion startled me. I wondered how I could vacillate from bliss to blubbery within seconds. In preparation for the tests, I was off of my daily thyroid pills. My manic mood swings were a direct result of my lack of meds. When hypo in a flash, one can be as poignant as a poet or as nutty as a bag of trail mix.

Dr. Smith went on to say, "Go right to oncology for the injections. I will call you with the results. Lorna, while I have you, I have to let you know that I am taking somewhat of a career turn. I will be leaving Massachusetts for Atlanta, Georgia in June. It's been wonderful having you as a patient. I want to assure you that you'll be in great hands." **THUMP**...***thump***...**THUMP** ...***thump***...*Did he just say what I think he said?* As I reached into my soul trying to grab out my best actor self, I forced down the boulder in my throat. With an instant pounding on the sides of my head I said, "Oh, my gosh, that's a <u>big change</u>. I am very happy for you. Congratulations!" At that point he said, "I'll see you before I go."

Dr. Smith was the first man to ever dump me. The enormity of our breakup froze my body. On the verge of losing someone very dear to me, I found myself feeling unbelievably helpless. Other than my husband and my surgeon, there was more intimacy in my relationship with Dr. Smith than with any other man in my life. Dr. Smith found my lump. Dr. Smith held my hand through each step on my road toward wellness. Dr. Smith called my home during my radioactive hell to make sure I was okay. Dr. Smith called my cell at 8:00 P.M. some days during the week to give me lab test results. Dr. Smith tolerated my eccentric manner and never made me feel as if he didn't get me. Dr. Smith was my family. On a truly innocent level of connection - I truly loved him.

That Monday, I went into Boston with my cooler, vials of Thyrogen pig secretion, and brave face. As I entered the oncology department, I was greeted with, "I've nevAH seen anyone come in heAH with a coolAH! How the hell'd that happen?" Nurse June had a Boston streetwise smoker's voice. As she directed me to a little curtained-off area, she said, "One leg up on the chayAH (chair) and bend ovAH. I have to stick 'ya in the behind. They told 'ya that, right?" "Yes, and I've been looking forward to it ever since I got the news. I used body lotion with sparkles so my back side would shine for you," I replied. "You spaHHkled ya' ass for me?" She asked. "My butt isn't as cute as it used to be, but it still likes to make a good impression." I replied. "She's a friggin riot, this one." She replied. "Comes in with a coolAH and spaHHkles on her ass."

On the way home from the injection, I felt sleepy. I wasn't too sleepy to drive, but I felt heavy. The injection seemed to add a sense of weight to my body. My imaginary back-pack filled with rocks forced me to bed soon after I arrived home. I returned to Boston the next day for my second injection. After the second shot, I felt even more bogged down. I remember trying to pick a few things up at the grocery store. My arms were weak. It felt as if each food item was a circus elephant trying to balance itself in my hands. With my cart half empty, I parked it at the courtesy booth and walked out of the store. Grocery shopping was out of the question, but I did go into the office every day. To summarize how I felt on Thyrogen- Each moment felt like I had just woken up after a terrible night's sleep. That constant state of murkiness engulfed my body for about a week.

That Saturday, I attended my first Thyroid Cancer Survivors' Association, Inc. (ThyCa) meeting in Boston. Since my diagnosis, I had become very familiar with their web site www.thyca.org. It wasn't until I noticed a posting about the Chernobyl Anniversary Convocation in Boston that I actually wrote to one of the local members. Thrilled to have an educated person to chat with about thyroid cancer, I sent her daily emails about my life pre and post-cancer. She was a great resource. I could hardly wait to meet her in person. As I walked through the court yard of the huge hospital in Boston I saw the face of the woman whose emails I had been drinking in for weeks. "You must be Lorna!" she said. "Come on in, Love. We are just about to get started." Her Aussie/English accent (as she calls it) was both charming and entertaining.

The meeting opened with each person sharing their name, their type of thyroid cancer and how many years they were out. I'll never forget how initially exhilarating it was to sit with a group of people who truly understand my new normal. Suddenly, typical salutations turned into group members using numbers and formulas to explain their health status. Radioactive iodine radiation treatment levels were shared, along with thyroid globulin levels, T4 and T3 levels, tumor sizes, and the dates of their last round of labs. The topic of new thyroid cancer research was discussed followed by a round and who was pissed off at pharmaceutical companies for offering science museums more money than thyroid cancer research groups. I learned who in the group had Hashimoto's disease, who still felt hypo, and who felt hyper. My head was spinning. Just then, it was my turn to speak.

"Hello, my name is Lorna Brunelle. I'm 35 years old. I am a year and a few months out. I had radioactive iodine radiation therapy on March 17th, 2005. I am ashamed to say I do not know my exact dosage. It was under 100. Maybe around 50? Was it 53? I completed Thyrogen injections this week. Forgive me. I am still a little foggy. Unfortunately, I cannot tell you any of my numbers. I guess that makes me one uniformed patient. On the subject lacking information…I don't even know what Hashimoto's disease is. So far, my doctor calls and says, "Everything looks fine." Then he mails a lab slip with numbers on it. I put the slips in a folder marked CANCER. Until today, I never realized that I needed to track each slip." (Uncomfortable pause.) "Thank you for having me."

After a small speck of silence, a man in the group said, "Lorna, we will help you. You have to keep track of your numbers. You are your best advocate. You need to watch your numbers and chart how you are feeling. You need to bring that information to your doctor. Who is your endo?" As soon as he asked the question, I felt my eyes well up. Through tears induced by a week without meds, I rambled, "Well you see, my endo is moving to Atlanta, so after researching all of the endocrinologists in the area, I'm switching over to Dr. Lang who incidentally, was the mentor to Dr. Smith." Suddenly the circle became a buzz with elation! Compliments over the amazing Dr. Lang filled the room. I was in the presence of a Dr. Lang fan club. Every person at the meeting was in her care. The votes of confidence made me feel great about my decision to select her as my new thyroid cancer B.F.F. (best friend forever), but silently I mourned the near end of my relationship with Dr. Smith.

After the love fest over Dr. Lang ended, a man in the group said, "Lorna, your homework is to bring in all of your paperwork. We will help you chart your numbers. It's really easy. In time you'll find it very empowering." His caring eyes and audibly damaged vocal chords pierced my heart. I left the meeting overwhelmed by what little knowledge I had about my true medical state. I was living the life of a lazy and irresponsible thyroid cancer patient. I was vaguely familiar with terms like thyroid globulin and tumor marker, stimulated and non-stimulated testing, and thyroglobulin antibodies, but didn't really understand the need to take matters into my own hands. This seems so old school to confess, but I assumed all of my numbers were Dr. Smith's responsibility. If he said I was good, I was good.

In the beginning of my recovery, I focused my energy on things like making it through each day without crying. My numbers never even penetrated as precedence. To make matters worse, I was unable to regularly attend the meetings. My job at the casting company fell during the exact same hours the ThyCa group met. I was only able to attend that particular meeting because the casting office was closed for school vacation.

A few hours later, I found myself on the bleachers at my nephew Tyler's baseball game. My head still spinning from the meeting, I could hardly focus on what was happening on the field. PRIVATE came up on my cell screen. *Could this be Dr. Smith calling me during his Passover? No way.* "Hello, Mrs. Brunelle, it's Dr. Smith. Your tests were fine. Everything looks great! Your levels are perfect. Everything is exactly how we want it to be." Then I heard him say, "You have zero thyroid blah blah bah dee blah blah." *Ughr, he is spitting out my numbers! I don't I have a pen in my bag. Shit, I need those numbers.* He concluded with, "Things look super! Enjoy your weekend!"

I blurted, "You are the *BEST*, Dr. Smith!" Sort of laughing it off as if he didn't warrant such praise, he said, "Well thank you, Mrs. Brunelle. Have a good weekend." I hung up the phone saying, "I love that man!" for everyone on the bleachers to hear. I meant it. I truly loved his soul. He went the extra mile for me. He called the day before Easter on a weekend to ease my mind. How many doctors would do such a thing? Gone were the days of Dr. Smith's hand holding. I'd lost my guardian of light. It was time to buy a flashlight and fly solo into the dark thyroid numbers territory.

May 6th, 2006, had arrived and my first public address on the topic of thyroid cancer was only hours away. I was consumed with self doubt. *What if they don't get my humor? What if my dirty bombshell joke is a bomb? What if my honesty about The Bow Tie Bastard offends the doctors?* Just as my insecurity tried to get the best of me, a little voice inside my head said, *What if by sharing my story, I help someone? What if this is the beginning of a whole new adventure on the thyroid cancer public speaking circuit? What if today I change someone's life?* As I sat in for the tail end of the doctors' panel, I heard my surgeon Dr. Randolph welcomed Dr. Lang to the front of the room. As the elegant Amerasian woman began sharing her information, I couldn't help but wonder whether or not we were the right match. She was very serious as she went through her presentation.

Dr. Lang put a slide up on the screen. The text read, "The fastest growing cancer among women is NOT what you think. Ask your doctor to check your neck for thyroid cancer." The most stimulating part of the slide was the photo. The audience assumed we were looking at a breast, half of a nipple and a woman's waist. Once we closely looked at the photo, through the help of Dr. Lang, we realized the breast was really the side of someone's face, the nipple was really one half of someone's lip, and the waist was really someone's neck. The brilliant photo can be seen on the checkyourneck.com site. She held the room in her hands. Her dramatic delivery was strong. When the doctors broke for recess I introduced myself to my new endo. "Hello, my name is Lorna Brunelle. I am a patient of Dr. Smith. I've contacted your office and will be seeing you this fall. I really appreciated your presentation today." She graciously responded and wished me luck on my speech.

Each remaining doctor on the panel took a turn at the podium. The data was very clinical and technical. For hours I heard about cells, antigens, formulas, and ratios. The last doctor to speak was Dr. Paul Konowitz, an ear, nose and throat specialist who works in the same hospital as my surgeon. He is the founder of "Doctors as Patients." His riveting story about his life as both a physician and a patient intimately walked the audience through his journey. He was a thriving doctor who became a suffering patient once diagnosed with a rare and potentially fatal autoimmune disorder called Pemphigus Vulgaris. The disorder affects the skin and mucous membranes. As his story unfolded, we realized how becoming a patient forced him to look within, closely examining the type of doctor he had been during his career.

On the edge of my seat, I listened to the successful and well respected doctor confess all of his medical shortcomings. Before being afflicted with his disease, he passed judgment on patients who were on anti-depressants. He didn't always pay attention to and listening to his patients if he didn't agree with what they were saying. He took some cases less seriously than he should have. He never truly absorbed the domino effect illness has on a patient's life. He passed judgment on people who requested pain medication. He often lost sight of the fact that each patient was a parent, wife, husband, partner, sibling, child, mother, father or grandparent. He had a lack of consideration for the impact illness has on patients- never realizing that each patient was at risk of losing their work, their wages, their homes, their security, their identity and their self-confidence. Until he got sick, he thought he was an excellent physician.

Infused with an almost haunting guilt about his medical disservice, he vividly recounted the turning point of his career. With gut wrenching detail, he walked us through the halls of his own personal disease induced hell. An ominous cloud of crude truth hovered over the conference room, as he bravely and bluntly spoke about his lost wages, his loss of identity, his excruciating physical and emotional pain, his lost self-confidence, his loss of self-worth, his family in crisis, his dependence on pain meds, his depression, his time spent in therapy, and finally, by the Grace of God, his strength to pull through.

He added that once he became the patient he understood what it felt like to be a number. He knew how it felt to have someone only half listen. He knew how it felt to see the face of a doctor who didn't really grasp the intensity and the enormity of the situation. His presentation was filled with a vulnerability hardly ever publicly displayed by people in our country -let alone by doctors. His words filled my soul with a sense of hopefulness for the future of medicine. His message, (which has since become part of the curriculum at the Harvard School of Medicine) was insightful, riveting, tender, crucial, and poignant.

Throughout this book, I have talked about how magnificently empowering it is to transfer all of your negative experiences into a positive place in your life. My epiphany came during my quest with cancer. For Dr. Konowitzit, his turning point seems to have surfaced while battling his disease. He has taken his story on the road. He is educating young doctors to see patients as people. In time his willingness to bring change will result in a generation of empathetic doctors treating and nurturing communities across the globe. Dr. Konowitz is a modern hero on a mission to improve the quality of care in medicine. His work reminds us that it's never too late to make a difference.

I was next in line to share my story at the podium. For a quick moment, I became the fourth grade student with the shitty Show and Tell item. I was the kid who had to speak in front of the class after the kid who passed around rocks gathered at the Parthenon on their family holiday in Greece. How could I possibly follow Dr. Konowitz?

As I situated my speech on the podium, the rhinestone heart on my bracelet caught the light and glistened back at me. The heart shaped sparkle filled my mind with Lynn Ahrens' lyrics from the song "Part of the Human Heart" from the musical <u>Once on This Island.</u> *Of all who took the journey, and managed to endure…The ones who came before you, the others yet to come…And those who you will teach it to…And those you learned it from…You are part, part of the human heart.* My cancer was revealing the good hearts of the people all around me. It was time to share my story. Time to teach what I had learned.

I had years of public speaking experience yet had never addressed a crowd of physicians. My heart (which seemed to be pounding out of my chest) reminded me that I was in new terrain. With the opening line of my speech only seconds away, the heart on my bracelet continued to twinkle up at me. I pretended the luminosity of the heart charm was a spot light. Like any veteran performer, I embraced the light, took a huge breath from my diaphragm and began my speech. When I looked up at the crowd I saw Dr. Randolph's humane face. I knew I wouldn't fail. I was a product of his fine work. My journey was worth recounting.

The audience was silent while I spoke. Laughter from the crowd rushed in as I recounted my thoughts about the radiation therapy. I said, "In my twenty's I was a bomb shell. At thirty-four, I became a human dirty bomb! Guess that makes me a dirty bomb**shell**!" I noticed my new endo Dr. Lang laughing. Her sense of humor sealed the deal. She wasn't Dr. Smith, but she got me.

The speech was a success! Audience members congratulated me as I triumphantly returned to my seat. Dr. Konowitz walked to the podium and said, "Wow. All I can say is WOW!" Then he looked over to my section of the theatre and said, "Thank you for sharing your story with us." Again, the lyrics of "Part of the Human Heart" flooded my mind. The surgeon who saved life and my career, the endocrinologist who discovered my cancer and held my hand during my recovery, Dr. Konowitz, and all of the strangers, friends, and family who made a monumental difference in the way I saw life after my diagnosis; were all part of the human heart. They were all part of the universal rhythm of life. As the applause for my speech continued, I said a prayer thanking God for bestowing his angels of heart upon me.

Two days after the convocation, I found myself at the casting company surrounded by a forest of professional football players. In my high heels, I was shortest person in the pre-audition room of testosterone and athleticism. We were working on a big picture about a fictitious famous football player raising his newly acquainted nine-year-old daughter. The star of the picture was a very well known actor and wrestler. I must confess I'm not a huge football person. I had no idea who the team members were standing in front of me. All I knew was how vulnerable the athletes were. The guys could play on the field, but very few knew how to play a scene. They were in search of guidance on how to succeed in the audition. My job was to coach each person on a short two-page scene until they felt prepared enough to go on camera and deliver the lines. I accompanied a few of the all stars into the casting room and read opposite during their screen tests.

The casting world is extremely busy. Within seconds an hour can turn into the entire day. I worked through lunch neglecting to cancel the tentative birthday lunch plans I had with my sister Liz. I coached straight through my morning shift completely unaware of the time. During a small lull in the chaos, I made a note to call my sister to explain my absence. My sister is a colossal football fan! Working with members of the NFL would have been one of the best days of her career. For me it was just another day at work.

"Happy Birthday!" I said on her voice mail, "I'm sorry I didn't make it home in time to take you to lunch, but I have a GREAT reason. I'll call you when I get home to explain." A very famous player overheard my message and said, "It's your sister's birthday? And you are here with US? You didn't take her out to lunch? That's not right. Does she like football?" I let him know the word **like** was the understatement of the year. "Hey, call her back. We'll sing Happy Birthday to her." I responded by saying, "No, thank you, I cannot do that. I don't want to distract anyone. But thank you so much for offering. That's really sweet." Then he said, "It's my decision to use <u>my</u> phone and call anyone I want, right? Okay, so give me your sister's number. I'll call her and sing." Calling my sister had become a marvelous distraction from his pre-audition nerves. The customer is always right, right? I said, "Okay, call her. But remember - this was YOUR IDEA. I cannot lose my job over this!" He dialed the number. She answered. He introduced himself to her, wished her a Happy Birthday, and sang the song.

The serenade broke up the anxiety in the waiting area. Several players became privy to my sisters birthday. One of their managers (yes, most of the boys came in with managers, it was VERY Jerry McQuire) said, "Your sister loves the Patriots, huh? Well, why don't you get a few autographs for her from the guys?" Again, I was extremely professional and said, "Oh, I couldn't. -Office policy. They are here for the audition- it's not like we are at a public signing. We respect that." Just then the manager said, "I'm sure a few of these boys would love to sign an autograph for your sister." So within a few seconds, about five members of the New England Patriots autographed a page of the movie script. Most signed their names but a few boys wrote "Happy Birthday, Liz" and added their jersey number and signature. I was beaming over the idea of seeing my sister's face when she read the paper! It was a very cool day at work! If only I watched football, it would have been even cooler!

Moments after, a <u>very well</u> known member of the Patriots asked me to work a scene with him. It tickled my funny bone to see so many colossal men (who spend their time on the field ramming into each other) so petrified over saying a few lines. I congratulated every one of them for trying something so new. At one point a player said,

"Wow, you should work at the stadium! You are a GREAT COACH! I really appreciate your help and your patience." *Okay, now my day is looking even better...I have big ol' famous football men complimenting me... BRING IT ON....Thank God I'm having a good hair day!* Then in a quiet corner around the bend from the casting door, two of the most famous players asked how I ended up in the biz. I told them that I started out as a singer/actor and quickly walked them through my career path. Again, normally this type of thing doesn't come up with actors on big casting days, but for the most part these men were totally out of their element.

My job was to keep them calm and happy, so I indulged each question. One of my new famous friends said, "You are singer, huh?" "Yes, I have even sung the Anthem at your little playground over at Gillette Stadium," I replied. By then several tall and wide oak trees wearing men's clothes gathered around me. Outwardly amused by my comment, one trunk said, "Oh, you sang at our playground, huh? Well, sing somethin' for us now."

Totally familiar with how unfamiliar the casting event was, I politely told them that performing for them in the hallway of a casting call would most likely get me fired. "Oh yeah, I see it, you're all asking us to do our thing over here reading this script and messin' up lines for you all over the place. We're going in all nervous and acting on the camera. Makin' fools out of us. But you won't even sing for us? You won't even do *your thing* for us! Okay, I see how you are." Again, the customer is always right, right? They asked me to sing. I didn't want to misrepresent the company by seeming rude. My job was to prepare the clients, and keep them comfortable and stress-free until their audition. I pulled them far away from the casting door. After a few minutes of contemplation over being fired, I said, "What do you want to hear?" Another famous player said, "Sing something soulful. Something with soul, feelin', and heart."

For lack of a better song on the spot in the hallway outside of the casting room, I sang a verse of "Amazing Grace". As I sang, each gigantic football star listened. I noticed their shoulders shrinking and their breathing patterns change. They were being soothed by song.

It was one of the COOLEST moments of my career! Being fired no longer entered my mind as I concluded the song with the line "Was blind, but now, I see." After a second of silence one of the players said, "No! No she <u>didn't go all old school on us</u>, brinin' in Jesus! Uh Hum, PRAISE HIM...***PRAISE*** **HIS NAME**." I could tell through his southern dialect that he was from another part of the country. Each player told me where they were from. For the record, I wasn't slacking on the job. The men had worked their scenes a dozen times over. They had signed off on prep with me and were waiting for their time in the casting room.

The true power and healing effects of song rejuvenating a room full of stressed out giants. "Amazing Grace" transformed famous millionaire football stars (who were nervous about auditioning for a major motion picture) to everyday people talking about their lives. The players began sharing their stories. I discovered how each person came to Boston. Just then the conversation took a serious turn. Two of the men shared their medical tribulations. Each of them had undergone extremely serious surgeries to preserve their knees, arms, and legs. One of them was scheduled for another arm or shoulder surgery and had to sit out the upcoming season. As I listened completely relating to their pain, one of the players (who had his own month on my sisters football calendar) said, "You just have **no idea** what it's like to have a surgery that may take away your entire career. It's just not right. It's just crazy. You have to put it up to Jesus and hope He's lookin' out for you. That's all ya can do."

Seeing the fear in his eyes, I said, "Actually I <u>do</u> know what it's like." Somewhat shocked by my response, the players looked me. "Why? What happened to you?" one asked. I pointed to the thyroid cancer scar on my neck and said, "See this scar smiling back at you? (the shape of my scar is a smile) Well, that smile marks the spot where cancer used to live. When they removed my cancer I was at risk. I could have lost my singing voice. So I *really do* know what it's like to walk into a hospital for surgery and wonder if you'll wake up with your career or world as you know it, in tact." With the utmost respect and empathy, a larger-than-life famous ball player said, "Wow, Miss. You really DO know."

There it was again…the special connection that can only be made with like-minded people.

On the way to the parking lot after the session, I saw two members of the ball team chatting curb side. "How'd it go in there?" I asked. "Good. Felt good about it," one of the players replied. The other player said, "Hey, you take care, and thanks for all your help. You made it real easy in there. God Bless 'ya and <u>keep singing</u>. You got **HEART** <u>girl.</u> It's a beautiful thing." When he mentioned my heart, he placed his hand over his chest and smiled. On the way home, I opened the sunroof allowing the gorgeous early-May sun to shine down on me. Reflecting on my time with the famous athletes I realized that we are all part of the human heart. We are all here trying to live, learn, thrive, survive, evolve, and grow. We are all tested. We are all challenged. Despite all of our lessons, all of our tests, all of our highs and lows- by the grace of God, our hearts keep beating. We walk on stronger, smarter, and more aware of our blessings.

Maybe our heart beats are the echoes of encouragement from heaven? Perhaps the rhythm of every beat of every heart is the sound of God clapping for us on the side lines as our angels cheer us on in the stands?

Saying Goodbye Again

$\mathcal{S}$HORTLY AFTER MY TIME WITH THE football players, Rose and I went to a phenomenal spa on the ocean in New Hampshire called Wentworth by the Sea. Several years back, I saw a story on a type of healing treatment called Shirodhara. The spa offered the treatment. The description on their spa menu ended with, "May Serenity walk with you." Lickety-split, I signed up to be transformed.

As we pulled into the grand entrance way of the Great Gatsby-esc harbor resort, I felt my lungs expand. I was hours away from transcending into a deep state of relaxation. For days, we sat in huge Adirondack rocking chairs overlooking the bay. We listened to the sounds of the roaring 20's and big band music of the 40's. We ate luscious treats, swam in the picturesque pool, and dozed between spa treatments. Finally, it was my turn to meet "Miss Shirodhara". During my pre-Shirodhara discussion, the therapist said "Oh, you've had cancer. Your body stores that trauma. This treatment will expel all of the emotions and trauma you have connected to your cancer out of your system. This will help you release or say goodbye to the baggage cancer has a way of leaving behind in your psyche."

For the first forty-five minutes or so, the therapist lightly massaged my body. Her goal was to bring my energy down to a relaxed state. Next I heard her move the oil dispenser (a very cool looking brass Indian- style pot or chamber) over to the bed. Before long, I felt the incredible warm-scented oil drizzle onto the third eye of my forehead. After a few minutes I drifted into a surreal state. With my eyes closed, I saw beautiful cranberry crimson colors with hints of vibrant orange and golden yellow swirling above my head. The galaxy of jewel tones engulfed my body. I felt the warm glow of each hue wash over me.

Just as quickly as the colors rushed in, they faded away. I saw a long dirt road amidst hills of lush emerald and jade grass. Wildflowers and mustard seed covered the horizon. The scene took me back to my time in England. The rolling hillsides resembled my trip to Stonehenge. *Is this memory recall?* I wondered. *Am I seeing the places I've been in my life? Is this treatment opening up the place in my brain that stores memory?* Next I saw a magnificent bird fly over my head. The wing span reminded me of a hawk, but its body was massive. The bird flew right above my face and took my breath away. I actually felt the wind from the bird's flight on my nose as he soared over. *Where am I now? I've never had this memory...this is not part of my past. Where am I? Am I the bird? Am I flying freely above the countryside? Above cancer? Above death? Above pain? What is this?* Soon after the hawk-like bird flew away from me, in the corners of each side of my landscape, I saw the wings of several birds. The odd thing was that none of the birds had bodies. I only saw masses of graceful fluttering wings. *Are you my angels? You are beautiful.*

Once the wings slowed down, the entire scene faded back into the colors swirling around my canvas of Shirodhara heaven. Just as the colors began to lighten and change from reds and golds to pinks and purples the therapist said, "Take your time and be very careful getting up. Move slowly and be sure to drink the water I have left for you." *No! It's too soon. I want to go back. Don't I have more cancer to purge from my subconscious? That wasn't long enough.* I looked at the clock in the room. I had been in her care for nearly two hours. The time passed felt like thirty minutes. For years I've heard about people seeing colors and having visions during various treatments like cranio-sacral work and Reiki. I have never been able to let go enough to experience such a release. Our spa visit was a flawlessly rejuvenating get-away.

The following week I loaded my car with gifts for Dr. Smith. The time had come to say goodbye to my darling doctor. In search of the perfect farewell trinket, I stayed up the night before writing a list of adjectives and words best describing the man who changed my life. The left of the page had each initial of his name printed in a large bold font. Example: D for doctor. In the line following the letter, I listed the words. For "D" I wrote: **D**edicated, dependable, determined, dynamic, debonair, devoted. My masterpiece was printed on blue paper and framed in a gold frame with cream matting.

In addition to the framed testimony to his greatness, I purchased the Dr. Seuss book called "Oh, the Places You'll Go." I wrote a few words on the inside front cover. On his card I wrote: "To the only man who has ever dumped me-best of luck on your new adventure!" I tried to keep everything funny and light, but my mind was consumed with sadness over the idea of closing that chapter in my life. I placed my best pageant smile on my face and walked into his office.

Before long, Dr. Smith walked into the room wearing a very sweet brown suit. As soon as our eyes met, I felt the impulse to sob. Rather than embarrass myself, I went right in for the humor and handed him my presents. "What's all this?" he said. "You didn't have to do this, but you know that, right?" First he opened the book. "Oh, great, we don't have this one. Thank you," he said, referring to his family. Then he read the card and chuckled. "This is perfect!" he said. As quickly as the paper was off of the framed description of him, he burst into laughter as he read each word. For a perfect moment, both of us were laughing over the silliness of the gift. *This is exactly how I wanted this to be,* I thought. *I want to remember him laughing. I want him to remember me as the girl he made well ...the girl whose laughter he restored.* Then he said, "Would you mind if I circulate this in the office? The ladies are going to get a real kick out of this! You are too much."

When he returned from the desk area, our final moments became more serious. I thanked him for everything he had done. I tried to convey the impact knowing him had on my life. He wished me well and offered up a few beautiful sentences about wellness and happiness. On the verge of tears again, I threw out another funny sentence. With all of my might, I tried to prevent a deluge of tears from splashing over his sweet brown suit coat. "Well, I guess that's it," he said. "It has been an absolute pleasure treating you. Best of luck to you."

Like so many times before, Dr. Smith walked me to the front desk. Holding my file in his hands he said, "I've made a copy for Dr. Lang. If you have any questions, call the office. They'll take care of you." As he spoke, he sifted through my file and stopped on a page. With his finger pointed to October 21st, 2004, (the day that he found my lump) he said, "That is when this all began." Taken aback by his moment of nostalgia, I (holding back the tears) said, "It's hard to believe so much has happened and changed in such a small amount of time. It's been amazing. **You** are amazing. Thanks again." Then in my cheerleader voice I said, "Break a leg in Georgia!" After a momentary pat of his hand on my arm, he turned and walked away.

As soon as my body cleared the corner of the hallway I started to cry. At first I cried gentle controlled tears that lasted the duration of my elevator ride. On my way to the parking lot, I openly sobbed while stumbling through my pocket book for my keys. As I sat in my car trying to catch my breath, I couldn't help but recall that day in October 2004 when from the very same paved lot, I called my husband crying. So much has happened on the hospital grounds. *This lot of pavement is a cemetary now…a part of my soul was buried here the day Dr. Smith felt the lump…my past…my history… is in this ground…I will never visit this graveyard again. I am walking into the future.*

As I made my way onto the highway, I broke down with audible sounds of sorrow. Tears and nasal discharge seeped out of my face as I tried to find a napkin. I was saying goodbye to someone I loved all over again. The loss of Dr. Smith hurt as much as losing my grandfather. He was more than just my doctor. He was my family.

May 23rd, 2006, was the last time I saw Dr. Smith. Since my diagnosis, over a period of only fifteen months, I had bid farewell to nine people. Call me selfish, but I was tired of saying goodbye.

Discovering Why

I MET A LOCAL TV PERSONALITY WHO spoke passionately about the Chernobyl Children Project U.S.A. He mentioned how the group desperately needed summer host families to house the children who were in need of medical care in the United States. I began talking up the project. I was in search of a few wonderful Massachusetts dwellings for the children of the Chernobyl region. I went into high gear and pitched my C.C.P. plea to just about everyone I met. As I've said before in this book, thyroid cancer is prevalent in the Chernobyl region. As a thyroid cancer survivor I considered it my duty to raise awareness for the next generation of children in need of help twenty years after the disaster.

At breakfast, Rose and I discussed the possibility of her hosting two children from Belarus. The C.C.P. was my way to give back and extend my story into the community. It was my chance to turn thyroid cancer into something positive. I became fixated on finding the children summer host families. The more I talked up the C.C.P. program, the better I felt about my recovery. The idea of doing good things for the C.C.P. helped to make sense of my hardship.

The last week of June, Alexis and Masha landed at Logan Airport. They traveled some twenty-four hours to get to the United States from Belarus. Both children (under the age of ten) left their homeland in search of four weeks of fresh, clean air and food, free medical treatment, and a sublime American experience. With presents, balloons, flowers and massive teddy bears in hand, hundreds of people lined the corners of a conference room in Boston to welcome the children. We anxiously awaited the arrival of the children we hadn't met, yet already loved. The welcoming ceremony was the happiest I had seen my friends since they lost their son. I will never forget how radiant Rose looked as she watched the doors, hoping to catch a glimpse of the two children God had sent to her for the summer. My heart raced in anticipation of meeting the little Chernobyl cherubs.

Before long someone announced that the children had landed. They were on the bus headed our way. The room was a buzz with excitement. Just then a female voice said, "The children are almost at the curb outside." By that point, my heart was fluttering. It was truly one of the most electrifying moments of my life. Suddenly, a parade of extremely brave, fatigued, and frightened bodies marched in. They made their way through a crowded room filled with cheers, applause, smiles, laughter and love. My eyes, immersed with tears of unadulterated amazement and bliss, fixated on the new generation of queens and kings from the greatest environmental catastrophe in the history of humanity.

Before long the children were presented to our friends. I had the honor of watching them embrace the children for the first time. As Rose hugged the children, I thanked God for bringing thyroid cancer into my life. After over a year of saying goodbye to so many people in my life, I was finally saying hello.

I couldn't get my cancer out of my mind. Thyroid cancer and all of the research, networking, conversations, speeches, and people connected through my illness; brought those children of the Chernobyl region across the map to the front door of my healing heart. That moment in my life was by far the most profound correlation I have ever made with my cancer. *This day...right here in Boston surrounded by all of these children...this may be why all of this happened to me. A few lumps in my road thanks to cancer were certainly worth seeing these children in our country. In the presence of these beautiful children, I am restored. I have made peace with my illness. These two children came here to receive lifesaving care. If I had anything to do with improving their health…it has all been worth it. Perhaps on this night I have finally discovered WHY cancer happened to me.*

For the first two weeks of their stay, I spent every day with the guests from Belarus. We ate cheeseburgers and chip-seezzz (that is what they called French fries), shopped for American fashion, drove go-carts and hit a local carnival. We loaded our things on the ferry and headed for Martha's Vineyard. We were hours away from a Cape Pogue summer get-a-way.

About five minutes after boarding the ferry, the sky turned black and gray. Every piece of the sun was masked by threatening clouds. The waves beneath our vessel were enormous. Before long we were being tossed up and down. Swells were crashing over the top of the now seemingly-tiny toy boat. Water was all over the floor and was seeping in through a crack on the large metal door of the first floor. I heard the bartender say she had never seen the water so rough.

As I walked through piles of families seated in water on the floor, I glanced out of the window. Each pane of glass was completely submerged in water. Sounds of panic were everywhere, as the smell of spilled beer and vomit permeated the cabin. The boat tossed up and down throwing its' passengers onto the floor whenever they tried to walk. I grabbed hold of the bathroom door knobs and shimmied myself across the side of the boat in search of Rose and the children. I found a pale-white version of my friend huddled around a pair of bright-eyed and bushy-tailed children from Belarus. They were speaking Russian at the speed of light. My initial thought was that they were petrified. After really listening, I realized they were excited!

The first floor of the ferry was intolerable. The stench of tossed belly and the movement of the boat were too much for us to handle. We forced our way back up the stairs and sat in the seats closest to the center of the boat to ride out the storm. Each time a wave crashed over the boat, the kids cheered as if they were on a rollercoaster ride. I wondered why the children of Belarus were so fearless. Every other child on the ferry was hysterical, all the while our two international travel-mates remained stoic. For some reason their audacity struck a cord with me. There was nothing ordinary about these children. They were like little mystics filled with wisdom. Each child had a mile-long rap sheet of medical misfortune. Each child was a cancer survivor. They were fighters. They were fearless.

After a few more blustery minutes on the ocean, our ferry docked in Oak Bluffs. From there we took a bus to Edgartown and hopped on the Chappaquiddick ferry. During the twenty-minute drive over the sand dunes to the house, the children of Belarus smiled and pointed out of the backseat windows. Their eyes twinkled as they locked on the beauty of the island. Without question, they were in paradise. The protected Cape Pogue wildlife sanctuary was boasting birds, dragonflies, butterflies, sea inlets, ocean waves and an endless horizon of white sand and pristine beach.

Once we got to the house, Rose and I began making the beds while our husbands took the children swimming. I could hear the laughter of each child with the constant underscoring of waves splashing around them. That night on the phone, they told our translator it was their "happiest place on earth." I'll never forget the enormity of that sentence! How gratifying to know that I, by talking up the C.C.P., played a small part in their joy.

The following days were spent with the children collecting crabs in buckets, eating hot dogs, swimming, going for canoe rides, catching fish, and floating for hours on boogie boards. One late afternoon I took the children swimming around the bend in a serene patch of still water. For about an hour they played in the water, laughing and giggling, having the time of their lives. Earlier that week, over thirty Portuguese Man of War jellyfish had washed up on Chilmark causing many beaches to close. The unexpected and out of place guests to the island were washed in from a storm. The night before the translator spoke to the children about the danger of coming in contact with a "Medusa." The fearless tots insisted on swimming each day just the same. As adults, we became the American hawk eyes constantly on watch for the jellyfish.

At one point a very unusual looking jelly swam by my leg. I gathered up the children and together we watched it make its' way to the shore. "Oh, Medusa," they said. "Ouchie Ouchie?" was their next question. "Yes, ouchie," I answered. The children picked up their boogie boards and walked along the shore line scanning for a clear spot in the shallow water. Their boldness made me think of my nieces and nephews. Would they have insisted on swimming after seeing what may have been a bad jellyfish? Would their apprehension have removed them from the water? The little children of Chernobyl wore the battle scars of cancer caused by contamination. The fearless soldiers came to America in search of a radiation-free stay. Their U.S.A. bliss was only a month long. They weren't about to allow the possibility of a "Medusa" spoil their fun. They were risk takers living in the second of each moment.

The children initiated a new game wherein they stayed perfectly still (side by side on one boogie board) allowing the water to take them into the beach. By tapping me on the arm and vigorously pointing to my boogie board, they made it clear they wanted me to participate. After about two minutes of not talking (silence seemed to be a prerequisite for their game) our boogie boards ended up nose to nose. Speechless, the three of us looked at one another as our bodies glided across the sea and onto the sand. Although we didn't speak during our game, their eyes pantomimed the story of their lives. Through a veil of ethereal delight, I felt the souls of two, small in body, vast in power, travelers. Undoubtedly they were sent to teach us more about ourselves and the way in which we should approach each day. Without any words they reminded me of the American abundance around me.

On July 19, I woke up with a heavy heart. The time had come to say farewell to my new little friends. Surrounded by a plethora of parting gifts, the Chernobyl children prepared for their long journey home. I hugged each cherub, kissed their tiny foreheads, and promised to keep in touch. My next stop was the cemetery. It was my grandfathers' first birthday back in heaven. He and my mother were born on the same day. I knew she, too, had an aching heart. On the way to visit his site, I stopped to buy him a pack of his favorite cigarettes. Ironic don't you think? I wanted to buy him the very same thing that took his life. I hated supporting his habit when he was alive, but felt the need to buy the butts in death. I brought a bouquet of yellow Heliposis from my garden.

As we decorated his headstone with flowers and candles, I placed the cigarettes down next to his name. "Those are the wrong ones!" my mother and sister said. "He didn't smoke that brand. You don't know that because you never liked buying them for him." My face must have shown total disgust over my blunder. My mother interjected with, "It's <u>PERFECT</u> that you didn't get the right brand! You never got the right brand unless you called us six times from the store to ask us what he smoked. Naturally, you'd buy the wrong brand. You were trying to surprise him. It's great, Lorna."

We sang Happy Birthday and laughed about old memories. During our visit, every member of my family (except my sister Liz) repeatedly lit up their cigarettes. It was as if we were sitting around his kitchen table smoking and shooting the breeze. Suddenly the overwhelming desire to share a butt with my grandfather came over me. I took a cigarette out of his wrong brand birthday pack and asked for a lighter. "WHAT?" My mother asked over shouts and gasps of disbelief from my nieces, nephews, husband, brother- in- laws, step-father and sisters. "<u>You have never had a cigarette in your life!</u> WHY DO YOU WANT ONE NOW?" mum asked.

I think I just wanted to make amends for all of the times I blew my grandfather off because I didn't want to leave his house smelling of butts. Maybe I felt guilty for all of the hours of good conversation I missed? Maybe I wanted to have a smoke with a man I loved on his 82nd birthday? Maybe I wanted to make everyone at the cemetery laugh on a sad day? After all, it was my mother's birthday. Decorating her father's site on the day they had always shared together must have sucked.

For whatever reason, I lit up the butt. I conversed with my family as if I had been a smoker all of my adult life. At the risk of sounding like a politician running for office, I didn't inhale. There was something very natural about having a smoke with my grandfather. With my cigarette in hand, I remembered how light I felt in his hands each time he picked me up. I thought about how stiff the box of butts felt in his shirt when I hugged him. I remembered the smoke rings he'd blow for me. I used to sit in awe as those rings magically floated through the air. Back then, none of us knew the socially accepted rings were taking minutes off of his life.

I held on to the mystical memory of the magical smoke rings. I put all of my shame and guilt concerning cigarettes and our relationship into the center of those childhood memory smoke rings. I allowed the rings to float my guilt right up to heaven for absolution. That was the last time I was to feel bad for all of the hours I missed with my grandfather during his life as a smoker.

A few weeks later, my husband pulled into his friends' beauty shop and placed his head under her sink. The time had come to give his long locks one final washing before being cut and donated to Locks of Love. About two years prior, he made a personal bet with himself that he wasn't going to cut his hair until he finished renovating our barn. For some reason, the idea of sporting a pony tail was an incentive for him to move quickly through the remodeling. Once I was diagnosed, he decided to go the twelve-inch distance and donate his beautiful board-straight, jet black Native American hair to someone in need of a wig. As the months went by, my husband looked less and less like the man I married, and more and more like someone who belonged at an open call audition for a fake butter commercial. Some days, I'd wake up forgetting he and I had the same length hair. For a sleepy second, I'd ponder who the hell was lying next to me.

The important part of the story is that the editor of our local paper ran a story with lots of before and after photos of Roger's road to wig making. Very few men in our community were photographed for donating hair. We hoped it would spark an interest in men who wanted to give back. I was really proud of him for completing the project. Each time I saw his shiny bald head, I was reminded of how many chemo patients were waiting to feel whole again with hair. Making the wig was one of the most selfless things he had ever done. His bald head was just another reminder of how much cancer had changed us.

At the end of the summer my cell phone rang. "Lorna, I'm calling to say that you have been selected as our Person of the Year! We'd like to honor you with a dinner on October 27th, 2006. We are so impressed with the work you have done in our community. We'd like to thank you and recognize you with this prestigious award." Speechless, and not exactly sure the call wasn't a prank, I said, "I cannot hear you very well. Do you need to me to make a speech on behalf of your person of the year?" "No, Lorna, you **are** the person of the year!" he replied, somewhat confused by my confusion. "Well, that's unbelievable," I said. "I'm only thirty-five years old. Isn't this award reserved for people who have spent their life working in the community?"

"Yes, Lorna, you are in fact the youngest person we have ever nominated. It was a unanimous decision. We are grateful for all you have done. We have been keeping track and following your successes, and couldn't be more excited to have you as our pick this year." He then went on to list all of the past recipients. Without question, I was in standing with some very giving people. "Well, my goodness, this is an honor," I said. "Thank you so much for your call and please keep me posted with whatever you need from me." *This is so interesting...I am coming off of the worst year of my life and I am being honored as person of the year! How freaking apropos is that?*

The worst year of my life was 2005. Cancer surgery in February, my friend passing away in March, radioactive iodine treatments a few weeks later, another friend passing in March, another friend passing away in April, Roger's grandmother passing away in June, my grandfather's diagnosis of lung cancer a week after that, his demise and death that August, the devastation of Hurricane Katrina that same week, rescanning of my body in search of more cancer that fall, changes in my meds, and being tired all of the time...without question, the year 2005 had sucked.

What I failed to remember was that I was **living** in **2006**. I was so wrapped up in 2005 I neglected to focus on 2006. Since January 2006, things were pretty great. I was back to working at the casting company, Roger's ninety-year-old grandmother had survived a risky surgery, my business was celebrating ten-years of success, I spoke in Boston about thyroid cancer, was offered a job as a booking agent for a modeling agency, was working on a big movie, helped two sick children from Belarus receive free medical care, went to Florida twice, hit a spa in New

Hampshire twice, had a beach house booked for a week in Falmouth, my family and friends were healthy, I was feeling a more like myself, and I had made peace with my illness. I was eager to manifest my cancer into good things. I was moving toward a life of meaning and intention. I had finally discovered why I had cancer. PERSON OF THE YEAR 2006-what better way to celebrate my evolution?

Nineteen Months

BEFORE LONG SCHOOL BUSSES PACKED WITH children were back on the roads. I was back in full swing of the fall semester. When I turned my office calendar from August to September, I was reminded of my appointment to meet my new endocrinologist at new hospital in Boston. For as long as I can remember, I have resisted change. I have driven a Jeep for the past twelve years. I use my cell phones until they completely expire or are submerged into a beverage of choice. I replace the same staples in my wardrobe when they are tired. Other than a few seasonal highlights, my hair always looks the same. So you can imagine how wired I was over the idea of a new hospital. Out of all of the doctors on "Team Lorna", the endo is one of the most important for follow up care.

I pulled down the road to the hospital. I drove past a sea of primary political signs with waving hands behind them. I questioned the coincidence of political events and my medical schedule. *Note to self, maybe I should run for Governor once all of this medical stuff is behind me. Every appointment seems to be on election or primary day. This must mean something.*

After about five minutes of screening with a fellow, Dr. Lang walked through the door. A striking tower of perfect health, my attractive Amerasian endo shook my hand and offered me a smile of familiarity. *My face does ring a bell to her. She remembers me from the convocation. -Props to her for being on the ball.* Eventually she asked if I had any questions. "I attended a ThyCa meeting back in April. I'd like to attend more meetings but I work every Saturday in Boston. Everyone in the room knew their numbers and charted out their progress after each lab or test. I don't chart. I don't even know how to chart. I left feeling very irresponsible. I understand my entire ThyCa group is in your care. Do you teach us how to chart?"

Her answer confirmed our long-term relationship. "Lorna, you don't have any homework with me. I will worry about your numbers. That is my job, you don't have to take that on. You have enough to do. You can leave all of that up to me. That is what I am here for." After a huge sigh of relief, I asked why some people chart. "Your thyroid cancer care is a co-operative effort between you and your physician. Some patients need to feel in control of their condition. Others feel just overwhelmed. In this type of situation, if your physician knows how to manage thyroid cancer, you can share the responsibility of your numbers by being aware of what they mean. But allow the physicians to do their job and take care of you. I do recommend that you keep a record of your results for future reference. I <u>don't think</u> you need to have them memorized." At least I was organized. Each time Dr. Smith mailed my results, I put them in a file. -Now for my least favorite part of my first date with my new endo.

I was trucking along feeling good (90% of the time) on the meds prescribed by Dr. Smith. I was on 200 mcg of Synthroid and 25 mcg of Cytomel per day. I felt pretty close to normal. No heart racing, no sweats, and no irritability. Remember how much I resist change? Well, you can imagine how unimpressed I was when Dr. Lang's fellow called me at 8:00 A.M. the following day. My labs were back. The plan was to change things up a bit. "We are cutting you <u>way back</u> Lorna. I think you'll feel <u>a lot</u> better," she said. "Do I have a choice?" flew out of my mouth followed by, "It's just that I hate change. Dr. Smith already has adjusted my meds a few times. I feel like my <u>ENTIRE LIFE</u> is being dictated by the little amber bottle from the pharmacy. The contents of that bottle literally decide how I feel each day. You change the dose, you change how I feel. I feel good. If it ain't broke, right?" The fellow paused and said, "Would you like Dr. Lang to call you?"

For the first two weeks on my new dose, (which incidentally was 150mcg per day of Synthroid and 12.5 mcg per day of Cytomel) I was back in bed after work. One night my husband walked me from the kitchen (fully clothed with a full face of make up on) and tucked me into my bed. After a two hour nap, I got up to shower and crawled back in my covers.

Five days later at 4:00 A.M., my alarm clock went off. By 6:30 A.M., I was on the set of the movie I had prepped the football players for. The shoot took place in the Emerson Majestic Theatre in Boston. By 8:00 A.M., I not only missed my thyroid, I was ready to walk around the corner to the old Combat Zone. I wanted to score whatever I could to stay awake. (I know, big talk from a girl who has never done hard core drugs and has only been drunk once!) I wondered how the papers would read. <u>Person of the Year Arrested for Scoring T3 Hormone in the Back Alleys of Boston.</u> When asked why Mrs. Brunelle turned toward a life of drugs and crime, she answered "I'm a thyroid med junkie." You should try living without a thyroid! Some days it's a real bitch."

I must back up and explain why we were on set. My boss had to fill a theatre with people who owned upscale apparel for a ballet scene in the movie. As a pageant coach, my closet has an endless supply of formal wear. My boss was aware of my wardrobe. A dozen students from my on camera acting class were scheduled to be on set the same day. It seemed like a cool experience to share with them. I called on my friend Katie. As a pageant girl, she had a killer wardrobe. Spending time with Katie is always a blast! I knew I was running low on my new dose of thyroid meds. What I didn't know was how quickly my body would check out.

As I sat, less than twenty feet away from the celebrities starring in the movie, my energy dwindled. Forget about star struck, I felt like I had been struck by a truck! About twelve hours on set, Katie and I began whispering a game of "I'd rather be (<u>Blank</u>) than sitting here." Filling in the blank was an amusing way to keep my energy at a functioning coherent level. Katie began with a list of awful things she'd rather be doing than sitting in the audience (on her thirteenth hour) serving as an extra for a movie. My relationship with Katie began in the late 90's when she was my voice/pageant preparation student. Since then, she had won five crowns and placed high at the Miss Massachusetts Pageant three times. Her competitive nature flew out as she consistently tried to top each of my "I'd rather be's." Finally, to show my sportsmanship, I said, "I'd rather be at home locked up in radioactive iodine quarantine recovering from cancer than sitting here." Bare in mind we were **whispering** the game.

Just then, the man on my right said, "Did I just hear you say you had cancer?" *Oh, shit, someone overheard me…I've totally offended someone… yikes! Well fess up. You did, after all, say it, Moron.* "Yes, I did. I'm sorry. To some, cancer humor is pretty inappropriate. We're just misbehaving over here in between takes, but we are whispering. I sincerely doubted anyone could hear us. I'm sorry if I offended you." His response jolted me. "Oh, I love cancer humor!" he said. "Do you like my suit? I bought it for my funeral but I haven't needed it yet. I picked out a casket too, but that's a little harder to lug around." As I gasped and laughed at the same time, he said, "Hello, my name is Dan. I am a Hodgkin's Lymphoma survivor. I'm a three-timer. I know all too well about being quarantined. I was in isolation for six weeks without human contact. Do you know what I'm doing after this gig? I'm going home to spell check my obituary."

As Katie and I laughed, he went on to say "Yeah so my doctor said, I have good news and bad news. The good news is you have two days to live, the bad news is, I should have told `ya the day before yesterday!" Soon after the joking subsided, he told us about a foundation he created. He explained that most families spend thousands of dollars on lodging, food and transportation while their children are treated for cancer. His foundation <u>Christopher's Haven</u> provides shelter, food and comfort to those families in Boston. I was blown away by Dan's mission to make his cancer a good thing. Without question, he had spent some time in hell on earth. Despite his months in the halls of cancer, he was able to reemerge centered and focused, able to shed some light into the dark world of disease. I told Dan about my passion for the Chernobyl Children Project U.S.A. In that moment, two lives influenced by cancer merged together for the better of mankind.

Conversing about hope and change with a cancer survivor is therapy. In a theatre packed with hundreds of well dressed actors, God placed Dan in the seat that touched mine. Perhaps I'm reading too much into this folks, but what do we see in the name Christopher's Haven? **Christ.** I believe Christ brought Dan to Massachusetts to create a better world for the children and families facing cancer. (For more information visit christophershaven.org)

The next day, I returned to New Hampshire for my final facial laser hair treatment. As I hoisted myself on the bed for the last time, I thought about all of the beds I spent time on since my diagnosis. The routine movement of lifting one leg up on the side of a bed and positioning back on the flat surface had become intrinsic to me. Many beds were rested upon for massages. Some beds were for laser hair removal. One bed was for a cranial sacral treatment. Three beds were for CT scans. A dozen or so beds were for body scans. One bed was for facials. Another bed was for a Shirodarah treatment. A few beds were for ultrasounds. One bed was for an ultrasound-guided fine needle aspiration biopsy. One bed was for surgery. Another bed was for my hospital stay during my surgery. Some beds were used to sit on and converse with my doctors. Other beds were used while the phlebotomist De Jour tried to find a vein in my arm and needed me on my back to extract blood from my ankle. (All of that ended when I met Cheryl. God bless her-she never misses.) Some beds were for napping on vacations at healing destinations. One bed nested under a canopy of princesses as I read a bedtime story to my niece Taylor. A hospital bed held my weight as I cared for my dying grandfather. Another bed was dressed in blue Tommy Hilfiger bedding as my niece Paige and I stretched across it to play with her new hamster. The floor of my office was used as a bed one night as my staff cast the show for our summer arts festival. (I was too hypo to sit upright in my chair.) Most of all, there was my king-sized bed adorned in butter cream flannel sheets, draped in a mountain of white bedding! That bed was eager to greet me at the end of countless hypothyroid days.

So many beds, with scenarios ranging from sadness to hope, had supported my body during every phase of my recovery from thyroid cancer. My preoccupation with my bed resume resulted in being pulled over by a New Hampshire police officer. From there, I was issued a speeding ticket. The cop handed me the ticket and said, "Next time you are in New Hampshire try to avoid driving like you are in Boston! Do you understand me?" Somehow this man knew I was a Boston girl. Was it my Red Sox baseball hat or the visible CITY OF BOSTON parking violation that gave me away? Enraged over not receiving a verbal warning, I took the $200.00 ticket from the cop. I stuffed it under my visor on top of my parking violation.

A chilling thought occurred as I drove away from the cruiser. For over twenty years, my uncle Ray was a cop in small town named Pembroke, Massachusetts. I received my speeding ticket in a small town named Pembroke, New Hampshire. Was my uncle telling me to slow down through that police officer? Seems too coincidental to overlook. I began thinking about the Mahatma Gandhi quote on a magnet in my kitchen. "There is more to life than increasing it's speed." Cancer had finally taught me to slow down. After nineteen months (since my surgery) of moving slowly, I was allegedly racing almost thirty miles over the speed limit down a windy back road in New Hampshire! Where the hell did I get off track? I said a prayer to my cop uncle Ray in heaven and asked him why he didn't intercept my misdemeanor with a warning. I didn't need a $200.00 smack down to get the point. I vowed to maintain the slow pace cancer had introduced to my life.

A few months later, I crossed the state lines to contest my speeding ticket in New Hampshire. The judge told me about his aunt **Lorna** and how much he loved her. He said he had never met another "Lorna Doone" until I stood in his court. From there, my ticket was dropped. My uncle had issued his warning from heaven. Message received!

The following week, we packed our bags for Venice, Florida. Roger's side of the family was celebrating a 50th wedding anniversary. The night before we departed, I approached my husband about staying behind. Needless to say, he was unimpressed with my timing. He promised to support me on the trip if and when I needed to rest. Ultimately, I didn't want to slow him or my in-laws down. On my new lower med dose, I was going to sleep (or at least get into bed) each night by 8:30 P.M. I needed to know rest would be an option in Florida. After witnessing my setback in energy, Roger knew what he was in for. Against my better judgment, I zipped up my suitcases and headed for a hypothyroid week-long stay far away from my own bed.

With **62.5 mcg less per day** of thyroid meds in my starving system this was by far the worst diet I had ever been on in my life. For the first time ever, I couldn't cheat. On Atkins, around the premenstrual days, I'd always nibble a corner of a slice of pizza or a sliver of a chocolate bar. On the "No Thyroid Diet" I couldn't slice myself a half tablet of Cytomel or have a sliver of Synthroid. Cheating would cause my prescription to run out too early. My insurance wouldn't refill my lifeline until the permitted calendar date. The concept of not being able to make myself feel better freaked me out. I wanted nothing more than to feel *right* in my own skin. Until then **right** had been 200 mcg of Synthroid and 25 mcg of Cytomel. I felt like a junkie in detox. I needed a thyroid cancer med fix.

Never before had I felt so desperate to feel normal. When I was recovering from surgery, my neck incision was bright red, I could hardly move, and I was weeks into my hypo thyroid stage, I understood why I was tired. My mind accepted the fatigue and pain as temporary. Nineteen months after all of that hell was behind me, I found it near impossible to accept feeling as tired as I was post-op. My fatigue seemed unfair, confusing and cruel. So what if my bones and heart were in danger on high amounts of thyroid meds? At least I could stay up and watch the news each night. At least I felt normal. On the lower dose of meds, each day begins with a hangover and ends with a coma. How the hell is this better for me? Shouldn't it be about quality of life? It should be my decision to feel good until I die.

The buzz of the alarm clock went off at 4:00 A.M. and I dressed for our trip. I made the mistake of taking my morning meds after I dressed. My meds mishap guaranteed a melt-down by 4:00 P.M. in Venice. I found (through mentally charting my energy) that my new meds only took me though the first twelve hours of each day. One can imagine how

I felt by 10:00 P.M. seated at a Florida steak house with my husbands' entire family! Trying to act normal, make conversation, and keep my head off of the table had never been so tough. At one point I gave in to the exhaustion. I stopped talking and disintegrated at the table.

The next day I strategically planned a way to survive the trip. Back at home, I take my meds at 7:00 A.M. on an empty stomach and eat an hour later. By 7:00 P.M. I fade away. At the hotel, I decided to eat breakfast early, wait for the two hour time span (after meals) to pass, and take my pills for the day. The breakdown: Breakfast by 8:00 A.M., pills by 10:30 A.M., ENERGY until 10:30 P.M.

I was sluggish each morning. The first day I was able to sit on the beach in Venice void of any physically draining responsibility. The beach was steps away from the car and Roger held my chair and beach bag. I spent the entire day floating in the ocean. It was divine. The second day we drove to Siesta Key Beach. I offered to hold my beach chair, bag and noodle. By the time I made it from the parking lot to the shore, I felt like I had run a marathon. "How are you doing?" Roger asked. "I'm pretty damn tired." I said, pretty damn shocked by how much the walk had knocked me out. "I really miss Dr. Smith. I HATE this new medication dose. I feel like I did during the weeks I weaned off my meds for the radiation." Once I realized I dumped too much on him during his vacation, I threw out an insincere, "It will get better though. I just have to get used to it."

Over an hour later, I was crawling along Siesta Key. I called on the blessed Mother Mary to restore my body and recharged my energy. Once my prayer was sent sailing on the sea winds, I called Reenie to bitch about cancer. As always, speaking to her made me feel lighter. As soon as we hung up a pod of dolphins swam by. *Things will get better. God came to me again in nature…I just have to keep the faith and keep my new chins up.* I wasn't joking about my chins. On my new low dose of meds, I had gained fourteen pounds within two weeks. -To me, yet another sign that I was once again hypo.

The next day we returned to Caspersen Beach. I read, prayed, walked, sang, and floated. Don't ask me why I do this, but whenever I'm in water, I sing. As I was singing, a dolphin appeared on my right side. Completely thrilled, I looked on the shore to confirm whether or not my in-laws and husband saw my new friend. As I sang, the dolphin swam very close to me. My husband estimates we were about ten feet apart. *God, is this another sign or does this a dolphin enjoy music? How will I know?* Just then, the dolphin swam even closer to me. I could clearly make out a mark on a fin. It looked like something took a bite out of it. The dolphin began jumping out of the water and doing playful stunts. My date with the dolphin was one of the coolest moments in my hypothyroid life. (Actually, it was one of the coolest moments in my entire life, but since I felt hypo at the time, I marked all things hypo.) As I swam with my adorable friend, I thought *this has to be a sign. I've been to this beach many times. I've seen dolphins almost every visit. I have never had one swim so near to me. I'm considering this a sign of hope. And to think I almost stayed home and skipped this trip!*

The next day we returned to the beach. Once again, a dolphin swam with me. This dolphin was much smaller than my friend from the day before. I referred to it as Baby. Baby swam with me for quite a while, keeping a protected distance from the bright orange noodle I rested on. I serenaded my oceanic friend with water themed songs. My voice echoed on the waves all day. Just when I thought my dolphin kinship couldn't have become any greater, Baby looked right at me. With a turned head, Baby fixated on my eyes for a few seconds and then dipped into the sea. Through Baby, I felt a true spiritual connection to God.

In addition to connecting with dolphins and God on the trip, I became a lot closer to Roger. Somewhere between dating ten years and nine years of marriage, over the past nineteen years we had become one of those couples who only hang out with couples. You know- the couples who only vacation with other couples, who only dine at nice places with other couples, and who spend most of their time in the company of other couples. Ever the modern pair, on dates we occasionally traveled men in the back of the vehicle and the girls in the front or visa versa.

Pre-cancer, I made fun of the couples who took long walks on the beach. In my world, those couples had just linked up on an on line dating site and were treading through the newness of their unrealistic love. Somehow, cancer had slowly changed my unenthusiastic spin on love. Vacationing in Florida, in October of 2006, I found myself falling in love with Roger. For the first time since August of 1987, we went for a walk together. Not just any ol' walk, but a long walk along the breathtaking Caspersen Beach. During our excursion, we stopped to pick up prehistoric shark teeth. Occasionally, we kicked off our flip flops to dive into the water to cool our bodies. We held on to one another as we fought our way out of the waves and back on to the shore. We strolled (at hypo turtle speed) the entire shore line of the isolated beach.

That night at dinner, Rog asked his father one of my all time favorite questions! "Dad, can you move down a bit so I can sit next to my wife?" Even at his great uncle's 50th wedding anniversary party, in a room filled with his family, Rog asked his father to move down one seat so he could park himself beside me. *What a lovely change this is,* I thought. *I can totally deal with this nice new cancer sparked change in our relationship.*

That night we had sex with *kissing*. To most couples, I'm sure kissing seems like no big deal. For us, it was. All of my life, I have been somewhat of a germ-o-phobe and a lot of a claustrophobe. Throw that on top of ten years of dating and nine years of marriage. I found it rather easy to lose the art of kissing. That night in Venice, I *wanted* to kiss my husband. After our romantic encounter, I returned to my bed. (I said I wanted to kiss him not spend the night in his bed! Baby steps, please.) A host of questions buzzed around my recently kissed head. *Has disease made us appreciate our time together? In his eyes, am I back to my old self again? After nineteen months of being lost, am I home? Am I kind again, considerate again, doting again? Is that why he wants to be near me? To what address shall I mail my thank you card for bringing this change in my marriage? If kissing, walking, holding hands, hugging and sitting near each other are all the perks from having cancer, I can live with that.*

Our delightful dolphin filled trip had filled my heart with love. "Amen!" I whispered a bed away from my lover. After knowing Roger for nineteen years, it took nineteen months of thyroid cancer recovery to know myself enough to let him in. My epiphany was both sad and encouraging. *Bring on the kissing and all of the other positive things inflicted by cancer! But most of all- bring on LOVE!* **Bring IT!** *BRING- IT- ON! Amen.*

My Catholic Bat Mitzvah

*T*HAD BECOME A HUMAN MOLASSES, A condition I had no intention of sticking with. When I returned from Florida, I emailed my new endo. She needed to know how unimpressed I was with the new dose of meds. As for my experiment with taking the meds later in the day during my vacation, my energy seemed to last longer into the evening on the trip. My Massachusetts lifestyle is not conducive to feeling hung-over all morning waiting to take meds. My new endo asked me to stay positive. She reminded me that I needed to be patient and give the new dose time to work its' way through my body. I was sick of waiting. Although her message of hope was meant to keep me focused, all I felt was contempt for her lack of consideration. I had a hunch that she would be an all numbers and no ears doctor, but I had secretly hoped my instincts were off mark. "The numbers say you are fine" method of care wasn't working for me.

I awoke on October 21st, somewhat blue. It was the day Dr. Smith found my lump. My LUMP-iversary. I sat in the parking lot of the

Boston hospital crying on the phone to my husband exactly two years prior. So much had changed in twenty-four months.

I dressed for my Boston job trying to shake my edgy attitude. Call me crazy but I was certain two years after my doctor found my lump I'd be feeling like my old self again. Upon diagnosis, I kept asking doctors and thyroid cancer survivors how long it takes to feel normal again. Most people said the first year was about surgery, radiation and recovery. The second year was about adjusting the medications. So in my mind, within twenty-four months I'd be fine. The fact that I was still adjusting my meds and trying to feel normal put a real kink in my panties. Was my Catholic guilt getting the best of me? Rather than bitching about feeling tired, should I have been praising God for sparing my life? Regrettably, some 730 days after my diagnosis, an indeterminate state of hypothyroid despondency was all I felt.

Without question, October 21st, is forever going to be a significant day in my life. That particular afternoon, it was about to become a monumental day for my friend Nellie. Nellie is a Non- Hodgkin's Lymphoma Stage Four cancer survivor. She has been to hell and back. We had more than cancer in common. Nellie is the niece of my breast cancer-surviving friend Reenie. While pregnant with her son, Nellie was told she had cancer. As her unborn son nested in her belly, she began radiation therapy beneath a big lead blanket. Once he was born, she began chemo. After several weeks in the hospital, a complete bone marrow transplant, chemo, and radiation, she was on her way to recovery. After work, I was going to watch her walk down the aisle. Her miracle wedding day was reason enough to abandon my disheartened feelings toward October 21st.

Nellie asked me to help select happy joyous music for the ceremony. On the way over to the church, I repeated lyrics to one of the songs. *This is the day that the Lord has made, let us rejoice and be glad for, this is the day that the Lord has made...Hallelujah, Hallelujah.* I had sung the words too many times to remember, but on that crisp autumn afternoon, I finally understood their meaning. There truly was so much to rejoice over and be glad for. Sure, I was tired but in the big picture, Nellie the Miracle was getting married! After a stunning parade of bridesmaids, it was time for Nellie to make her entrance. My eyes welled up as I watched her grown up son (once the baby in her belly when cancer tried to win) walk her toward the alter.

When it came time for Nellie to say "In sickness and in health", she paused for what felt like an eternity. Through tears, in an almost inaudible tone, she said, "In sickness" and continued crying though "and in health". I felt the damp drops escape from my conservatory trained eyeballs. It was indeed a cancer survivor's catharsis. Nellie's Blessed Sacrament was more important than any other wedding I had ever witnessed. Her exchange of vows flushed my heart and soul into overdrive, forcing me to praise God, The Blessed Mother Mary, the saints, the angels, the stars, the moon, Mother Nature, chocolate, and all things divine, great, and powerful that help to pull us through. Nellie defied the odds. Her wedding was a perfect manifestation of faith, hope, and the will to love and live. For every cancer survivor across the globe, Nellie's nuptials symbolized a second chance at life. After losing a little piece of my soul to disease, Nellie's wedding made me crave a long life filled with love. From that moment on, the twenty-first day of the tenth month of each year will be remembered as the day Nellie reminded me that anything is possible.

The following week was spent preparing for my person of the year event. Despite a closet full of clothes, I hit a few stores in search of a signature piece that would make me feel special on my special night. I walked away with a martini-olive green, crushed velvet fitted jacket with a dramatic necklace that boasted a large green gem stone. I loved being wrapped in the color of the heart chakra. My only question was whether or not to wear black or winter white under the green. After a session of "do I wear my hair up, down, or back in a low pony" I called on my former student, now stylist. Weeks prior she offered to experiment with my ever thinning (once lush and thick) locks. She set my hair in huge rollers and placed me under a dryer for nearly an hour. When it was all said and done, I had hair any super model would envy. We'd recreate the look for the party.

The only thing left to do was write my speech. The topic was "Giving Back". I had less than nine minutes to convey my passion for helping people. The day before my dinner, I scrapped all of the fluff from the text and wrote from my hard-core true heart. Truth: we struggled financially growing up. Truth: my community helped us when we needed it the most. Truth: I was the face of a hard-working, thirty-five-year-old woman who survived cancer. Truth: I had been working since the age of eleven. I babysat on the weekends to buy expensive hip school clothes to fit in. Truth: those who come from humble means should never turn their back on their roots despite how successful they become. Truth: To me, giving back is the definition of success.

The body of the speech gently addressed my childhood and conveyed how incredible it felt to be the recipient of so much goodwill and kindness. I included a story from November of 1985 when a stranger (or anonymous friend) left a box filled with a Thanksgiving dinner outside our door. I shared how overwhelming it was to open a graduation envelope to find that I had been awarded a full scholarship to college in honor of a local artist. As I typed the end of the address, I prayed my simple and honest words would be enough to penetrate and inspire.

That week, my weight got the best of me. As I dressed for the party I kicked myself for not dumping all of the weight I had gained since my surgery. I went in for surgery in February 2005 after a near forty-pound weight loss. I lost thirty-seven pounds. (I round it up to forty, thank you very much.) Post-surgery, all of the weight returned. I found the pounds impossible to shed after my thyroid was removed. As I beat myself up for being plus size, it occurred to me that I never had such unhealthy thoughts about looking so unhealthy. *This must be the new dose of meds talking...Big or small, I have always been a confident girl.* It crushed me to look so crushed in my crushed velvet jacket. I felt like a ball of puffed rice wrapped in seaweed. It's true folks, I looked like a piece of human sushi.

As I greeted my guests I tried to dump the fear of someone poking me in the eye with a chop stick, or saturating me in soy sauce, wasabi, and pickled ginger. I tried to give myself a pep talk. *This is a celebration of the work you have done in the community. This night is about all of the good stuff that makes you YOU...it's not about your idiosyncrasies or imperfections. So, smile, Sushi Smile!* Around 6:15 P.M., almost everyone I love took a seat in my honor. When I sat down, I felt the crushed velvet jacket crush my upper body. *Not to self, always sit in an outfit before purchasing it!* I wanted to crawl under the table. In fact, if my black pants and black v-neck sweater were beneath that table, I would have crawled under to change. Without question, my new low self esteem was brought on by the new low dose of thyroid meds. The important thing was that I recognized the change and tried to work through it. Normally (well, I should say when things were normal) I'd eat up a night of festivities with friends. I freaking love my birthday! It usually lasts the *entire* month of February. High in weight, or low in weight, I have never hidden from a good time. *Breathe, repeat, breathe, repeat! You look fine… No one can see how crowded you are in the jacket. You are behind a table. Breathe, repeat… have FUN! Smile!*

Without any warning, the coordinator of the event walked over the podium. He welcomed my former student (now friend and co-worker) to the mic to sing the National Anthem. As soon as she finished the song, he began reciting the story of my life. *Holy research!* I thought as he listed paragraphs of memories and moments that defined over three and a half decades of a life, MY LIFE. Before long, his timeline brought him to the word **CANCER**. As this virtual stranger (we had only met a handful of times) spoke about how I dealt with cancer, I, seated less than a foot away, tried to smile. *No, no, wait- Cancer wasn't invited to this party! I cannot have cancer here tonight! Dear God-I am not up for cancer talk tonight! God knows, I've given away too many of my tears to cancer. My vulnerable cancer underbelly will not be exposed this night. My hair looks fantastic! No one with good hair should cry in public!*

All eyes were on me. I tried to use every acting class I had ever taken to hold back my tears in fear of: **A**-Getting eye make up on my contacts and wrecking my make up less than fifteen minutes into the evening, and **B**-seeming like a hypothyroid sick person emotionally destroyed by cancer, and **C**-Soaking my velvet. Crying cancer creampuffs had no place at the head table. The night was about honoring girl power and strength.

When he finished briefing the crowd on my life, I stood to thank him. He came in for a hug. The smooth velvet sleeves of my jacket unexpectedly slid my arms around his body like toboggans. The full embrace allowed my lungs to expand for the first time since he began reading his note cards. Soon after my two State Rep friends were introduced. They praised and roasted me over a number of things bestowing an incredible sense of their impression of me on the audience. *Fantastic! No words about cancer. Bravo Boys. Thank you. I can do this…I can be honored for something other than surviving cancer gracefully in my community.*

As each new person spoke, I tightened my shoulders hoping the word cancer would refrain from upstaging my night. Just then, another former student (now friend and co-worker) took over the mic. *Oh, thank Heaven…she will not work the C…She's almost twenty-one years old and brings a fresh perspective to life. Cancer is not part of her world…she'll be lighthearted and funny.* She opened by saying that although I was named person of the year, in her world, I had been her person of the year for the past ten years. After a few moments of sharing comical stories about the things we have in common such as abbreviating words, and shopping for oversized sunglasses, she read the following profound words: "In my experience, we all meet people along the way who truly understand us, who share an inexplicable connection with us. They give us comfort in knowing that there is someone in this big world who can look at you and understand how you feel, can finish your sentences, and always knows how to make you laugh. Some people find it in a childhood friend, some find it in a sibling, and some are lucky enough to find it in a significant other. I myself and many of you here tonight are blessed to have found that person in Lorna. I believe that one of the most precious blessings in life is finding someone who understands you in that way. You may call it luck, fate, serendipity, or destiny. I call it the grace of God."

My tired, hypo, and on new meds soul melted as I listened to her adult spin on a relationship that began when she was a ten-year-old child. We met long before cancer left its' monogram on my neck. Could it be that our relationship was never compromised by cancer? Her words about spiritual connection truly moved me. I allowed myself to cry a little during her speech. I trusted in that context, my tears wouldn't wash me away.

Next up to the mic was a relatively new friend. The crowd heard his interpretation of a girl he had only met a few months prior. After a near two hour interrogation on what kind of state rep he'd be, I put everything aside to help him win the seat on Beacon Hill. Until that night, I'm pretty sure my new acquaintance had no idea I ever had cancer. Cancer never came up during the coffee hours covering taxes, education, health care, and gay marriage. I loved that my cancer had no place in our newfound relationship. He considered me to be a woman of merit. Cancer couldn't take any credit for his claim.

A friend who I've known for years was next in line to speak. She mentioned being "lucky enough" to be on my email list during my recovery. She said it was an "extraordinary privilege" to receive weekly updates on my progress. Her assessment: my witty emails were a way of keeping everyone at ease. Even in sickness I was taking care of others. She was right. I didn't want anyone to lose sleep over my illness. I wrapped each email in humor and sent it along the internet waves praying my words would make my friends feel better about <u>my</u> cancer. During the most terrifying time of my life, it would have killed me to let others know the extent of my fear. How *sad* is that? After sitting in my sushi suit over two hours listening to people say how brave I am, I appreciated her commentary on how humanly flawed I am. Not letting the people who love you **in** to help, is a flaw.

My mother–in–law presented the final speech. Here is a small passage from the text. "Your caring nature has been bestowed on both family and friends, coming through as a kind word, a caring touch, a thoughtful card or gift or a bouquet of flowers. Not just for a special occasion, but just because you wanted to do something nice. You faced your own personal health crisis, with unmatched strength and courage. Never once did you look for sympathy or outwardly show fear, only a strong determination to win the battle, which you did."

Her words sparked a correlation between how I initially dealt with cancer, and how I dealt with my childhood. The similarities stunned me. I never plastered the true gore of my domestic violence childhood to anyone. I never shared how often my mother was smacked around, or how often the cops came to my house to protect us. It simply didn't seem strong, appropriate, or attractive to discuss such ugly things. I wanted people to see a girl who was persevering and thriving. When first diagnosed, I approached people the exact same way. I didn't want anyone to see me tired or afraid. No one knew how much I doubted the longevity of my life span. It simply didn't seem strong, appropriate, or attractive to discuss such ugly things. I wanted people to see a girl who was persevering and thriving.

I had to ask myself the big question. Had I been acting since the earliest years of my life? Was I hiding the truth? Was it all a cover up? Or had I spent my entire life trying to protect people? After lending a hand so many times over the years, why didn't I ask for help when I was diagnosed with cancer? At the core I was a girl who grew up on a shoe-string budget constantly working harder for a better life. In my case, hard work led to hard independence. Perhaps my self-sufficiency is why I found it so impossible to reach out?

The quality of a person has always mattered more to me than their monetary value. At the end of the day, it doesn't matter if we grew up poor, or rich, gain a ton of weight, or stay hot, are blessed enough to remain healthy or survive cancer…What matters is what we do to make life matter. Judging by the amount of people sharing the night with me, my life mattered.

If someone you know is making a difference let them know it matters. In our society, there is always a long line of people waiting to tell us when we have screwed up. How often do people tell us when we've done something right? People don't usually hear about the mark they have made until their life is almost over. Catholics seem to save great praise for funerals. Years back, I attended a Jewish Bat Mitzvah for my student. At the reception, her family spent hours sharing how much her life mattered. As a thirty-five year old Catholic girl, my person of the year dinner felt like my Bat Mitzvah.

Within a few hours, the wine glasses were cleared from the tables. The colossal celebration in my tiny little corner of the world left me with a new perspective on giving. The importance of helping others and receiving help during times of need are key elements to survival. My dinner celebrated the positive impact regular people can make on the lives of others simply by lending a hand. Helping each other flourish nourishes the spirit. After years of being an independent woman, I finally understood the power of partnership.

In time, cancer jack hammered through my cement exterior skeleton and taught me how to ask for help. In time, cancer made me understand the power of honesty. I urge you to reach out and share your true self. Life is certainly more splendid in the company of real people. Above all, when hardship falls on your shoulders, remember to love yourself. Even when you are hypo, looking in a mirror at a body you hardly recognize, remember to love yourself. At least once a day, compliment yourself on something fabulous you've got going on! Your expedition to enlightenment is best illuminated by self adoration.

Osmani

HE DAY BEFORE HALLOWEEN I HAD a breakfast date with my niece Taylor. I called to confirm picking her up within the hour. Life was typical when we hung up the phone. Less than thirty minutes later life changed. My brother-in-law found his fifty-eight year old mother dead. A massive heart attack. The spiritualist in me believes that we each have a planned time to leave the earth. The realist in me knew my extra weight was bad for my heart. Since my new endo lowered my meds, I had gained an additional fifteen pounds. I joined the local YMCA after the funeral service.

A few weeks later, Roger and I went to the Museum of Science in Boston to see the BODY WORLDS 2 exhibit of "REAL HUMAN BODIES". Dr. Gunther von Hagens, renowned German anatomist and creator of BODY WORLDS, is the inventor of Plastination-the pioneering technology that makes contemporary anatomical exhibits possible. To date, over twenty million visitors in thirty-five cities in Asia, Europe, Canada and the United States have experienced the exhibitions of real human bodies thanks to his progressive vision. To some this may seem dark and unnecessary, but to a girl who studied voice and lost her thyroid, it was a must see.

About three-quarters of the way into the exhibit, I finally found what I was looking for. Standing right in front of me, was the body of some lucky bastard who got to keep his thyroid until death. My brain could not grasp how something so tiny could serve as the on-site boss or "Godfather" of our bodies. It seemed inconceivable that the diminutive gland could control so much of my life. In the human body drawing room God must have given the thyroid a Napoleon Complex full-well knowing it would want to over compensate for its' small stature. The next cadaver showcasing his thyroid was magnificent! The display was called DRAWER MAN. A section of muscle was pulled away from the thyroid framing out the exact nesting spot of the gland. It was breathtaking. The next exhibit was called RING MAN. This cadaver was displayed on gymnastic rings. Sections of the body were ringed out to show the layers underneath the surface. This was the most exhilarating and telling exhibit for a singer who had undergone a thyroidectomy. THE RING MAN'S body still had all of the nerves wrapped around the thyroid. His thyroid was gorgeous!

I walked right up to the neck of the man who donated his body to science and drank in the intricate journey each of his nerves made as they mapped their way around his thyroid. Completely awe-inspired by my surgeon, I thought, *how on earth did Dr. Randolph save my voice?* I actually asked that question out loud. Like a crazy person, I spoke to myself in the gallary. "Good God, Dr. Randolph truly is an artist of medicine." I vowed to write him yet another note praising him for saving my career. Motionless, I stood a foot away from the nerves, muscles and glands, fascinated that I could still talk let alone sing. With so much going on in such a small amount of space to work, I marveled at my surgeon's precision.

In a glass case in the center of the room, I saw an enlarged thyroid next to a normal thyroid. The contrast between the two glands was freaking amazing. The singer in me made a point to find the diaphragms, epiglottises and larynxes in the display cases. My husband and I bought the voice-guided tour device. The thyroid narration basically implied that the thyroid is **bad ass**. In a gallery full of people (both dead and alive), I found myself mesmerized by the ever-so-serious voice over talent summarizing the gland that changed my life.

The exhibit also showed a profile section of an obese body. Once I saw the fat protruding off of the muscle, I thought about my recent commitment to exercise. I swam at the Y every day following our visit to the museum. For weeks, I swam. Determined to drop the pounds cancer had invited back to my body, I pushed my frame through the water. One day I woke up and found it unbelievably difficult to move. In desperate need of an oil can, I, like the Tin Man, tried to go about my day dreaming of the moment when I'd be able to stand up straight again. *Well, isn't this a kick in the ass, for the first time in years I'm trying to make an honest attempt at weight loss through exercise and now I cannot walk…this is just perfectly plus-sized peachy.*

After two ibuprofen tablets and a gloss of biofreeze across my lower back, I stayed in bed from sun up to sun down. My goal was to restore my busted ass. The amount of pain I felt made me want to reject my plan to become healthier through exercise. When I was hypo and sick with cancer I could still lower myself to the toilet seat. Since my newfound fling with fitness, I needed the sides of the sink and tub just to position my ass properly on the John without pain shooting down my legs. (I'll refrain from discussing the arduous and torturous task of having a bowel movement.) I couldn't help but wonder if my lower thyroid med dose was causing my muscles to behave so poorly again?

So there I was, at the highest weight of my thirty-five year life span, wondering what the hell it was going to take to feel and look normal again. My level of frustration left me feeling glum. My over-use (or misuse of) muscle injury was so severe I lost about two weeks at the gym. Back in high school when I prepared for a pageant, I had terrible shin splints. The physical fitness routine involved about twelve minutes of jumping jacks and skipping. The constant pounding forced me to walk around with rulers taped to my shins on top of layers of sports cream for days. Imagine my surprise when at 124 lbs (ahh-the good ol' days) my body was upset by jumping around. My point is that my body healed quickly back then. Unlike my thirty-five year old busted ass, my seventeen-year-old shins found it in their heart to forgive my radical behavior. They quietly resumed their non-aggravated place on my legs. My thirty plus year old ass held a super-sized grudge for weeks.

In time my broken ass mended. The year 2006 was coming to a close. For the first time in my married life, we stayed in our P.J.'s for Thanksgiving dinner. For years I had wanted to ban the tradition and order out Chinese food. **Gasp!** (I don't need a turkey to remind me of all that I am thankful for! I am perfectly capable of counting my blessings over an egg roll.) Half of my wish came true that November. I stayed home, ate a traditional meal in my P.J.'s, and wrote pages and pages of this book. Speaking of books and food, each night Rog and I read together in bed. It was my latest way of avoiding late night snacking. On the subject of reading, my thyroid meds seemed to be changing the prescription for my eyes. My eye doctor told me I will never be a candidate for Lasik surgery unless my level of thyroid meds stays the same for two years. She said vision is influenced by pregnancy, too. Who knew?

"I Feel Bad About My Neck" by Nora Ephron was my next read. I bought the book for my menopausal mother after falling in love with the title. I felt bad about my neck months following my thyroid cancer surgery. The idea of reading about someone else that fell out of love with their neck tantalized me. Five pages into the story of Nora's relationship with her neck, I read an amazing tale that paralleled a memory in my life. **I'm going to pull right from her book in quotes**. "My own experience with my neck began shortly before I turned forty-three. I had an operation that left me with a terrible scar just above the collarbone. It was shocking, because I learned the hard way that just because a doctor was a famous surgeon didn't mean he had any gift of sewing people up. If you learn nothing else from reading this essay, dear reader, learn this: never have an operation on any part of your body without asking a plastic surgeon to come stand by in the operating room and keep an eye out. Because even if you are being operated on for something serious or potentially serious, even if you honestly believe that your health is more important than vanity, even if you wake up in the hospital room thrilled beyond imagination that it wasn't cancer, even if you feel elated, grateful to be alive, full of blinding insight about what's important and what's not, even if you vow to be eternally joyful about being on the planet Earth and promise never to complain about anything ever again, I promise you that one day soon, sooner than you can imagine, you will look in the mirror and think, I hate this scar."- Nora Ephron.

In that passage, Nora became the voice of every person in the world who has been left with railroad tracks of scars across their body. Do you remember how insulted The Bow Tie Bastard was when I asked him if I could bring in a plastic surgeon? He nearly fell victim to spontaneous combustion. If you cannot find a surgeon who is secure enough to allow you to bring in a plastic surgeon to close the deal, then you may want to find another surgeon. You may have to pay out of pocket for this luxury (most insurance companies will not cover this) but **you are worth it!**

If you love your surgeon, and are too embarrassed to ask about bringing in a person from plastics, you can seek out a plastic surgeon after the operation. Remember, everyone heals differently and some scars may be harder than others to repair. Rest easy knowing you have options. I heard that most surgeons haven't studied plastic surgery outside of the few hours covering this topic in med school. Asking a podiatrist to do the work of a plastic surgeon, would be like asking a country and western singer to perform an Italian aria. Without studying opera, a singer cannot deliver an aria in a foreign language merely because they can carry a tune. One plastic surgeon in Boston told me he could improve a scar up to four years after surgery. Another Boston-based plastic surgeon told me he could rework any scar at any time. He promised to give each patient with a more aesthetically pleasing appearance. Since we are on the topic, here is an update on my scar. I am writing to you today twenty-two months after the surgery. My scar has pretty well faded. Most people say it is one of the best scars they have ever seen. After over a year of massaging my scar with silicone gel, "cross fibering" or breaking up the scar tissue daily, I am happy with my results.

On the eve of December 1st, I removed the decorative autumn splendor from my property. The window boxes were adorned with winter greens and cranberry velvet bows that had a touch of gold light catching glitter in them. The front porch was wrapped in garland. Wreaths were hung on all of the doors. As I set up the Sci Fi 2006 Christmas tree, I marveled at how easy Christmas had become. Soon after my tree was trimmed, I placed the candle lights in the windows. For the final touch, I set the TV remote to the Holiday music channel. Non-stop carols from Thanksgiving until New Years Day. In less than thirty minutes, Christmas had arrived. Ah, the true joys of stress free Christmases after cancer. I told you, cancer can bring you clarity.

For the first time since I began writing this book, I am writing in real time. I am no longer cutting and pasting old emails and journal entries into this now quite lengthy Word Document. Today, on December 3rd, I write hoping that together we will come down the home stretch of my twenty-four month adventure. After careful consideration, I am going to stop writing on December 15th, my cancer-versary. One might say my new cancer-free life began on February 2nd, 2005, when the cancer was removed from my body. The second Dr. Smith confirmed my cancer, my life changed. And so that frigid December night marks the real beginning of my story. Let us walk down the final days of my first twenty-four months with thyroid cancer.

December 4: After record-breaking warm temperatures in New England, the ground was covered with snow when I woke up this morning. What is it about the first snow fall that makes me so full of hope and forgiveness? With each flake of snow second chances and new beginnings seem obtainable. Then, just when the frozen ground begins to soften, and the crocuses make their way to my feet, I feel reborn.

This afternoon, I met with a man who once worked with my mother. Now he is a writer for the Boston Globe. All of his life he wanted to pursue acting and voice-over work. After raising his children and being a well established writer, he felt it was the right time to dust off that dream. During our meeting he asked about my cancer. Turns out, his girlfriend is a breast cancer survivor. He said, "I find that some people have cancer and never ever want to speak about it again. They want to move on without looking back. Then some people, like yourself, well, they get this disease and literally become crusaders! Each day they try to raise awareness or come to terms with what has happened by making something good come out of it. I just find it fascinating how differently people deal with cancer."

I quickly said, "I'm not a crusader. I fall somewhere in the middle. I want to raise awareness for groups like the C.C.P., but I am not the leader. The leader is the crusader. Not that crusading is a bad thing-again. I just don't warrant the title." The man laughed and said, "Look up the word. Trust me...you're a crusader." The sound of the word crusader coming out of his mouth energized me! I loved the idea of having a new BIG "C" in my life! I couldn't wait to meet with the president of the C.C.P. to sink my teeth into crusading for her cause. Before long, I'd serve as her solider on the front lines helping children with cancer.

December 7: A few hours ago I was queen of the treadmill! I walked for sixty minutes and feel amazing! I intend to show up at least four times a week to walk on the mechanical road to skinny. I shall do this until I notice a weight loss. Yes, I just typed "until I notice a weight loss" which most likely implies that subliminally I plan to discontinue using the treadmill once I shed a few pounds. -Do I know myself or what? In all seriousness, I have found an amazing support circle at the Y.M.C.A. Every time I walk into the fitness room, I am proud of myself for making this change in my life. The meeting with C.C.P. president went extremely well. She loaded me up with hand outs, and walked me through what it takes to bring the children of Chernobyl to the United States each summer. During our conversation she mentioned my surgeon. Dr. Randolph had recently operated on a small child from the Chernobyl region. The child had thyroid cancer. How frightening must it be for a child to leave their family and fly to America for (of all things) surgery? Guess what they call thyroid cancer scars in the Chernobyl region? -The Chernobyl Necklace. I couldn't imagine a better way for me to volunteer my time.

A few days ago, I met a man named Osmani. He was at a party for my former boss at the modeling and talent agency in Boston. When I asked the man of Cuban and Lebanese descent the meaning of his name he said, "Messenger of God." "Well, it doesn't get much better than that!" I replied, while echoing the pronunciation of his beautiful name in my head. I believe Dr. Randolph is a messenger of God traveling the globe raising awareness and saving lives. The magnitude of the impact he is making on the world will be felt for years to come.

At 10:30 P.M., mum appeared in my bedroom to parade her newly highlighted hair. After praising her stylist for being a genius **and** an artist, mum felt compelled to drive over to my gallery to display her latest purchase. Her hair looked like a piece of art. The next day, mum called at 9:00 A.M. to see if I'd like to take her hair out for a day of shopping and lunch. Unable to refuse the power of a good hair day, I promised to be at her house within an hour. Mum said, "My hair looks so gorgeous, I have already been to a few stores this morning." As if her hair actually motivated her to run early errands.

On the way to lunch mum said, "I heard on the news they are distributing pills to residents within ten miles of the Pilgrim Power Plant to prevent thyroid cancer if there is an accident or terrorist attack." *Note to self,* I thought *research this as soon as you get home. Everyone in our country within forty miles…no, fifty miles…no, 100 miles of a power plant needs those pills.* There are reports stating that radiation from the Chernobyl disaster hit places as far as Germany. With that in mind, it seemed rather silly that the pills were only being distributed to residents within ten miles. As soon as I got home I pulled up articles on Potassium Iodine pills.

I discovered that only 10% of residents in Plymouth, Massachusetts (home to a nuclear power plant) picked up the Potassium Iodine pills. The owners of the Pilgrim Plant have offered to pay for the medication! It's FREE! Life without a thyroid is tricky folks! If you live near a power plant, I urge all of you to go to your state web site (my state is www.mass.gov) to research this topic. The subject of Potassium Iodine pills may seem a bit radical. I get it. Thing is, I feel like it's my responsibility to get the word out about this cancer. According to the Light of Life Foundation (checkyourneck.com) the incidence of thyroid cancer in women is rising faster than any other cancer in the United States. This year, at least 35,000 new cases of thyroid cancer were diagnosed and treated. Because of the excellent overall survival after treatment for thyroid cancer, there are at least 350,000 thyroid cancer survivors living in the United States.

This purpose of this book is to share all I have learned from my disease. God may have saved my life so that I could be one of his messengers. Osmani. As I said before, it doesn't get much better than that.

Or As Happy As You Can Be

MESSENGERS OF GOD HAVE SURROUNDED ME all of my life. Through both subtle and blatant signs, they have guided me in the form of family, friends, parents, children, teachers, grandparents, students, acquaintances, nature, and yes- even strangers. I firmly believe that nothing is random. I got cancer near the one spot of my body that I have communicatively relied on every day since I was born. It's not like I got cancer of the elbow, friends. I got cancer of the thyroid. The thyroid and all of the nerves around it live on the same block as my voice. It's just too perfect to be a coincidence. I'm convinced this was a case of good old fashioned guardian angel kismet ship forcing me to wake up and appreciate the work I have to complete while I'm here. Once I became conscious of how much was at stake, I knew if spared in surgery, I would spend the rest of my time on earth using my voice to bring positive change to the world. Like a butterfly, I am ready to soar. Eager to share my story. Eager to use my spared voice to revolutionize the way people approach cancer.

This December 15, 2006, I write to you as a survivor of cancer. With my diagnosis exactly twenty-four months behind me, one would think I'd have cancer all figured out. Although I have undeniably learned a lot, I find myself just as befuddled by the complexities of cancer **now** as I was when I got the news nearly **730 days ago**. On January 22, 2005, just before the disease was removed from my body I wrote a mantra that ended with: <u>This may change me, but I will not allow this to define me</u>. How naive were my expectations? How can a dance with cancer **not** change or define a person? Each time I open a bottle of Synthroid, pick up a prescription for Cytomel, or look at my smiling scar, I am reminded that once upon a time, cancer lived in my body. I have an ongoing recurrence preoccupation. Every time I catch a cold, feel a lump in my neck, or experience an odd sensation in my body, I wonder if it's cancer. That type of paranoia changes people.

<u>Confessions of a Girl with Cancer</u>

Paranoia: Since having cancer, I find myself less trusting. I never stand near the microwave now when its' in use. I try to heat my food on the stove. If I choose to heat food in the microwave, I never heat the food in plastic or Styrofoam. I try to avoid Styrofoam all together. (The sound of it makes me crazy.) I always try to put my cell phone on speaker and keep the receiver far away from my neck when talking. Some say cell phones emit radiation. Like I need that? I no longer freeze water bottles in the freezer for fear of the plastic (like the Styrofoam and plastic) breaking down in my food during the extreme change in temperature. I totally avoid dental X-rays and encourage others to pull the protective bib <u>all the way up to their mouth</u> when they are having dental X-rays. UPDATE ON THIS: Today mum had a dental cleaning. A special thyroid protector x-ray bib was used. Let's all toast the person who designed that gadget! I will never live next to high tension wires or power lines. I will never live next to a power plant. I will never buy a house near an old military base. I seek out cancer hot spots in my state trying to piece together the correlation to cancer.

I read a report called "The Coming Water Crisis" which refers to Bourne, Massachusetts (right near mum's house) as a hot spot connecting perchlorate in the water to thyroid gland dysfunction. The source being a component of solid rocket fuel, munitions, and fireworks; has leaked from at least fifty-eight U.S. military bases and manufacturing plants with contamination confirmed in twenty states (listing by name) including Bourne, Massachusetts. Let us not forget that I live fifteen miles away from a nuclear power plant. How's that for a double whammy?

So where was I? (Hold on, is someone trying to hack into my computer?) Oh yes, some of my paranoid changes in my life since having cancer. I've read the Johns Hopkins University studies connecting cancer to sugar and red meat. I've cut way back on my consumption of those foods. Some people believe that radiation and radon gas hazards are associated with granite countertops. I will never have granite in my kitchen. I will never show up for a scan, blood test or ultrasound and trust that the results will be negative. If I seem crazy, forgive me.

Energy: Dare I say that I have noticed a slight improvement in my stamina over the past few days? On September 25, 2006, I changed the dose of my meds. By October, I was unable to stay up to watch the 10:00 P.M. news but I needed a nap to make it through the day. By November, I no longer needed the nap. Now in December, I can watch the end of a 10:00 P.M. program, have a little intimate time with my husband after the 11:00 P.M. news, and still function the next day without feeling hung over! Can I get an AMEN?

After transitioning through the lower dose of meds, I know I can make it through a five-star, busy day without falling over. On this new dose of thyroid meds, I can live a safe life. My heart and bones will be happier for it. By safe I mean, I can put in a normal day and expect average results. If I need to put in a **super hero** day I have to take precautions. I have to either **A.** pace myself, and rest as much as I can; OR, **B.** take my meds later in the day; OR, **C.** try drinking a cup of caffeine and risk the elevated heart palpitations; OR, **D.** try avoiding sugar and carbs and eat more protein throughout the day; OR,

E. double up on my Cytomel and hustle my way through midnight! (Totally kidding)

Recovery: As cancer survivors, I believe we have suffered post-traumatic stress disorder. I'm certain our recovery from both ailments will last a lifetime. We need to set realistic goals. We can no longer behave like *constant* super heroes. We can, however, accomplish super hero feats in small batches. On a super hero day, I can: work, shop for food, put all of the groceries away, prepare a lovely meal, do a load of laundry, stop by an event, and have sex with my husband. On my not so super hero days (especially when I am due for my period or under great amounts of stress) I can: leave the breakfast dishes in the sink, work, fold a load of old laundry still sitting in the dryer, take a nap in an unmade bed, and order take out for supper. The sky is not going to cave in if we neglect to make our bed each day! It took my recovery to get that through my head.

Weight: Without a thyroid, I think my weight is going to be a constant battle. I'm not the kind of woman who leaves hot and sexy photos from her youth around the house for inspiration to lose weight. Half of the time when I look at the girl in those photos I don't even know her. I will never cut out a super model from a magazine and tape her to my fridge to help me reconsider a carrot stick. (Yes, on some low carb diets, even a carrot is the enemy. They are, after all, a carb.) If you check in on me in a few years, I'm sure I'll be relatively plus-size, smelling of Biofreeze; limping around with my broken ass trying to figure out why burning calories seems like a form of ancient torture. Speaking of Biofreeze, I still experience leg cramping. At the end of an exhausting day, I can almost guarantee I'll have leg twitches. When my leg cramps start, I reach for an ibuprofen, a banana, and a calcium pill. Works every time.

After a few weeks at the gym, I have lost seven pounds. If you'd like to mail me a congratulatory box of chocolates, my address is in the phone book. Dark chocolate (with nuts) is my favorite.

The space between diagnosis and recovery. Looking back, I wish I had been more selfish immediately following my diagnosis. I wish I had done more of what I needed. "Cancer affects the whole family" was a catchphrase I became stuck on. I felt guilty for having cancer. The last thing I wanted to do was worry the people I love. Upon diagnosis, there were times when I wanted to stay in bed and ignore the phone. That behavior would have made me the depressed girl with cancer. Instead, I went over the top to seem normal. I stayed busy, tried to laugh, made jokes, returned calls, made dinner, did housework, and went out to lunch with friends. On very few hours of sleep, I behaved "normal" for weeks. Keeping up that act was exhausting! I'm pretty certain I should have gone away for a few days to be still. Quiet time, was probably exactly what I needed. (Either that or an Ativan.) For anyone newly diagnosed, I recommend conceding to quiet time. There is a healing power in stillness.

Not too long ago, I had breakfast with a neighbor who had just been diagnosed with thyroid cancer. She had a large mass that looked like an Adam's apple protruding from her neck. I tried to explain the power of merely pondering and being contemplative during her days leading up to surgery. At the time, she, too, was in the "I'm fine!" mode. I recognized myself in her. I could not help but wonder if that manic behavior is a form of denial or simply a method of coping.

If I had to it all over again I would have taken more naps, read more books in my P.J.'s, laughed through funny movies, and sat in a chair to watch the birds in my yard. Those moments of quiet contemplation flooded me during my quarantine when I had no choice but to stay home. I only wish I had welcomed time for those healing hours when my entire body was still in tact. On the road through cancer I think it's important to slow down and read the billboard messages. Life lessons are on those billboards.

Metamorphosis: Cancer allowed me to experience a metamorphosis. Up until my diagnosis, I was a happy little worm. Everything in my adult life seemed splendid. I had a great marriage, successful business, beautiful home, healthy and true friends, and wonderfully supportive family. Most of my days were spent laughing with the people I love. I felt very blessed. Once the lump was found, I retreated into a dark cocoon. In there, I closely examined my marriage, my relationships and my lifestyle. For years, I had been looking through rose-colored glasses.

Pre-cancer, I compartmentalized everything I was feeling. I stuffed the unresolved issues onto my **to do** list, and moved along through life in an automaton over-drive fashion. Staying busy was the key to never having time for the **to do's**. Masquerading as a workaholic, I thought I was happy.

All of that changed after my surgery when I was forced to slow down. In many ways, cancer became my speed bump, letting me pause long enough to tune in. My solace was the certainty that after a winter of cancer-induced reflection, I was going to resurface from my cocoon. In the spring of 2005, I was to become a breathtakingly beautiful butterfly! I couldn't wait to soar high above my pain and longed to be filled with a newfound clarity. My awakening would define exactly what I wanted to get out of my new life, leaving all of my bullshit bad habits behind.

Truth: My metamorphosis didn't happen as quickly as I would have liked. Over time, I transformed. One by one, I crossed items off of my **to do** life list. Thanks to cancer, I was no longer afraid of change. I urge you to use the power a life-altering situation bestows upon you. While at that crossroad, you can work through just about anything.

Anger and Hope: As cancer patients we share the same givens: We are scared. We are vulnerable. We are grateful. We are uncertain. We are hopeful. We are brokenhearted. We are angry. Pre-surgery, anger consumed me. I was beside myself with rage. Had I only slowed down a bit during the weeks leading up to my thyroidectomy; I may have been more rested. I may have been more grounded. I may have been less angry. It's hard to juggle anger and hope. Maintaining a balance of anger and hope is a sacred art. Right now, focusing on the things I know to be true keeps my anger at bay.

I know cancer tried to kick the shit out of my spirit. I know it failed. As cliché, "I think I just threw up in my mouth" as this seems, I know cancer made me the woman I am today. I know cancer made me want to work harder. I know cancer made me want to have a better life. I know cancer made me want to give more, get more, love more, be loved more, feel more, and listen more. I know cancer made me want to live.

What I wanted then: Two years ago, I wanted to wrap everything I had learned from cancer in a big box. I wanted to tie all of that knowledge up in a pretty bow made from hope. I wanted to make certain the secret to withstanding and making peace with cancer would be inside that box waiting for you. I wanted to be your time line for recovery. I wanted to be your "in sickness and in health" friend. I wanted to help you heal. I wanted to raise awareness for an unknown cancer. I wanted to prove to you that within twenty-four months of being diagnosed with thyroid cancer you'd feel normal again. I wanted to write the book that wasn't on the shelf when I got sick.

Now that I have come to the end of my two year adventure, I am convinced my excursion with the cancer will not end until I take my last breath. Cancer is going to be a part of me all of the days of my life. I didn't know that when I began writing this book, of course. I wanted to leave you with a solid confirmation that your life would be **normal** two years into your cancer tour of duty. I now realize how relative normal is. Although I didn't crack the case, I don't regret purging my story. I know this book has helped me put my experience into perspective. On the days when I didn't want to talk, the computer was my best friend. Writing about disease helped me extinguish the fire cancer tried to burn in my soul.

A life with cancer doesn't stop and restart. In sickness and in health, our lives keep going on day after day. Therein lies the miracle of this cancer. We, the thyroid cancer survivors, are permitted to live long joyous lives filled with archaic stories capturing decades of memories and boundless moments of laughter. Time is the number one thing that makes this cancer so good. Despite our life-altering dance with mortality, most often thyroid cancer survivors live long lives. Time affords us days rich in happiness.

What I want now: After twenty-four months of writing almost every day, my goals have changed. Two years ago, I wanted to be able to fix you. By recounting my story I thought I had the power to mend your cancer brokenness. I've always fixed others when I've felt especially broken. Now, I want people to know about thyroid cancer. I want everyone to have regular neck exams. I meet countless people who say, "Oh, my neck always feels funny when I swallow." Or, "I have a lump in my neck." Or, "I'm tired all of the time and have this lump…I'm sure it's a goiter." After urging those people to have a neck check or thyroid labs, I walk away certain they'll need another messenger to repeat my words. I want **you** to be a messenger.

We have all seen a wall of medical pamphlets (on subjects such as breast cancer and diabetes) in physician's waiting rooms. I want you to ask your doctor why there isn't any information on thyroid cancer. After they give you an answer, I want you to ask them to order and display a few hundred pamphlets. I want you to know you have the power to ask questions when you are diagnosed with cancer. I want you to know you have the authority to change doctors. I want you to know that you have the right to obtain Potassium Iodine pills if you feel unsafe near a power plant. I want you ask your legislatures to protect our communities from the environmental toxins that are making us sick. I want you to realize you have the strength to **survive**.

It is going to be okay. It's okay to put stock in the inconceivable and believe in miracles. It's okay to be aware of your blessings and still want more. It's okay to write a book in your pajamas, unashamedly ignoring a sink full of dishes. It's okay to hire someone else to clean your home. It's okay to run to the store braless, without a stitch of make up. (Quick! Call the loony bin, Lorna has lost her marbles!) It's okay to use paper napkins from your car glove box as toilet paper on rainy days. It's okay to travel a lot, and spend a little more money than you think you should on a nice hotel. Comfort is key before and after cancer. It's okay to be imperfect. It's okay to have a few weeds in your garden. It's okay to forget the birthdays of your friend's children. It's okay to be more honest, your loved ones and real friends will be able to handle it. It's okay to love more deeply. If you get hurt you now know you have the strength to bounce back. It's okay to trust again. It's okay to have a brownie sundae with your best friend more than once a month. It's okay to be a little selfish even though your life was spared. You mustn't feel indebted for being cured, that was God's choice. It's okay to ask for help. It's okay to say NO. It's okay to set energy-reserving limits. It's okay to wear flat shoes to work in a comfortable pair of pants with a wrinkle free shirt that doesn't require dry cleaning. It's okay to have big plans for the future. It's okay to shower without your cell phone and house phone on the toilet seat in the bathroom. You can return your missed calls when your skin is dry. It's okay to cut yourself some slack. (In most cases, if you don't, no one else will.) It's okay to nap. Napping doesn't make you lazy. It's okay to sample a grape before you buy the bunch. It's okay to fantasize about your dream vacation as you cover your body in self-tanner and apply a whitening strip on your teeth. It's okay to laugh. Having fun won't bring back your cancer. It's okay to deem yourself invincible. It's okay to proudly walk around the house naked. Isn't it time we felt comfortable in our own skin? It's okay to miss your thyroid and your old self as long as you love your new self. It's okay to live a full, joyous, and fabulous, life. I implore this of you!

The Next Step: It would be difficult to walk away from writing simply because this deed to healing has been completed. Writing has become my therapy. Once my over-typed forearms became used to feeling like pieces of tightly pulled ship rope, I found great solace in the click of the keys. (Incidentally, this book rubbed away most of the letters on two keyboards.) I'd love to write a children's book about cancer or a cookbook for people with thyroid cancer. God's decision to spare my voice launched my indelible commitment to positive change. I will carry on my volunteer work at the Massachusetts Eye and Ear Infirmary. I plan to host a thyroid cancer walk through Boston. I will continue to support thyroid cancer patients daily through my web site dirtybombshell.net. I will remain committed to the children of the Chernobyl region. There is nothing more American than helping people in need. God willing, I have only scratched the surface of my work.

The Good Cancer: Some folks are offended by the term good cancer. I mean, after all, cancer isn't good, right? In the book "Thyroid Cancer: A Patient's Guide" by Doctor Douglas Van Nostrand, Leonard Wartofsky, and Gary Bloom, the authors seem to dismiss the good cancer misnomer as they point out that there is no good cancer, just one where a lot of the time doctors succeed. For most people the concept of a good cancer is absurd. Although Dr. Smith introduced my type of cancer **as good**, I remain focused on all of the goodness cancer has brought to my life.

Her Secret: I'd like to leave you with a story that is taken out of chronological order. On June 11th, 2006, mum and I invited my friend

Reenie to join us for a day trip in Watertown, Massachusetts. With my grandmother Concetta in toe, we attended the annual Armenian Festival. Once we finished eating the best Armenian food in Massachusetts, we made our way to the bathroom. A stunning elderly woman wearing a pink suede suit with pink high healed shoes stood in front of the mirror. In a very shapely brazier, she adjusted her stylish wig and applied hot pink lipstick to her beautiful face. Reenie signaled my attention to the Fashionista. We took in the splendor of the gorgeous creature who seemed to exude a certain vibrancy and wisdom.

"You look *fabulous!*" I exclaimed, unable to hold back my adoration. My compliment opened an inundation of praise from a posse of admirers. "Well, thank you," she said with the eyes of a 1940's Hollywood screen actor. "Guess how old I am?" she asked, in a flirty, yet challenging voice. In fear of being too polite or insulting, we each mentioned an age between seventy and eighty. With a tennis match bop, her face darted side to side while we spouted out numbers. As proud as punch, she stopped our guesswork and boasted, "I am <u>ninety-three</u> years old."

After a round of "You go, Girl!" and "You look A-M-A-Z-I-N-G, Sistah!" mum asked the question of the hour. "What is your secret? Do you have a secret you can share with us? How have you done it? You are my hero!" We waited on baited breath. With a devilish look and brazen Armenian accent, she revealed fountain of youth. **"Happiness!"** she exclaimed. "You have to be happy." Then, after a pause, she turned back to us and said, "Well, as happy as you can be."

A few moments later, we saw our new-found idol chatting with her fans in the lobby. "We never got your name," my grandmother said as we approached her. "Well, you see, here is the thing with my name…it has been more of a burden than it's been worth. I always feel like I have so much to live up to. My name is Angel."

In that moment, we knew we were in the presence of a messenger of God. She was an angel sent to share the uncomplicated secret to a long and fabulous life. ~Happiness!

With Christmas ten days away, I find myself reading holiday card inscriptions. "Here's to good health and happiness in 2007!" My wish for you extends well beyond the holiday season. My eternal wish for you is a luscious life filled with perfect health, phenomenal friends, a fortress of family, a bounty of blessings, and hours upon hours of joyous laughter and happiness. I went through hell and ended up stronger, happier and more fabulous than I have ever been in my life! If cancer or any other dark cloud hovers around your door, please remember my story. I can guarantee the sun will always return to shine upon you. Most of all, no matter how overpowering life becomes, please try to be happy. Or, in the words of an angel, be, "As happy as you can be."

Afterword

On May 16, 2008, my alarm clock went off at 5:00 A.M. The birds were chirping through my bedroom windows as I prepared for surgery. Three years after my thyroidectomy I was scheduled with Dr. Randolph in Boston for another thyroid operation. On May 16th, I wasn't the patient. I was a guest observer in the O.R. It was fascinating to witness the very same surgery, with the very same surgeon, in the very same hospital. At one point during the operation, Dr. Randolph allowed me to step up on a stool to get a better view of the thyroid region. It was one of the most exhilarating moments of my life! I think I missed my calling. Are there any thirty-seven year olds in med school?

I have become a lot more adventurous since I finished writing this book. I have snow tubed down a mountain, started eating sushi, gambled in Vegas, and even flew into the Grand Canyon in a helicopter for a Champaign luncheon. Speaking of alcohol, I have even been seen drinking dirty martinis. Doesn't every dirty bombshell deserve a dirty martini every now and again? I love my new energetic, risky, and daring life! My endo increased my Cytomel and Synthroid. (Yeah!) Each day at

2:00 P.M., my phone rings reminding me that it's time for my mid-day dose of happiness. I work out at the YMCA close to five times per week. I am up to thirty minutes on the elliptical, and an hour on the treadmill. I hired a personal trainer for weight training. The numbers on the scale have not changed, but my butt looks better! I am a lot stronger. I can even open a jar of pickles on my own! A lifelong goal.

I am now on the management team and serve as a community coordinator for the Chernobyl Children Project U.S.A. Twenty-two children and two adult translators from the Chernobyl region stayed in my neck of the woods last summer. On February 6, 2008, I heard the Russian voice of the boy I collected crabs with on the shore of Martha's Vineyard. In perfectly rehearsed English, he called to sing Happy Birthday. A serenade of that magnitude would serve as a near impossible feat for a young boy living in an impoverished village in Russia. In July of 2008, I received the Chernobyl Children Project U.S.A. *Joyce Feeley Award* for my work with God's children of the Chernobyl region. My student won the Miss Massachusetts pageant. In 2008, I accompanied her to Miss America. From my seat in Vegas at the Planet Hollywood theatre, I watched her win the talent award and the Children's Miracle Network Award. The circle of loving, learning, teaching, and giving goes on. Fascinating gifts, opportunities, and blessings grace my doorstep every day. Who knows? I may even embark on a new career. The Singing Surgeon has a nice tone to it.

Life after cancer is good. Really good. Actually, it's better than good, it's **FABULOUS!**

Lorna J. Brunelle

A graduate of the Boston Conservatory, Lorna J. Brunelle has dedicated her life to fostering creativity and self-expression through art. As the owner of The Burt Wood School of Performing Arts and The Alley Theatre, a teacher and casting associate at Boston Casting Inc., the official vocal coach for the Miss Massachusetts Pageant and a member of the National Association of Teachers of Singing, Lorna spends most of her days behind a camera or music stand. She is active in the Massachusetts Eye and Ear Infirmary's efforts to support thyroid cancer patients and research, and was featured in their 2008 documentary, and several issues of their magazine. In 2010, The Boston City Council proclaimed October 22 **Lorna J. Brunelle Day** for her community service and humanitarian efforts. Lorna lives with her husband Roger in the Ebenezer Soule House in Middleboro, Massachusetts.

For information on Lorna, or to learn how to volunteer time or make a donation for cancer research, visit www.DirtyBombShell.net

My grandmother Concetta "Connie" was selected as a
finalist in a beauty contest held on the USS Franklin Delano
Roosevelt Air Craft Carrier in the late 1940's. All of the
men submitted photos of their wives and girlfriends.

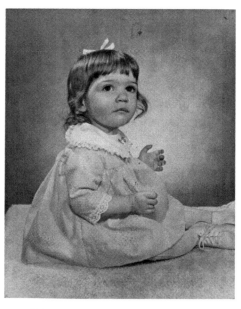

Me at 13 months old in 1972.

Me as a toddler.

With my sister Elizabeth "Liz" in the early
1970's in Belmont, Massachusetts.

In high school with my sister Tahlia.

Junior year of high school.

My high school senior picture 1989.

With mum in May of 1993 on my college graduation day.

With Roger in May of 1993 on my college graduation day.

With my niece Paige on June 14, 1997, at our wedding.

June 14, 1997, Our Wedding Day.

Me and my nephew Tyler on October 19, 2002,
at my sister Liz's wedding.

My mother Wanda with my niece Taylor the fall of 2002.

My mother Wanda with my niece Paige and nephew Tyler.

My nephew Trey with my students Alyson Levy and
Amanda Kelly the fall of 2009. The local paper ran
this photo. The caption read "Ladies Man."

The last photo of my perfect neck taken in January
2005, a week before my surgery.

Photo credit: Imagemakers Photographic Artists,
New Bedford, Massachusetts.

With my sisters Liz and Tal, and my nieces Paige and
Taylor, at Tal's wedding September 20, 2008.

My mother with all four grandchildren, Paige, Tyler,
Taylor and Trey on Cape Cod the summer of 2009.

At the ribbon cutting for my new theatre
"The Alley Theatre" October 2010

Photo credit: Karen Foye

Helpful Sites:

ThyCa: Thyroid Cancer Survivors Association
www.thyca.org

"I'm Too Young for This!" Cancer Foundation
www.imtooyoungforthis.org, www.stupidcancer.org

The American Thyroid Association
www.thyroid.org

The Thyroid Foundation of America
www.allthyroid.org, toll free phone line: 800-832-8321

The Light of Life Foundation
www.checkyourneck.com

Stop the Madness Thyroid Natural Wellness Site
www.stopthethyroidmadness.com

American Association of Clinical Endocrinologists
www.aace.com

The Hormone Foundation, affiliated with The Endocrine Society
www.hormone.org

Johns Hopkins Thyroid Tumor Center
www.thryroid-cancer.net

Thyrogen
www.thyrogen.com

Web Md
www.webmd.com

American Thyroid Association
www.thyroid.org

Make donations or volunteer time:

Randolph Thyroid Research Fund
(Gregory_randolph@meei.harvard.edu)

The Mass Eye and Ear Infirmary   **Boston, Massachusetts**
email: development@meei.harvard.edu

Development Office
Massachusetts Eye and Ear Infirmary
243 Charles Street
Boston, MA 02114   617-573-3345
Or make a gift on-line at www.masseyeandear.org/donations/.
Please be sure to indicate Randolph Thyroid Research Fund.

The Chernobyl Children Project USA
www.ccpusa.org

Light of Life Foundation
www.checkyourneck.com

Thyroid Cancer Awareness Bracelets
www.checkyourneck.com or call (847) 372-5333 or write to:

Expressions of Hope, LLC
618 S. Northwest Highway
219
Barrington, IL 60010 info@expressions-of-hope.com

ThyCa: Thyroid Cancer Survivors' Association, Inc.
thyca@thyca.org
www.thyca.org   *877-588-7904 (Voice – Toll-free)*

ThyCa: Thyroid Cancer Survivors' Association, Inc.
PO Box 1545
New York, NY 10159-1545
tel: (877) 588-7904 (toll-free)
fax: 630-604-6078
thyca@thyca.org

I'm Too Young For This! Cancer Foundation
40 Worth Street
Suite 1318
New York, NY 10013
Main/Fax: 646-861-2565
Toll Free: 877-735-4673

Locks Of Love
www.locksoflove.org

Relay For Life
www.cancer.org

American Cancer Society
1-800-ACS-2345 (or 1-866-228-4327 for TTY).
24 hours a day seven days a week.

Christopher's Haven Fund, Inc.
c/o Middlesex Savings Bank
150 Commonwealth Road
Wayland, MA 01778
www.christophershaven.org
"A Home for Kids when cancer hits home"

Things to read:

Surgery of the Thyroid and Parathyroid Gland
Dr. Gregory Randolph

Surgery of the Thyroid and Parathyroid Glands Second Radiation
Dr. Gregory Randolph

Thyroid Cancer: A Patient's Guide
Dr. Douglas Van Nostrand, Leonard Wartofsky, and Gary Bloom

The Anatomy of Hope: How People Prevail in the Face of Illness
Jerome Groopman

Why I Wore Lipstick : To My Mastectomy
Geralyn Lucas

Women's Bodies, Women's Wisdom
Dr. Christiane Northrup
Creating Physical and Emotional Health and Healing
www.drnorthrup.com

I Feel Bad About My Neck and Other Thoughts On Being A Woman
Nora Ephron
www.randomhouse.com

Prepare for Surgery, Heal Faster-A Guide of Mind-Body Techniques
Peggy Huddleston
www.healfaster.com

On Death and Dying (Kindle Edition)
Elisabeth Kubler-Ross MD
www.elisabethkublerross.com , www.ekrfoundation.org

Healing Through the Dark Emotions: The Wisdom of Grief, Fear, and Despair
by Miriam Greenspan